# Developing Instructional Units

# Developing Instructional Units

## Applications for the Exceptional Child

Second Edition

**Edward L. Meyen**
University of Kansas

Wm. C. Brown Company
Publishers
Dubuque, Iowa

This book is dedicated to the memory of the late Dr. Tony D. Vaughan, under whom the author studied as a beginning teacher, and to Sigurd B. "Bernie" Walden, who was a true advocate for the classroom teacher.

# Contents

# List of Figures

# Preface

An author encounters many temptations when revising a book. There is the temptation to revise every chapter and, in essence, to produce a new book with little resemblance to the first edition. There is also the temptation to add additional chapters to illustrate what you have learned since the previous edition was published. In seeking direction on revision, advice was sought from several persons currently using the book in teacher training programs and in inservice training. In general, the feedback suggested that as a practical guide for teachers, no major revisions were necessary. A number of specific suggestions were received and most have become a part of this revision.

The most frequent comment from reviewers related to the book's appropriateness as a guide to regular class teachers in unit preparation. Although the examples and the general emphasis of the book continue to be oriented toward teachers working with retarded children, a number of changes have been incorporated to illustrate its application to regular class teachers. Certainly, the steps employed in writing units are generally applicable regardless of the target student population. The author remains firm in his belief that unit teaching is a viable instructional method for most children, particularly for children with learning problems. As the trend toward "mainstreaming" exceptional children in regular classes increases, many teachers will find it necessary to include the needs of exceptional children in their instructional planning. An attempt has been made to increase the book's use as a reference for regular class teachers without reducing its effectiveness as a source of direction in planning instructional units specifically for exceptional children.

The most significant changes in this edition are those made in Chapters 1 and 2 and the inclusion of a new chapter on *Organization and Curriculum-Based Unit Planning.* In place of the introductory chapter is a detailed discussion on unit teaching and its implications for teachers. Chapter 2 has been strengthened to include a more extensive curriculum frame of reference for the reader. This author feels very strongly that the classroom teacher makes major contributions to curriculum through unit development, and that he or she should understand the curriculum development process. The revision of

Chapter 2 was not an attempt to discuss curriculum development comprehensively. It was intended to provide additional information on the curriculum development process so that teachers would better understand the implication of preparing instructional units that, when made a part of a child's instructional program, become part of that child's curriculum.

The new Chapter 8 is also a curriculum-related chapter. It builds on the information presented in Chapter 2 by applying curriculum development principles to unit planning. In this chapter, specific attention is given to procedures for the identification of skills and concepts to be taught through units. Emphasis is also given to procedures for organizing units into long-range plans.

In completing the revised edition, the author's primary goal was to retain the practical flow of the first edition and its focus on the systematic preparation of units. The obvious new feature of the revised edition will be its increased generalizability to regular class teachers and the additional emphasis on curriculum development. Although occasional reference is made to teaching style and methodologies, the "how to" aspects of unit teaching are not stressed.

Edward L. Meyen

# Acknowledgments

The author is sincerely indebted to the many teachers who have shared their ideas about unit teaching and who through their candid observations have kept the author's attention focused on the classroom. Appreciation is also expressed to the several anonymous reviewers whose comments were extremely helpful in preparing this revision; their influence is apparent.

Specific mention is due Sue Elkins for editing assistance, Judy McCracken for her insightful revisions, and above all, Judy Tate, Rita Shields, Julie Chappell Neubauer, and Sherry Muirhead for their patience and tolerance in typing the manuscript.

To my wife, Marie, and my children, Brad, Brett, Joy, Blake, and Janelle, "thanks" again.

# 1

# Unit Teaching
# in Perspective

Among the instructional methodologies that a teacher may elect to employ, unit teaching is probably unique. This method's uniqueness is not related to its complexity nor to its application to specific learner deficits. It relates instead to the method's comprehensiveness and the array of teaching skills required to use it. When unit teaching is analyzed from the perspective of skills involved, it becomes apparent that the method is eclectic. A teacher must be able to construct an instructional unit as well as implement it. Unit implementation places the teacher in the roles of an instructional manager, a monitor of individual progress, and an extemporaneous developer of learning experiences. Unit teaching features that contribute to its uniqueness include the following:

- Units must be developed.
- Unit development entails curriculum decisions.
- Unit teaching is particularly applicable to group instruction, but individual differences must also be accommodated.
- Unit teaching is temporal, that is, teachers must capitalize on current events to maintain interest and to reinforce instruction.
- Teacher-made supplemental materials are important ingredients.
- Pupil assessment on a scheduled and cumulative basis is required in unit teaching just as in other instructional modes.
- Units of instruction represent curriculum elements. Thus, teachers must continually monitor unit content in reference to established curriculum.
- Unit teaching allows teachers to be sensitive to the needs, interests, and backgrounds of students. It also calls for on-the-spot decisions in terms of what to teach and what not to teach, when child-related events occur. Such events may include social problems experienced by a particular child or an expression of interest by a group.

1

The list could be extended, but it is sufficient to illustrate the range of teaching skills involved. The skill that obviously stands out pertains to development. While most teachers modify and occasionally design teaching materials, unit teaching requires independent material development. There is no alternative. It is not the need to develop units so much as the consequence of teacher-developed instructional material that accents the necessity for development skills.

For example, when a teacher modifies a lesson, designs a work sheet, or builds a series of activities to supplement instruction, the emphasis is generally on a particular skill or concept. Units are much more inclusive. When a teacher develops a unit of instruction and subsequently teaches the unit, the content includes a variety of skills, social concepts, and considerable information. In other words, the unit represents a larger portion of the child's instructional program—the curriculum. This is particularly true if the teacher implements several units during the year. In essence, the unit represents a substantial portion of the child's curriculum. Thus, teachers should take the developmental process of constructing units seriously. If units were readily available as instructional packages, teachers would not need to be concerned with their development. As this is rarely the case, most teachers find it necessary to produce their own units to meet their pupils' instructional needs.

Unit teaching is by no means a new instructional approach, but is probably one of the oldest teaching methods. It has been extensively utilized by classroom teachers in social studies and in language arts. As a total instructional approach, it has been most popular among teachers of self-contained special classes for the mentally retarded. Here again, the unit method has a long history.

The characteristic problem in the use of units relates to the arbitrary manner in which they have been developed. In general, teachers have constructed their own units, taught them, evaluated them, and, in turn, revised them for use with subsequent groups of children. Each teacher has used his or her own format and steps in unit preparation. They worked well but were unique to the developer and of little use to other teachers. Although considerable curriculum content was covered by units, there was no curriculum accountability in terms of unit contributions to the curriculum. To determine what curriculum aspects were included in units, it was necessary to review the completed units after the fact. There has also been the problem of teachers' failing to capitalize on the unit's potential. They have often designed activities around a theme without fully exploring the implications of the unit topic. Consequently, many skills and/or concepts that could have been taught as an integral part of the respective units were not. The teacher did not consider them in the unit development process.

These concerns represent the rationale for this book. The application of the unit method described in subsequent chapters may not be substantially different from other discussions. But the stress placed on the systematic development and organization of units does fill a void in the literature.

## Unit Teaching: Appropriate for Whom?

The first edition of this book was oriented toward teachers assigned to self-contained special classes for the mentally retarded or teachers in other instructional settings interested in unit teaching. The reason for this was the author's concern for the quality of units being incorporated into Special Education programs. When appropriate, the application of unit instruction to other populations was stressed, but in general, the first edition was narrow in its suggested application of unit teaching. The intent was not to restrict the application of unit teaching to a particular group but to accent its relevance to the mentally retarded. In this edition, an attempt has been made to broaden the perspective. Although the application of the technique has been enlarged, the emphasis on systematic development procedures remains the same. In other words, units to be used with students in so-called regular classes should be no less well-designed and effectively implemented.

Unit teaching is a desirable instructional approach for any student population. Certainly, arguments can be made in favor of applying the method to groups of specific students. But in reality, unit teaching is a highly generic instructional approach that allows skills and concepts to be couched in the context of themes meaningful to students. Thus, units take on both informational and skill development missions. The question of application to varying student populations is not a question of appropriateness, since the content is teacher-pupil determined. Rather the question is two-fold: the amount of emphasis to be devoted to unit teaching, and the organizational format in which unit instruction is offered. The most extensive use of units (in terms of time allocation) occurs in social studies and language arts in the regular class and in special classes within Special Education. "Extensive use" means a continuous series of units of sufficient scope to provide approximately one-third to one-half the instruction offered. In other settings, units are more likely to be included as separate instructional units than as part of a unit-based curriculum. In both cases, unit teaching is important to the curriculum, but the difference in the emphasis tends to be related to the student population and/or the setting. The organizational format question also relates to the amount of emphasis to be given to unit teaching. In situations where occasional units are taught, teachers are more likely to be less formal in their approach to constructing units. The opposite is true when a substantial portion of the curriculum is committed to unit teaching.

From one point of view, the question of whom unit teaching should be used with depends more on teacher variables than on learner characteristics. Teacher skills in terms of teaching techniques and preferred teaching styles probably affect the decision to use or not use units more than information about the target student group. This does not negate the importance of considering pupil data in selecting teaching strategies. However, it suggests that unit teaching applies to children in general, and that the primary factor relates to teacher capabilities in employing the unit technique. Circumstances in which pupil variables dominate the decision to use units occur when the student target group has characteristics that demand serious consideration of the unit method. Such children might include the mentally retarded, disadvantaged, disturbed, or hearing-impaired. The primary learner characteristics that make units highly desirable relate to the need for embedding the teaching of skills and concepts in information and experiences highly meaningful to the learner and to the need for applied experiences. Units also provide more options for students requiring concrete instructional techniques.

## Instructional Trends and Unit Teaching

It would be presumptuous to suggest that there is a national trend in the popularity of unit teaching. A review of the literature would reveal that little attention is being given specifically to this technique. The predominant emphasis is on individualized instruction, specifying behaviorally stated objectives, and employing criterion measures as an approach to pupil assessment. However, if unit teaching is viewed as an eclectic approach involving a variety of techniques, then most of these educational trends have implications for teachers interested in unit teaching. Moreover, if the current trends are viewed from the perspective of the conditions they create, then much can be gained by teachers' examining these trends as they relate to unit teaching. Obviously, teachers should examine educational trends regardless of their instructional orientation. However, in analyzing new approaches, trends, or ideas, it is helpful to have a frame of reference. Teachers can use their teaching style, teaching assignment, or a particular methodology such as unit teaching as a frame of reference. This is not to suggest that a teacher should seek to evaluate each trend only in terms of its application to his or her situation. Rather, the trend should be approached from the perspective of what it represents and the implications for a particular reference in teaching style or methodology. For purposes of illustration, selected trends will be commented on in terms of their relationship to unit teaching.

*Open School Models*   The movement toward the open school concept of education places considerable emphasis on pupil initiative and places the teacher in an "engineer" role. Individual learner performance is closely monitored, and the student is given considerable freedom in pursuing personal interests. Instructional approaches that allow pupil-initiated experiences to occur are encouraged. The implications for unit teaching of the open school model are two-fold. First, in most open schools the climate is highly conducive to unit-related activities. Pupils are encouraged to create products and to work cooperatively on mutual projects. Thus, teachers willing to modify units for small group efforts and capable of guiding students as participants in unit design will be able to use units effectively in the open school model. On the other hand, teachers who feel that they must control the instruction through their unit teaching will not be as successful, or they will find themselves distorting the open school concept and employing traditional methods under the guise of the open school model.

The second implication pertains to the team teaching often found in this model. Participating teachers may find it necessary to restrict the skills and concepts included in unit teaching to those instructional areas for which they are primarily responsible on the team. However, this restriction is compensated for by their having access to the experience and expertise of other team members in unit design. An additional related feature of the open school model is the frequent use of classroom interest centers, which can be capitalized on to the advantage of units. The primary negative implication pertains to the necessity of monitoring individual student performance. This is often done at the behavioral objective level. In unit teaching, this task added to development responsibilities results in a major time commitment by the teacher.

*Due Process*    The due process issue relating to student rights may seem far removed from unit teaching. However, it must be noted that one of the major concerns of the due process issue is the question of whether a child's educational program is appropriate and efficient. The emphasis is on accountability. Few teaching methods provide so comprehensive a source of accountability evidence as unit teaching. For example, a well-designed unit clearly illustrates the content covered. Teachers who execute units effectively also systematically collect data on student progress. If the planning procedures described in this book are implemented, teachers will be in a position to provide complete information on the instructional program taught to the students assigned to them. This does not guarantee that the program is appropriate for every child, but it does clearly provide a source of information for making decisions on program appropriateness. This particular example is offered not as an artificial or contrived example, but to illustrate the point that a teacher need not withdraw from emphasizing unit teaching merely because of a trend toward accountability. Unit teaching provides an excellent approach to instructional accountability.

*Competency-Based Instruction*    The current emphasis on competency-based instruction represents a unique trend; its impact is on teacher training as well as on elementary and secondary education. Unit instruction is directly related to the objectives and the pre- and post-testing of performance against criterion measures used in competency-based instruction. Of all the trends, this probably will have the most significant influence on unit teaching, particularly on the design and construction of units, rather than the actual process of unit teaching. Most competency-based programs include the development of modules. If you examine samples of modules, it is apparent that they approximate mini units. The emphasis on module development should yield additional insights into the improvement of unit designs.

*Student Participation in Curriculum Decisions*    Although they are not necessarily part of a visible trend with its own identity, students are seeking and being given more of a role in influencing their curriculum. The impact goes beyond representation on planning committees at the secondary level. Teachers are being encouraged to employ more democratic procedures in selecting content, allowing students to elect options in satisfying instructional requirements. One of the strengths of unit teaching is that it allows for student participation in the planning process. Units can actually be designed so that students carry much of the instructional load through projects, interest centers, and planning activities.

*Mainstreaming*    The previously described general trends are not specific to particular groups of students or to specific instructional settings. There is a movement occurring that has implications for general as well as special educators. It relates to the current emphasis on alternative approaches to educating exceptional children. For several years, the self-contained special class has been the primary instructional model for providing educational programming to exceptional children. Recently, it has become apparent that this has been a narrow approach. It has been sufficiently demonstrated that a variety of instructional alternatives is appropriate to exceptional children and that no one approach is best. Although this may be an oversimplification of the legal and social history leading to this position, it is clear that there is a trend in Special Education to move away from considering the special class the primary instructional option for exceptional children and to view it as merely one of several options.[1] Integral to the trend is a shift of responsibility for exceptional children from special educators to regular classroom teachers, with Special Education personnel assuming a support role. The popular term for this trend is "mainstreaming." It implies that all children, to whatever degree possible, should remain in the mainstream of education. For exceptional children, it suggests that the focus be on assisting the regular classroom teacher, through training, consultation, and instructional resources, to meet the exceptional child's needs within their regular class. The exceptional child may, if necessary, attend a resource room or receive tutorial assistance part-time. But the child's primary identification remains with the regular class, and the regular class teacher assumes primary responsibility for his or her instruction. The self-contained special class becomes an option for those children whose learning problems are sufficiently serious to preclude their benefiting from regular class affiliation. As a result, the special class is used less frequently as an instructional option for mildly handicapped students, while it remains a viable option for children with more severe learning problems. Even in the latter situation, the special class option is viewed as tentative, and the child's placement as temporary. When appropriate, the emphasis is on shifting the child's participation from the self-contained to the regular classroom. The implications of this trend are many; it is mentioned here simply to illustrate the implications for unit teaching.

The obvious implication of mainstreaming is the increased instructional responsibility assumed by the regular class teacher. The range of abilities in the regular class will probably not be extended, since many exceptional children have always been assigned to regular classes. However, the number of children with severe learning problems requiring specialized instruction will increase. Instead of having an occasional student who is difficult to program, regular class teachers can anticipate having many classes with students having a full range of abilities. The principles of mainstreaming call for the provision of support services to the teacher and, if necessary, directed to the child. The intent is not merely to place exceptional children in regular classes. The provision of support services necessitates the participation of additional personnel. In most cases when exceptional children are returned to the mainstream, the child's instructional program will involve at least two teachers—the regular classroom teacher and the resource teacher. This arrangement in itself does not significantly affect the application of unit teaching. However, there are a series of related effects of mainstreaming that do have implications for curriculum and for the unit teaching method.

Figure 1 compares the characteristics of self-contained classes with alternative models—mainstreaming. A review of this figure shows two major implications for unit teaching: more restrictive time-frames available for instruction, and increased need for attending to the specific instructional needs and performance of exceptional children who are mainstreamed. The time restriction is the result of moving from a self-contained situation, in which the teacher not only was assigned to the same group of children full-time but also exercised considerable control over the curriculum, to a situation in which the exceptional child is integrated with other children and no longer separated for instructional purposes. Where the special class teacher de-

---

1. A detailed bibliography of references pertaining to mainstreaming appears at the end of this chapter. The author elected not to discuss the trend fully because the subject is covered more extensively in several other sources available to most readers.

| Self-Contained | Feature | Alternative Models | Curriculum Consequence |
|---|---|---|---|
| 1. One teacher has primary responsibility for instruction. | *Teacher Variable* | 1. Responsibility for instruction is shared by at least two teachers. | 1.1. Each teacher has a different area of instructional responsibility.<br><br>1.2. Coordination in programming and material selection is essential.<br><br>1.3. One teacher is always a regular class teacher who must make changes in his/her regular curriculum to the degree possible.<br><br>1.4. Control of curriculum variance is more difficult to accomplish. |
| 2. Placement is basically full-time. | *Time Variable* | 2. Placement is part-time for designated periods of time. | 2.1. Decisions must be made on what instruction takes place where and when.<br><br>2.2. Time restraints preclude use of curricula in resource rooms which are integrated and require large time-frames.<br><br>2.3. The restricted time-frame reduces the teacher's option for reinforcing skills and concepts throughout the day which were previously introduced through specific lessons. |

| Self-Contained | Variable | Alternative Models |
|---|---|---|
| 3. Focus is on a total instructional program. | *Curriculum Variable* | 3. Focus is more on specific skills and concepts with instructional responsibility shared among teachers.<br>3.1. Local curriculum planning and development are more complicated because of having to relate areas of instruction to different settings and teachers.<br>3.2. Need for teachers to gain access to instructional activities within curricula or materials that relate to specific skills and concepts increases. |
| 4. Administrative control more aligned with Special Education director or person designated responsible for Special Education. | *Administrative Variable* | 4. Administrative responsibility more directly aligned with building principal.<br>4.1. More control of curriculum by regular education.<br>4.2. Loss of flexibility for applied instruction such as field trips, etc. |
| 5. Reasonable homogeneity of pupil characteristics in class. | *Pupil Variable* | 5. Broad heterogeneity of pupil characteristics in regular class; more resources specific to the instructional problems of children served.<br>5.1. Decision-making of regular class teacher increases and becomes more significant. Resource teacher requires more diagnostic information. |

**Figure 1. Characteristics of Self-Contained and Alternative Models—Curriculum Consequences**

Reprinted with permission from E. L. Meyen, G. A. Vergason, R. J. Whelan, eds., *Alternatives for Teaching Exceptional Children* (Denver, Colo.: Love Publishing Co., 1975).

signed units specifically for exceptional children, the regular classroom teacher must now incorporate activities into units that also accommodate the needs of exceptional children. If districts truly develop mainstreaming programs and do not merely integrate exceptional children into regular classes, sufficient resource people should be available to consult with teachers in the design of instructional units. Regular class teachers are likely to find that exceptional children, particularly mildly mentally retarded students, will require considerable remedial instruction in the skill areas and that unit instruction will become a major vehicle for reinforcing the application of such skills. Teachers in mainstreaming situations will also find that units provide an excellent means for providing meaningful repetition. Consideration should also be given to peer teaching techniques in using units in mainstreamed classrooms.

It would be inappropriate to suggest that the trend toward placement of exceptional children in regular classes will lessen the difficulty of preparing units or create a better climate for unit teaching. It will require more planning and more emphasis on evaluating pupil performance. In the process of developing units for mainstreaming programs, teachers should experiment with planning procedures and group instructional techniques that are applicable to classes whose range of abilities and behavioral characteristics vary extensively.

## Prerequisites to Unit Teaching

Although it is not reasonable to suggest that there are ten rules to good unit teaching or that there are absolute prerequisites which must be met by teachers desiring to teach units, certain teaching behaviors do enhance the effectiveness of unit teaching. These behaviors are not unique to unit teaching. In many ways, they are essential to good teaching in general. Individually, the behaviors may be insignificant, but collectively they result in successful unit teaching.

*Teacher confidence* is extremely important. Unless teachers have confidence in themselves, the responsibilities of making curriculum decisions, designing units, and guiding the behavior of students may be too much. Some teachers are more comfortable in employing techniques that do not require them to construct material. Still others prefer more individualized approaches.

*Knowledge in curriculum content* in the subject area(s) involved in unit teaching is essential. The teacher's personal knowledge often becomes a primary resource in structuring unit content. Thus, unless the teacher is reasonably knowledgeable about curriculum skills and concepts, difficulty will be encountered in the selection and sequence of skills within units.

*Sensitivity* to the personal needs and behavioral patterns of students is always important, but is particularly so in unit teaching. Units allow teachers to alter instructional plans to accommodate current events and to orient units to the specific interests of students.

*Group teaching skills* represent probably the single most important teaching skill applicable to unit teaching. Included in the skills are questioning techniques, the ability to differentiate reinforcements when working with a group, being a good listener, ability to organize instruction and learners for participation in instruction, and being responsive to students in a convincing manner. The last skill is important. Students need attention and, above all, need to feel confident that the teacher is attending to them personally.

*Flexibility* becomes a virtue in unit teaching. It is not feasible to maintain a rigid time schedule. Teachers will encounter situations in which plans must be changed in order to gain closure on an experience. In other circumstances, students may not be responsive to a particular lesson, and, with little notice, the teacher must shift to a relevant but contrasting activity.

These behaviors describe mature teaching behaviors. To a degree it is true that unit teaching requires a skilled teacher. Beginning teachers will find that the challenge of developing and teaching units is a good route to developing these essential skills. Once skilled in unit teaching, the teacher can probably be successful in implementing almost any teaching technique.

## Summary

The intent of this chapter was to assist the reader in gaining a broad perspective on the process of unit teaching, not to develop any particular set of skills relative to unit teaching. The purpose was to convey the view that unit teaching requires a variety of teaching skills and that, because of the curriculum implications of unit teaching, the development of units warrants systematic planning.

SELECTED REFERENCES FOR ALTERNATIVE PROGRAMMING
FOR EXCEPTIONAL CHILDREN

ABESON, A. "Recent Developments in the Courts." *The Right to an Education Mandate.* Minneapolis: University of Minnesota, Leadership Training Institute/ Special Education, 1973.

ADAMS, C. "A Program for Mainstreaming at Stevens Point." Bureau Memorandum 13 (1972):9-11.

ADAMSON, G. and VAN ETTEN, G. "Zero Reject Model Revisited: A Workable Alternative." *Exceptional Children* 38 (1972):735-738.

ANDERSON, B. R. "Mainstreaming is the Name for a New Idea; Learning Resources Center for Special Education." *School Management* 17 (1973):28-30.

BEERY, K. E. "Mainstreaming: A Problem and an Opportunity for General Education." *Focus on Exceptional Children* 6 (1974).

———. *Models for Mainstreaming*. San Rafael, Calif.: Dimensions Publishing Co., 1968.

BEERY, K. E., et al. *The Guts To Grow*. San Rafael, Calif.: Dimensions Publishing Co., 1974.

BESSANT, H. P. "Mainstreaming in Education." *Educating and Training of Mentally Retarded* 9 (1974):96-97.

BIRCH, J. W. *Mainstreaming: Educable Mentally Retarded Children in Regular Classes*. Minneapolis: University of Minnesota, Leadership Training Institute/Special Education, 1974.

BLATT, B. *Public Policy and the Education of Children with Special Needs*. Proceedings of the Conference on the Categorical/Noncategorical Issue in Special Education. Columbia: Special Education Department, University of Missouri, 1971.

BRENTON, M. "Mainstreaming the Handicapped." *Today's Education* 63 (1974): 20-25.

BROOKS, B. L. and BRANSFORD, L. S. "Modification of Teachers' Attitudes Toward Exceptional Children." *Exceptional Children* 38 (1971):259-260.

BRUININKS, R. H. *Problems and Needs in Developing Alternatives to Special Classes for Mildly Retarded Children*. Paper presented at 1st Annual Studies Conference in School Psychology, Temple University, Philadelphia, June 1972.

CHAFFIN, J. "Will the Real 'Mainstreaming' Program Please Stand Up! (Or . . . Should Dunn Have Done It?)." *Focus on Exceptional Children* 6 (1974):1.

CHRISTOPHERSON, J. "Special Children in Regular Preschool: Some Administrative Roles." *Childhood Education* 49 (1972):138-140.

COUNCIL FOR EXCEPTIONAL CHILDREN. *Regular Class Placement/Special Classes; A Selective Bibliography*. Arlington, Va.: Information Center on Exceptional Children, 1972.

DAILEY, R. "Dimensions and Issues in 74: Tapping into the Special Education Grapevine." *Exceptional Children* 40 (1974):503-506.

DENO, E. N., ed. *Instructional Alternatives for Exceptional Children*. Arlington, Va.: Council for Exceptional Children, 1973.

FINE, M. J. "Attitudes of Regular and Special Class Teachers Toward the EMR Child." *Exceptional Children* 33 (1967):429-430.

FOUNTAIN VALLEY SCHOOL DISTRICT. *Handicapped Children in the Regular Classroom*. Fountain Valley, Calif.: ESEA Title III Project 1232.

GOODMAN, H.; GOTTLIEB, J.; and HARRISON, R. "Social Acceptance of EMR's Integrated into a Nongraded Elementary School." *American Journal of Mental Deficiency* 76 (1972):412-417.

GOTTLIEB, J. and BUDOFF, M. "Attitudes Toward School by Segregated and Integrated Retarded Children: A Study and Experience Validation." *Studies in Learning Potential* 2 (1972):35.

———. "Social Acceptability of Retarded Children in Nongraded Schools Differing in Architecture." *American Journal of Mental Deficiency* 78 (1973):15-19.

GOTTLIEB, J. and DAVIS, J. "Social Acceptance of EMR Children During Overt Behavioral Interactions." *American Journal of Mental Deficiency* 78 (1973): 141-143.

HARTUP, W. W. "Peer Interaction and Social Organization." In P. H. Mussen, ed., *Carmichael's Manual of Child Psychology,* vol. 2. New York: John Wiley and Sons, 1970.

HOFNER, D. "A Shift in Emphasis in Programming for Handicapped Children." *Exceptional Children* 39 (1972):59-60.

JONES, R. L. "Labels and Stigma in Special Education." *Exceptional Children* 38 (1972):553-564.

———. "Student Views of Special Placement and Their Own Special Classes: A Clarification." *Exceptional Children* 41 (1974):22-31.

JORDAN, J. B. "Invisible College on Mainstreaming Addresses Critical Factors in Implementing Programs." *Exceptional Children* 41 (1974):31-35.

MAJOR, I. "How Do We Accept the Handicapped?" *Elementary School Journal* 61 (1961):328-330.

MANN, P. H., ed. *Mainstream Special Education.* Proceedings of the University of Miami Conference on Special Education in the Great Cities, Council for Exceptional Children, 1974.

MARTIN, E. W. "Individualism and Behaviorism as Future Trends in Educating Handicapped Children." *Exceptional Children* 38 (1972):517-526.

———. "Some Thoughts on Mainstreaming." *Exceptional Children* 41 (1974):150-153.

NOVOTNEY, J. M. "The Principal: The Key to Educational Change." *Catholic School Journal* 68 (1968):68-73.

PALMIERI, J. C. "Learning Problem Children in the Open Concept Class." *Academic Therapy* 13 (1973):305.

PEPE, H. J. "A Comparison of the Effectiveness of Itinerant and Resource Room Model Programs Designed to Serve Children with Learning Disabilities." Unpublished doctoral dissertation, University of Kansas, 1973.

PERTSCH, C. F. "A Comparative Study of the Progress of Sub-Normal Pupils in the Grades and in Special Classes." Unpublished doctoral dissertation, Teachers College, Columbia University, 1936.

PORTER, R. B. "If Not Special Classes, What?" *Training School Bulletin* 65 (1968): 87-88.

REGER, R. "Let's Get Rid of Special Classes, But . . ." *Journal of Learning Disabilities* 5 (1972):442-443.

REYNOLDS, M. C., and DAVIS, M., eds. *Exceptional Children in Regular Classrooms.* Minneapolis: Department of Audio-Visual Extension, University of Minnesota, 1972.

SIMCHES, R. F. "The Inside Outsiders." *Exceptional Children* 37 (1970):5-15.

VACC, N. A. "A Study of Emotionally Disturbed Children in Regular and Special Classes." *Exceptional Children* 35 (1968):197-206.

VAN ETTEN, G., and ADAMSON, G. "The Fail-Save Program: A Special Education Continuum." *Instructional Alternatives for Exceptional Children,* pp. 156-165, Reston, Va.: Council for Exceptional Children, 1973.

WALKER, V. S. "The Efficacy of the Resource Room for Educable Retarded Children." *Exceptional Children* 40 (1974):288-289.

———. "The Resource Room Model for Educating Educable Mentally Retarded Children." Unpublished doctoral dissertation, Temple University, 1972.

WARNER, F.; THROPP, R.; and WALSH, S. "Attitudes of Children Toward Their Special Class Placement." *Exceptional Children* 40 (1973):37-38.

YATES, J. R. "Model for Preparing Regular Classroom Teachers for Mainstreaming." *Exceptional Children* 39 (1973):471-472.

# 2

# Curriculum Development
# in Perspective

Historically, teachers have served on curriculum planning committees. Numerous curriculum guides, courses of study, and, more recently, assortments of behaviorally stated objectives have been produced. Typically, the focus has been on producing a product, and insufficient attention has been given to training teachers in curriculum development skills. Consequently, teachers frequently approach participation on such committees with only a vague idea of how they are to complete the assignment, although they are fully cognizant that something will be produced. This product orientation has tended to interfere with providing teachers needed preparation in the area of development skills. Master teachers are not necessarily expert in the curriculum development process, although in general they possess the appropriate frame of reference and readiness to acquire development skills. Too often, administrators assign teachers to curriculum planning committees without considering what is required to complete the assigned tasks. This author strongly supports teacher participation in curriculum development but believes that certain skills and information should be prerequisite to their participation. To delegate curriculum development responsibility to teachers without providing them the necessary support in the form of resources, training, and leadership places them at an unwarranted disadvantage.

Although this chapter presents an orientation to the curriculum development process, it is not a short course in curriculum development. Throughout this book, references are made to systematic planning relative to designing instructional units. In this chapter, unit teaching is placed in the curriculum context. This is an intentional attempt to remind readers that whenever a teacher organizes content and then constructs a teaching activity, curriculum development is taking place.

The cumulative effect on a child participating in several instructional units is that the experiences taught via units become a major portion of his or her curriculum. Thus, teachers must be aware of the collective impact of units on a child's curriculum. Those who employ the unit teaching method must be extremely sensitive to the overall curriculum implications of unit teaching. Readers are encouraged to pursue additional study in curriculum development. (Selected references on curriculum planning appear at the end of this chapter.)

The terms *curriculum, instructional program, courses of study,* and *curriculum guides,* to mention a few, are sometimes used interchangeably to describe what a particular student population should be taught. Although precise definitions for all processes and activities that educators engage in while carrying out curriculum development may not be necessary, it is important to differentiate between methodology and curriculum. This concern relates primarily to the confusion that surrounds instructional planning for students in situations where teachers are required to make major curriculum decisions. These occur whenever a child does not profit sufficiently from the regular established curricula. In some cases, these children are retarded, learning-disabled, or emotionally disturbed. In other cases, these are children without handicapping conditions who are experiencing learning problems to a degree that the originally planned instructional program needs to be modified.

Most of the educational decisions teachers are required to make are instructional in nature; they pertain to remediation of identified deficits and to techniques for enhancing the child's acquisition of particular skills and concepts. Only when a teacher encounters a child whose learning problem is serious is he or she called on to make major decisions regarding how that child is to be taught and the sequence in which the skills are to be presented. For the most part, teachers work from a base of prescribed curricula inherent in either guidelines or basal series and make their decisions to modify the program to meet the needs of individual children. This is also true in terms of teaching the majority of mildly handicapped children. For example, the child with a speech problem may receive therapy from the speech therapist and/or participate in activities aimed at speech improvement that are provided by the regular teacher. The curriculum, in terms of what will be included in the child's education, will probably not be altered by the need for speech therapy. In the case of children with sensory defects, the task becomes one of employing techniques and materials designed to maximize their learning of the regular curriculum. The sensory defect in itself will not substantially alter the curriculum content, although the rate of learning may be affected. The situation is quite different, however, when the child is limited intellectually, as in the case of the mentally retarded. Here we encounter the problem of having to make major curriculum decisions on *what* is to be taught as well as *how*.

As long as we are concerned with children whose learning problems are remedial in nature, or children who can progress in the regular curriculum with specialized instruction, the responsibilities for curriculum development are shared among regular and special teachers and curriculum consultants in general.

In situations where students are grouped for instruction because of learning characteristics that warrant special attention, additional responsibilities for curriculum decisions fall to the classroom teacher assigned to that group. As more exceptional children are placed in regular classes, teacher involvement in curriculum decisions also increases. Merely placing exceptional children in regular classes will not reduce the need for curriculum planning.

The importance of teachers' being familiar with the curriculum development process is best illustrated by the history of Special Education in planning educational programs for the mild mentally retarded. In this area, the tendency has been to establish special classes and to delegate responsibility for curriculum development to the special class teacher. Each teacher, in turn, has developed a curriculum based on what he or she felt was most appropriate to the needs of children assigned to the special class, thus producing a curriculum unique to the teacher. Other special class teachers in the same system repeated the process of planning curriculum individually. In the resulting situation, the retarded child encountered a new curriculum as he or she was transferred to other special classes or progressed through special class programs in a particular district. These circumstances should not occur. They have happened because of the general lack of investment in curriculum development and the insufficient support being provided teachers in their curriculum development efforts.

Curriculum research and, in many cases, curriculum planning relative to what specific groups of children should be taught, and in what sequence, have not received sufficient attention. Too often, the teacher has resorted to a cut-and-paste approach to curriculum development, because of a lack of direction in curriculum development literature and the absence of good local support. Although the pattern has been somewhat different in the regular classroom, in that teachers have had access to commercially prepared materials, basal series, and extensive curriculum guidelines, as the responsibility for teaching children with learning problems is extended to regular class teachers, their need for curriculum development skills will also increase. Teachers, in general, must be prepared to participate in the process of curriculum development. Such participation will take at least two forms: first, responding to children whose needs dictate the development of a modified curriculum; and second, participating in subject, school, or district-wide curriculum planning.

## Defining Curriculum

The term *curriculum* is frequently and varyingly defined as the courses offered, the overall experience provided a child by the school, the program included in a particular subject field, or in some cases, the sum total of experiences afforded school-age children regardless of school sponsorship. The global nature of such definitions confounds the real differences among them. To merely talk about what occurs in an educational setting as being the curriculum implies that there is little order or planning involved. As one reads curriculum literature, it becomes apparent that while the term *curriculum* is often carelessly applied, the curriculum development process is complex, and the decision making that results in curriculum structure is by no means arbitrary.

It also becomes apparent that there are differing views on the relationship of curriculum and instruction as implemented in the classroom by the teacher. Some writers take a comprehensive perspective of curriculum and subsume instruction and teaching methods under that label, along with content specification. Others view curriculum as representing the input into the instructional program. This view suggests that given the input, teachers may select those methods that work best for them in teaching the curriculum. In other words, the curriculum may be standardized, but the instructional programs will vary by virtue of the different methods that teachers employ.

Contrasting views on curriculum are expressed in the writings of Phenix and Johnson. Phenix defines curriculum as

> simply a name for the organized pattern of the schools' educational program. A complete description of the curriculum has at least three components: (1) What is studied—the "content" or "subject matter" of instruction, (2) How the study and teaching are done—the "method" of instruction, and (3) When the various subjects are presented—the order of instruction.[1]

This comprehensive view of curriculum incorporates the instructional program along with structuring the content into a single curriculum concept.

Johnson has developed a model that conceptualizes curriculum as an output of one system and an input of another. He states:

> Accepted usage identifies curriculum with "planned learning experiences." This definition is unsatisfactory, however, if "curriculum" is to be distinguished from "instruction." Whether experiences are viewed subjectively in terms of the sensibility of the experiencing individual or objectively in terms of his actions in a particular setting, there is in either case no experience until an interaction between the individual and his environment actually occurs. Clearly, such interaction characterizes *instruction,* not curriculum. A concept of curriculum that limits it to a *post hoc* account of instruction is of little value. Surely,

---

1. Philip H. Phenix, "Curriculum," in *Contemporary Thought on Public School Curriculum,* ed. E. C. Short and G. D. Marconnit (Dubuque: Wm. C. Brown Co. Publishers, 1968), p. 9.

curriculum must play some role in *guiding* instruction. If so, it must be viewed as anticipatory, not reportorial. Curriculum implies intent.

Surely, too, a useful concept of curriculum must leave some room for creativity and individual style in instruction. In other words, decisions regarding the learning experiences to be provided are the result of instructional planning, not of curriculum development. The curriculum, though it may limit the range of possible experiences, cannot specify them. Curriculum must be defined in other terms.

In view of the shortcomings of the currently popular definition, it is here stipulated that curriculum is as a *structured series of intended learning outcomes. Curriculum prescribes* (or at least anticipates) the *results* of instruction. It does not prescribe the *means,* i.e., the activities, materials, or even the instructional content, to be used in achieving results. In specifying outcomes to be sought curriculum is concerned with *ends,* but at the level of attainable learning products, not at the more remote level at which these ends are justified. In other words, curriculum indicates *what* is to be learned, not *why* it should be learned.[2]

This approach encourages one to think in terms of a three-dimensional construct including (1) the developmental process, (2) the composite of learning experiences delineated and ordered through the development process, and (3) the instructional program which allows students to interact in the educational milieu of their environment. The second dimension would represent the curriculum. Differentiating curriculum from instruction makes it somewhat easier for teachers to identify their role in the educational process. While they have a role to play in curriculum development, as well as in implementing the curriculum through the instructional program, they may frequently find themselves in a situation in which they are asked to carry out an instructional program compatible with a curriculum they have played a minimal role in developing.

The curriculum should provide objectives and offer a basic design for the instructional program. However, teachers should be free to employ those methods that work best for them in accommodating the curriculum. The methods they use will also entail teaching content not specified in the curriculum, especially when they plan experiences that will allow the student to learn prescribed skills, concepts, and information. Teachers will find it necessary to couch the teaching of certain curriculum aspects in content relevant to the learner but beyond the basic curriculum requirements, for example, information on sports, orientation to specific job opportunities, or experiences related to something unique to a child's development.

For the most part, teachers are responsible for the instructional program. While the curriculum specifies the outcomes they should strive for, they are generally free to use methods of their choice and to select a major

2. Mauritz Johnson, Jr., "Definitions and Models in Curriculum Theory," *Educational Theory* (April 1967), p. 128. Used by permission of the publisher.

portion of the supplemental instructional materials. Most likely they will also have a voice in choosing the basal series that may be used in certain subjects. The atmosphere they establish and their general teaching style are their own and are not necessarily dependent on the curriculum. Consequently, although several teachers in a school system may be implementing the same curriculum, they may vary considerably in the instructional techniques they employ. Each, of course, must be familiar with the detailed objectives and content of the curriculum.

## The Curriculum Development Process

As a frame of reference, let's look at a general example of the curriculum development process. The major determinant in developing curriculum for children centers on the consequences of the child's deficits in terms of learning. For example, mentally retarded children represent a group whose primary educational problems relate to limited intelligence and social ineptness. In structuring a curriculum for them, consideration must be given to the influence these limitations will have on their curriculum needs. Figure 2 illustrates one way of looking at the relationship between the curriculum development process and instructional programs for the mentally retarded.

*Curriculum Sources* In Figure 2, we begin by looking at the universe of knowledge, skills, and values that could potentially be included in the school curriculum. It is apparent that if our target population is composed of retarded students, a circumscribed curriculum is required. If we are concerned with representative children in general, the content of what might be included in the curriculum would be more extensive. At the same time, it might not include some learning experiences which the representative child learns incidentally but which the retarded child must be purposefully taught.

*Curriculum Decisions* A number of decisions must be made in the process of circumscribing the curriculum. These decisions are not mere choices; they involve the task of giving the curriculum dimension in accordance with the educational needs of the population for whom it is being designed. These tasks include formulating objectives, delineating content in reference to the objectives, and ordering the content in a sequential manner. Each of these tasks is influenced by the known characteristics of the student population; in this case, the mentally retarded.

*Curriculum* The model illustrated in Figure 2 places curriculum as the product resulting from curriculum decisions. As a product, it includes the sequentially ordered content planned as input into instructional programs designed for a particular student population. Basically, it specifies the dimen-

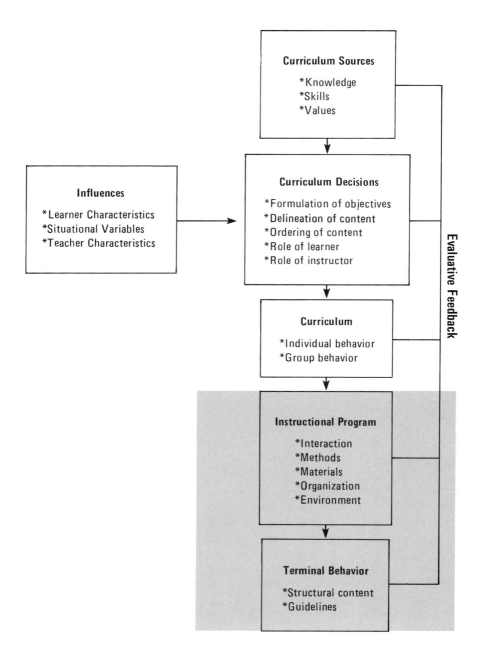

**Figure 2.  Example of Development—Evaluation Process**

sions of *what* and *when*. It may take the form of structured outcomes, which will serve as directives for teachers in carrying out their instructional programs. The curriculum places restrictions on the instructional program only to the degree that restrictions are inherent in the subject matter. These restrictions are not general, but certain subject matter areas or the nature of some skills do dictate a particular range of appropriate instructional techniques. For example, the teaching of multiplication facts would be difficult to accomplish through a discussion approach.

*Instructional Programs*    Operationally, the instructional program can be defined as the experience provided the learner in the educational setting. The teacher plans these experiences as a means of implementing the curriculum. Through the instructional program, learners interact with their environment. Within the learning environment, learners interact with their teachers, peers, and materials, as well as with aspects of the school's physical setting. The teacher manipulates environmental components to maximize the child's response to his or her environment. The emphasis is on facilitating the child's progress in attaining the outcomes specified in the curriculum. While teachers may extend their instructional program beyond the dictates of the curriculum, they should be sensitive to the curriculum based on goals for the student. Given the same curriculum, teachers will vary in the instructional methods they employ.

*Terminal Behavior*    The overall impact of the curriculum as executed through the instructional program is ultimately to influence the learner's behavior as he or she progresses through the system. This implies that there are certain accepted concepts about the general nature of learners who have completed the curriculum. These beliefs relate to what they are prepared to do in terms of additional learning, what they are capable of doing at the time they complete the curriculum, and the general social adjustment desired for the particular individual. The goals related to terminal behavior may change as new data are obtained on the group's capabilities and as more effective methods are found.

### Evaluative Feedback

Curriculum development is a continuous process. Successful development relies heavily on formative evaluation. As evidence is acquired that a change should be made in sequence, content, teaching strategies, or curriculum product format, this evidence should be considered. Evaluation is an important element of the development process. The primary evaluation technique employed in curriculum development is field-testing, that is, trying out curriculum activities in situations approximating the intended application. Such evaluation allows for product improvement during the development process. This procedure is typically referred to as *formative evaluation*. As illustrated in the model (Figure 2) evaluation occurs at each step in the development process. Most developers approach curriculum design with an evaluation frame of reference. In some cases, evaluation represents a separate component in the development process.

A second and less frequently applied form of evaluation is *summative evaluation*. This term basically implies testing the effectiveness of the curriculum product once it has reached final form. This is after the benefits of formative evaluation have been applied in the design of a prototype and in the field-testing. In the area of curriculum development, summative evaluation is often delayed until the product is available commercially. Under these circumstances, the teacher as a consumer participates in the summative evaluation. As long as the developer employs good formative evaluation procedures and uses the results to improve the product during the development stages, the final product should prove effective under summative evaluation.

The model presented in Figure 2 is intended to provide teachers with a frame of reference for the ways their instructional programs relate to the curriculum development process. In essence, what they do in their instructional program is dependent on the curriculum. Although teachers should participate throughout the curriculum development process, if they are special class teachers in a small district or even regular class teachers at small attendance centers, it is possible that they will fall heir to the task of determining the curriculum as well as implementing an appropriate instructional program. Under these circumstances, they will be likely to integrate developmental aspects with instructional program planning. The other alternative is to borrow the input resulting from curriculum planning done by other districts and select materials and methods to set an instructional program in motion. The immediate concern is to prepare for teaching their classes. For this reason, additional discussion on curriculum considerations and instructional models is warranted.

**Curriculum Considerations**

In examining commercial versions of curriculum, it is easy to overlook the effort and complex processing that are employed in developing quality curriculum. It may be apparent that a number of persons are involved in the project and that certain evaluation strategies are employed in testing the curriculum. However, the specific development steps are not so obvious. A brief introduction to the curriculum development steps applicable to unit teaching will be presented in Chapter 8. At this point, it is important that the reader be aware of certain factors that warrant consideration in curriculum development. Although curriculum development is not as situation-specific as the instructional program for a selected child, it is not feasible to develop curriculum and then assume it can be implemented without modifications in all settings. It is incumbent on curriculum developers to be sensitive to the conditions under which the proposed curriculum will be implemented. Teachers must approach the implementation of prepared curriculum with the awareness that they will need to make adaptations to apply the curriculum in their particular classroom. Figure 3 illustrates selected variables that must be considered both in curriculum development and in teacher implementation. Too often, teachers are disappointed in curriculum products because they have assumed that the curriculum could be implemented as packaged, and not be affected by local conditions so long as the directions were followed.

Although the variables warranting consideration in curriculum development and implementation are numerous, five basic factors have been selected for discussion: pupil behavior, instructional environment, external supports, established curricula, and teaching style. Although these factors interact considerably, each has its particular influence on curriculum development. In any curriculum development project, these areas should be carefully explored as prerequisites to curriculum development. Collectively, they provide the context in which most curriculum decisions are made.

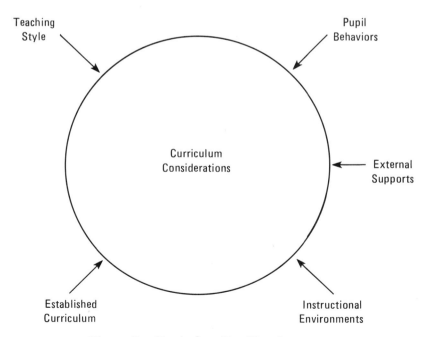

**Figure 3.   Curriculum Considerations**

*Pupil Behavior*    Except in unusual situations where instructional materials are developed around very restricted content, as in designing instructional packages about special events (for example, the 1976 Bicentennial), most curriculum development efforts are aimed at meeting the needs of a specified learner population. Thus, it is important to be maximally familiar with the target population. When classroom teachers prepare instructional units or develop curriculum specifications (see Chapter 8), they are familiar with the target population. It is incumbent on teachers who participate in curriculum development to keep the characteristics of the learner in mind as they make curriculum decisions. It is easy to be sidetracked into attending to the subject matter and focusing on creative ways of teaching while overlooking the unique needs of the target population. Even if you are familiar with the group of children for whom the curriculum is being produced, it is helpful to inventory their characteristics relative to the acquisition of cognitive, motor, and social skills. In addition to overt behavior, it is helpful to keep in mind those environmental factors in the child's history that have influenced current behaviors. These include the child's performance history in school as well as his or her home and community history.

*External Supports*    A serious consideration in any major curriculum development effort is the level of support offered by the administration, such as consultation, budget resources, free time for development, and general leadership. All these are included in the context of external support. A subtle but important support pertains to the reinforcement received by teachers for participating in curriculum development. It may be difficult to identify specific examples of reinforcement. However, with teachers who have previously invested energy in curriculum development projects, it is not difficult to determine their perception of the value placed on their contributions by the administration and by their colleagues.

*Instructional Environment*    The major environment to be concerned with in curriculum development is the classroom(s) where the curriculum will be implemented. In unit teaching, many activities frequently take place outside the classroom. One can determine, in general, the degree to which the classroom and the attendance center are conducive to implementing the proposed curriculum. If experiences are to take place outside school, though, the problem is a little more complex. It is first necessary to determine whether school policy allows for community resource utilization and whether financial reserves are available. These are important considerations that take on added significance when a proposed curriculum change requires unique environmental factors, such as introducing an open school model. Because of the extensive use that unit teaching makes of group and small group techniques, it does make demands on the instructional environment. These should be considered when planning a curriculum involving unit teaching.

*Established Curriculum*   Whenever a curriculum development activity is initiated at the school district level, the current curriculum must be examined. The emphasis is either on revision, replacement, or the addition of a new curriculum element. Thus, the departure point in development is the existing curriculum. Too often, a need for curriculum development emerges as a result of some attempt at assessment of needs. Or special interest groups observe a problem in what they consider to be the instructional program and present it as a major need. In reality the stimulus for curriculum development or revision may not relate to actual needs. A careful curriculum review will often reveal that the problem may not be the curriculum itself but insufficient skill on the part of teachers implementing it or, in some cases, lack of knowledge concerning the curriculum. In cases where the curriculum is clearly in need of revision, it is essential to know what is being revised. If the emphasis is on developing curriculum specifications for unit instruction, the task becomes one of determining which parts of the curriculum will be offered through unit teaching and which through other modes of instruction. In this case, knowledge of the existing curriculum will be a prerequisite to developing specifications for unit instruction. (See Chapter 8.)

*Teaching Style*   Teachers vary in the techniques they employ in their classroom. Given the same curriculum guidelines, two teachers may be equally successful in bringing about appropriate pupil outcomes while using contrasting strategies. Teaching style becomes a serious consideration only when the proposed curriculum requires that specific teaching strategies be employed or makes unusual demands on the teacher in terms of learning new skills or having to create particular classroom arrangements. In general, teaching style is important when selecting a curriculum or new instructional material. Teachers know their own teaching style and can readily determine whether or not a new curriculum or material will require a major change in their teaching behavior.

## Instructional Models

Because it is important for teachers to approach instructional program planning systematically, criteria are required for evaluating the various elements of such programs. The most direct method of determining relevant criteria would be to base decisions regarding the instructional program on directives inherent in the prescribed curriculum. In the absence of such a curriculum, teachers are forced to seek other alternatives.

One alternative is to employ basic criteria with general application to instructional models. Lembo states that an instructional model should meet three conditions; namely, diagnostic, prescriptive, and normative.[3] These criteria are more meaningful when stated as questions.

*Diagnostic:*

>Does your instructional program allow for assessing the functioning levels of individuals and/or the specification of instructional objectives appropriate to their cognitive abilities?

*Prescriptive:*

>Does your instructional program include procedures for individualizing instruction?

*Normative:*

>Do you have criteria that allow you to determine when optimal conditions for learning have not been met, as well as a means for assessing pupil growth?

These criteria are not earthshaking, nor do the results of applying them resolve our problem. But they do serve to focus the teacher's attention on elements in the instructional programs that merit close examination. They are the same elements that need to be considered during the curriculum development process.


## Curriculum Development and Project Procedures

The specific steps followed by curriculum developers in the process of designing instructional materials and curriculum will vary somewhat. In general, however, they are highly similar. The basic differences are in the resources available to the developer and the settings in which the development takes place. Most curriculum development is not done by individuals. Instead, it is carried out by project staffs which have financial support. Such projects may be established by local districts, state departments of education, universities, or autonomous curriculum development centers. Much of the curriculum development that has taken place in Special Education has resulted from funding by national or regional agencies. The setting in which the project is conducted generally influences the developer's philosophy. Thus, some curriculum development centers are oriented to hiring their own developers and centralizing the development process within their staff. Others centers may employ small development staffs and rely on writing

3. John M. Lembo, *The Psychology of Effective Classroom Instruction* (Columbus: Charles E. Merrill Publishing Co., 1969).

teams selected from the field to supplement their staff expertise. This increases the manpower source and creates a direct liaison with professional representatives from the field. The central development staff approach has the advantage of tight quality control over the development process. But it has the disadvantage of having to recruit a highly expert staff. On the other hand, public school-sponsored curriculum development will most likely be based on talent available within the district or accessible to the district through universities or consulting agencies. Generally, a skilled developer will be assigned responsibility for coordination, while teachers assume much of the development responsibility. To enhance teachers' development skills, districts will frequently invest in training them in needed skills as a process of project implementation. One advantage that districts have in curriculum development is that their development efforts are aimed at their own needs. They have a broad base of available talent and, over a period of time, they benefit from the residual values of conducting several projects. Their limitations relate to financial resources and the capability to commit groups of skilled personnel full-time to the development task.

Teachers become involved in curriculum development projects at the point of specifying objectives and developing content, or when it is time to field-test products. They rarely have an opportunity to participate in conceptualizing a proposal, securing funds, or carrying out the array of activities that go into curriculum development. It is not the purpose of this book to describe curriculum development procedures fully. Teachers, however, may find it helpful to be familiar with the major tasks typically involved in carrying out curriculum development projects. The approach will be to describe briefly selected tasks in the sequence in which they are generally encountered. The discussion is based on the assumption that the project is initiated as a result of needs assessment; it describes tasks, not operational procedures on how a task should be completed. It should be noted that the degree of formal attention given to each task varies with developers and the scope of the project, but in general the tasks are evident from the procedures employed.

## Needs Assessment

Most curriculum development projects undertaken by school districts result from some form of assessment of needs. This is not necessarily true of all major curriculum development efforts, most of which tend to occur when an individual (or individuals) conceptualizes a development project and seeks support. Under these circumstances, needs assessment involves confirming the priority status of the conceptualized proposal. This approach to initiate curriculum development relates more to project proposals on the national level than to locally created projects. In other situations, curriculum development projects may emerge from research on theory and again are not the result of observed needs on the part of local districts. Examples of such curriculum development efforts might include the "new math," open class curriculum, and behavioral analysis curriculum. Typically, however, locally conducted projects are derived directly from observed needs. Needs assessment studies are seldom conducted to generate a need for curriculum development. Instead, school districts attempt to monitor the curriculum program constantly to detect the need for curriculum development and/or revision. However, specific procedures can be designed to assist local districts in identifying the need for curriculum development or revision.

## Conceptualizing a Design Model

Most curriculum projects and major instructional products are based on a conceptual model. Development models vary in specificity from general commitments to a teaching approach—for example, discovery learning—to very complex schemata detailing interactions among pupil, environment, teacher, and material. The *importance* of the model is not inherent in its complexity but in how effectively it conveys the beliefs of the developers and the principles employed in the project. The development of a model serves a very useful purpose for the development staff. It requires the staff to specify clearly what they believe to be essential to the curriculum product they are developing. It also allows them to design a procedure that holds them accountable. In other words, once the model is complete, their views and the principles on which they propose to develop a curriculum product are open to examination by others. Curriculum developers begin to toy with the model early in the preliminary planning but wait to formalize it until they have subjected their informal plans to review by either proposed consumers of the element product or by the development staff that will eventually be recruited for the project.

## Rationale

The development of a rationale is somewhat analogous to writing a justification for the project. It involves formulating a clear statement of the project goal, a description of the target population, and an identification of the assumptions underlying the curriculum development proposal. The intent of the rationale is to relate the conceptualization of the project to the results of needs assessments, supporting literature, and the capabilities of the developer(s). The rationale is important primarily for those persons who must make judgments on the merits of the proposals, such as administrators, teachers, parents, school patrons, and possibly funding agency representatives. The rationale must be couched in a statement that communicates adequately the intent of the proposed curriculum. The emphasis should not be on formulating a complex statement, but on developing a very clear statement that can be easily understood without further clarification by the developer.

## Feasibility

A curriculum proposal may pass the test of a defensible rationale and still not be a feasible project. The variables that must be explored in determining the feasibility of the curriculum proposal are directly related to the capabilities of the district or center to carry out the development task and implement the final curriculum product successfully. It is best to test the rationale and feasibility questions separately. Ideally, the rationale question should be resolved first; however, circumstances sometimes exist in which the district has created sufficient development resources to have the luxury of experimenting with high-risk projects. Most districts will require that all proposals first be subjected to a rigorous test with underlying rationale. Feasibility decisions are based on available resources and needs. Obviously, rationale and needs assessment contribute to the feasibility decision.

## Organization for Development Tasks

It is at this point that decisions are made relative to putting the curriculum project into operation. Certain obvious decisions must be made, such as recruiting staff, determining the training they require, obtaining space, establishing time-lines, differentiating assignments, and establishing basic organizational procedures. There is also a more subtle task involved. It concerns establishing a commitment to the project on the part of staff members at a level equivalent to the commitment that probably is held by those who conceptualized it. Basically, the developers who conceptualize the project are dependent on staff members who are not part of the conceptualization to actually carry out development. Thus, very early in the organizational stage, orientation must take place. Somehow the staff members must feel a part of the conceptualization even though they were not actual contributors. Many times this means repeating some of the processes relative to needs assessment, conceptualization, rationale, and feasibility. For the most part, the decisions regarding organization are administrative and will take the form of the structured model.

## Prototype Design

Designing a prototype involves making an example of the product; that is, curriculum that approximates the conceptualization of what the final product will be. The prototype may take different forms. For example, it may be a product, such as a kit of materials, a book, or manipulative aids. At the same time, it may be detailed curriculum for a major subject area. In the latter case, it should be noted that curriculum content takes several different forms. For example, some curriculum products are skill-oriented toward the teaching of concepts and/or information. Still others are intended to influence attitudes. Regardless of what constitutes content, the emphasis should be on designing a process to facilitate content generation and experiences in a prototype form that can be subjected to evaluation. The task becomes one of refinement and production of a prototype. Typically, a prototype is developed, tested, and produced as a final product. If the preliminary development has been sound and the developer has selected good formative evaluative procedures, then there is likely to be little substantive change between the final product and the first prototype. On the other hand, if errors have been made in terms of analyzing the target population or in predicting the skills possessed by teachers, considerable change may be necessary. The purpose of designing the prototype is to provide an operational example of the final product and to subject the prototype to field-testing. The procedures for designing and evaluating prototypes represent a major task for any curriculum development project.

*Evaluation*

Evaluation is obviously inherent in the processes of defining a prototype. The development of curricula and/or curriculum products (materials) not only dictates the application of evaluation procedures but also presents a set of circumstances conducive to evaluation. In the realm of curricula, a considerable number of products emerge that are intended to bring about change on the part of learners. Consequently, evaluation can focus on the development process, the status of products at particular stages, and the subsequent effect on the learner. If designed appropriately, the evaluation process can serve to initiate a cycle procedure focusing on improvement of the product, that is, correcting its deficiencies. From this perspective, the evaluation becomes an attainable curriculum goal. However, it is apparent to teachers who have engaged in applied evaluation or research in the classroom that there are many variables which are difficult to control in curriculum evaluation. For example, it is not possible to control student attitudes, distractions within a classroom, or even prior experiences of students engaged in the activity being evaluated. To the degree possible, developers attempt to design evaluation procedures that take these variables into consideration. Their goal is to design an evaluation system that improves the product relative to the setting in which it will ultimately be implemented.

## Implementation and Dissemination

Local districts produce or revise curriculum with an intent to implement the results within their own programs. Depending on the scope of projects local districts carry out, they may also engage in broader dissemination efforts. Certainly major curriculum development projects are carried out by curriculum development centers with a commitment to dissemination and implementation. In general, curriculum development projects of this scope will develop dissemination procedures aimed at alerting the field to the availability of the curriculum product and to the nature of their design. Depending on the product, a project may also design procedures for training consumers (teachers) in the actual use of the curriculum to facilitate its adoption. Publishers frequently assume a major responsibility for the implementation and dissemination task. Since publishers have a commitment to marketing, it is important that potential users of the curriculum be familiar with the product and have sufficient information to make decisions on acquisitions.

The tasks previously described are representative of those encountered in the curriculum development process. They are presented solely for the purpose of adding to the reader's perspective on what constitutes curriculum development. It is not assumed that teachers will necessarily participate in all dimensions of curriculum development, but it is important that they be aware of the processes that ultimately create the products used in the classroom. It is also important that teachers recognize that development processes are very similar to the procedures they employ in designing teaching experiences and/or in actually constructing instructional units.

As has previously been pointed out, many teachers find themselves in the position of having to make decisions independently about what they are going to include in their instructional program. This is particularly true of teachers working with exceptional children. Special Education consultants or supervisory personnel may not be available. The building principal, while interested and willing to help, is likely to be overcommitted and not free to devote substantial time to assisting the teachers in organizing a curriculum that also accommodates children's needs. This, coupled with the lack of resources generally available to teachers working with exceptional children, places them in the position of having to make decisions based on personal knowledge about exceptional children. If they are oriented toward unit teaching, they may base instructional programs on the teaching of units. Since what takes place in the classroom becomes the child's curriculum, a curriculum based on the arbitrary selection of units is not a very sound approach to structuring a child's education. This is not to say that it is not feasible to develop a sound instructional program based on units. It can be done, but it must be related to a planned curriculum providing outcomes that the teacher strives to attain through unit teaching. Teachers may find it necessary to develop the curriculum as they teach units in their instructional program. This, however, does not make the practice a realistic approach. It results in the curriculum becoming what the teacher teaches, with little long-range planning involved. Another consequence is that, as children move from one special class to another, they encounter little continuity and may even encounter teachers with contrasting views about what exceptional children are capable of learning.

Because of the importance of a well-planned curriculum to the future of the exceptional child, teachers who choose to develop their instructional program around units should base their decisions about what is taught through those units on a sequentially planned curriculum. The teacher, then, is adhering to a prescribed curriculum but electing to use the unit method as the major vehicle for the instructional program. Those teachers who prefer to use units as a supplement to other methods must also be concerned with the relationship of the units they teach to the prescribed curriculum. In both cases, each unit must be well planned and executed. Teachers who base the instructional program on units have the additional task of building consistency among their units. If they are not working from a prescribed curriculum but emphasizing units in their teaching, they can reduce the risk of curriculum errors by systematic development of the units.

## Summary

The emphasis in this book is on the tasks inherent in writing well-designed units. This discussion of curriculum development has been presented to provide teachers with a frame of reference concerning what is involved in curriculum development and to encourage them to look at unit teaching as one possible instructional program method.

Attention has been given to differentiating instruction from curriculum. Curriculum here is the planned series of outcomes that the child should be assisted in attaining through the instructional program. The curriculum provides directives for the instructional program, but to facilitate implementing these directives, teachers should be given considerable freedom in determining their approach. In other words, a minimum of restriction should be placed on the methods a teacher may choose to use in the classroom, and teaching units may be employed either as a primary or supplementary method. In either case, this author feels that systematically developed units will be taught most effectively. The information presented in this chapter provides a background for reading Chapter 8, which is concerned with applying curriculum development principles to the design and organization of units. Because Chapter 8 is based on the assumption that the reader is skilled in the process of developing units, the reader is encouraged to study Chapters 3 and 4 first.

BIBLIOGRAPHY

JOHNSON, MAURITZ, JR. "Definitions and Models in Curriculum Theory." *Educational Therapy*, April 1967.
LEMBO, JOHN M. *The Psychology of Effective Classroom Instruction.* Columbus: Charles E. Merrill Publishing Co., 1969.
PHENIX, PHILLIP H. "Curriculum." *Philosophy of Education.* New York: Holt, Rinehart and Winston, 1958.


ADDITIONAL SELECTED REFERENCES RELATED TO CURRICULUM

BAKER, ROBERT L., and SCHUTZ, RICHARD E., eds. *Instructional Product Development.* New York: Van Nostrand Reinhold Company, 1971.
BANATHY, BELA H. *Instructional Systems.* Palo Alto: Fearon Publishers, 1968.
BURNS, RICHARD W., and BROOKS, GAY D., eds. *Curriculum Design In a Changing Society.* Englewood Cliffs, N.J.: Educational Technology Publications, 1970.
"Curriculum." *Review of Educational Research* 39:3. Washington, D.C.: American Educational Research Association.
"Curriculum Planning and Development." *Review of Educational Research* 33:3. Washington, D.C.: American Educational Research Association.
DRUMHELLER, SIDNEY J. *Handbook of Curriculum Design for Individualized Instruction: A Systems Approach.* Englewood Cliffs, N.J.: Educational Technology Publications, 1971.
GAGNE, ROBERT M. *The Conditions of Learning.* New York: Holt, Rinehart and Winston, 1965.
GOLDSTEIN, HERBERT. "Construction of a Social Learning Curriculum." *Focus on Exceptional Children* 1 (1969):2.
GWYNN, J. MINOR, and CHUSE, JOHN B. *Curriculum Principles and Social Trends.* Toronto: The Macmillan Company, 1970.
HANEY, JOHN B., and ULLMER, ELDON J. *Educational Media and the Teacher.* Dubuque: Wm. C. Brown Company Publishers, 1970.
KAPFER, MIRIAM B. *Behavioral Objectives in Curriculum Development.* Englewood Cliffs, N.J.: Educational Technology, 1971.
LENT, JAMES R. "Curriculum Development." Unpublished proposal, Bureau of Child Research, University of Kansas, 1975.
MAGER, ROBERT F. *Developing Attitudes Toward Learning.* Palo Alto: Fearon Publishers, 1968.
———. *Goal Analysis.* Belmont, Calif.: Fearon Publishers, 1972.
MAYER, WILLIAM V., ed. *Planning Curriculum Development.* Boulder, Colo.: Biological Sciences Curriculum Study, 1975.
SMITH, ROBERT M. *Clinical Teaching: Methods of Instruction for the Retarded.* 2nd ed. New York: McGraw-Hill Book Company, 1974.
STEPHENS, THOMAS M. *Directive Teaching of Children with Learning and Behavioral Handicaps.* Columbus: Charles E. Merrill Publishing Company, 1970.
THORSELL, MARGUERITE. *Kansas Plan: Conceptual Models for Development and Implementation of Curriculum Content Structures.* New York: Simon and Schuster, 1969.
WEIKART, DAVID P. "Curriculum for Early Childhood Special Education." *Focus on Exceptional Children* 6 (March 1974):1.
WHEELER, D. K. *Curriculum Process.* London: University of London Press, 1967.

# 3

# A Conceptual Base
# for Developing
# Experience Units

This chapter presents a point of view on how teachers can conceptually approach the design of experience units. The ideas discussed can be generalized to teachers in a variety of settings. However, the approach described is most appropriate for teachers who are assigned to the same group of children for large blocks of time and who are oriented toward experience-type units rather than units that may be rather narrow and restricted to a specific subject matter area. Teachers of mentally retarded students will find the guidelines offered in this chapter particularly helpful.

Units take different forms; consequently, when the term "unit" is mentioned, teachers vary in their interpretation of its implications. Some teachers associate resource units with those used in regular social studies programs, while others are oriented towards activity-centered units. Still others may view units primarily as a vehicle for allowing students to apply previously learned skills. Each perspective on unit teaching is accurate. No single structure for developing units is applicable to all situations.

There are, however, some features of unit teaching that are appropriate for use with pupils of average ability that are not applicable for use with children of limited intellectual ability. For example, in teaching resource units, the teacher typically plans the experiences around a central theme, introduces certain concepts, and involves the pupils in experiences that encourage them to seek information independently. Frequently, once the resource unit is operational, the pupils assume much of the responsibility for searching out information, reporting, and decision making. The teacher remains in control but accomplishes this through guidance, observation, and questioning. The pupil's role in the resource unit requires reasonable competence in reading and work-study habits. Children with limited intellectual ability, such as the mildly mentally retarded, are capable of considerable involvement in decision making regarding unit direction, but they do not possess the academic skills to work independently to the same degree as the average regular class pupil. At the same time, the activity-centered unit is not totally appropriate for those students. Most activity-centered units are of short duration and geared to holidays or special events; they are seldom coordinated with other aspects of the curriculum. In general, they are designed to involve the children in projects. The main objective of such units is frequently the teaching of information and social skills with a minimum emphasis on academic skills. Although this type of unit has merit, particularly as a change of pace, it fails to take full advantage of the opportunity to integrate the teaching of academic skills with social and activity-oriented experiences. Considering the shortness of the instructional day for many special classes and their slow rate of learning, the instructional program must make maximum use of each learning opportunity.

In contrast to an information-type unit, teachers are encouraged to consider an experience-type unit that is oriented toward the teaching of academic skills. The informational and social aspects of units will not be played down; rather the unit's potential as a vehicle for teaching skills and concepts will be stressed. The emphasis on skill development does not take unit teaching out of the realm of practical instruction. What it does is to capitalize on the relevance of unit teaching in making the teaching of academic skills meaningful. This approach to developing experience units will be developed more fully in the remainder of this chapter.

The emphasis on a "practical" approach to teaching academic skills and social skills to the mildly mentally retarded has resulted in unit teaching becoming a popular technique among special class teachers. In spite of its popularity, though, attempts to design and experiment with guidelines to assist teachers in writing and teaching units have been minimal. Suggested formats appear in a variety of publications. Because these are so general, teachers tend to develop their own unique procedures, and the units are of little value to other teachers. This is reflected in many units that have been published, as well as in the large number of curriculum guides developed by local school districts. They tend to be more informational than skill-oriented. Relevant information on a particular theme serves as the vehicle for most unit teaching in special classes for the mildly mentally retarded. The dimensions of such units are determined more by what the teacher knows about the topic than by the theme's potential for teaching or applying academic skills. The attention given to the systematic teaching of specific academic skills within the framework of the informational aspects has been minimized.

Administrators, researchers, and informed observers have been quick to point out the inadequacies of unit teaching as typically applied by many teachers. Criticism centers on the lack of internal consistency and sequencing of skills within units and on the failure of most teachers to formulate a structure for teaching units. These views are realistic concerns and warrant the attention of teachers and teacher educators who espouse the unit method of teaching. Unit teaching can be made more systematic if unit development is approached from a more structured orientation.

A conceptual construct will be presented along with specific steps for writing experience units. This material is not intended to suggest that unit teaching is a new concept in methodology, nor that the instructional skills required in teaching units to the mentally retarded are unique. Rather, the emphasis is on the systematic development of experience units. The suggested approach is based on the premise that the development of units should be more than the organization of information around topics.

Any discussion of unit teaching must acknowledge the significance of decisions made by teachers in the formulation of their instructional programs. Inherent in these decisions should be a clarification of the emphasis given to unit teaching in the instructional program. An equally important decision relates to the structuring of units that reflect both scope and sequence in the presentation of information and the teaching of basic skills. Prior to committing their energies to developing and teaching units, teachers must cope philosophically with the role they are going to give to unit teaching in their instructional program. This decision has implications for teaching style as well as for the overall organization of the instructional program.

The more emphasis given to unit teaching, the more important it is that each unit be planned in accordance with the content of previously taught units or units to be taught later in the program. It also becomes extremely important that the content covered in units be coordinated with other aspects of the instructional program.

**Organizational Construct**

The experience unit approach discussed in this book is based on the integration of skills and concepts from six core areas of learning into each unit taught. The core areas are communication, arithmetic, social competency, safety, health, and vocation. The emphasis is on integrating skills and concepts from all core areas into each unit, which requires considerable planning on the part of the teacher. The reason for the integrated approach is to capitalize on units' informational aspects to make the teaching of skills and concepts relevant to the learner. This does not necessarily deemphasize the informational aspects of units; rather, the information is made a more viable part of the unit. Frequently, in teaching units, teachers devote a major portion of the time spent on units to teaching information on the unit topic. For example, at the secondary level, a teacher might teach a unit on applying for a job. In doing so, he or she might center most of the activities on how to apply for a job. While this fulfills the need for information about applying for a job, a number of arithmetic and language skills can also be developed as part of the unit, if the teacher approaches the unit with a set toward using it in teaching specific skills.

Units are often developed with a concern only for teaching information relevant to the topic. The potential of units for teaching and reinforcing academic skills is too great to be ignored. If teachers merely select a topic and proceed to outline what they know about it into some teachable form, it is likely that the end product will be an informational-type unit with only minimal attention given to skill development. This is not to say that academic-type experiences will not be included. However, it is relatively safe to say that the academic emphasis will be secondary.

The approach suggested in this book gives attention to the informational aspects from two perspectives. First, it acknowledges the value of information about places, situations, and interpersonal relationships in unit teaching. Secondly, it places value on utilizing the informational content as a vehicle for teaching academic skills. Unit teaching allows the teacher to build on the student's repertoire of experience. The student is able to keep the content within a familiar realm. Consequently, it is logical for the teacher to capitalize on the student's interest in the unit subject matter to teach academic skills.

The six core areas collectively represent most curriculum areas. Figure 4 illustrates the relationship of the core areas to unit topics.

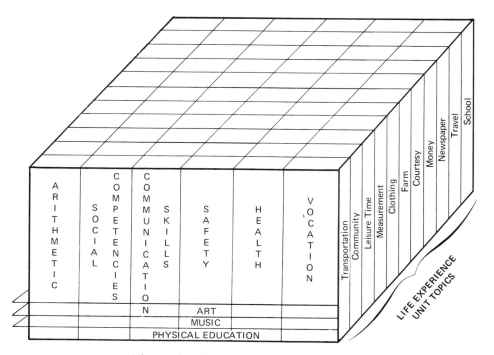

**Figure 4.   Organizational Model**

Experiences in each of the six core areas are incorporated into each unit taught, as illustrated in Figure 4. The unit topics listed on the right side of the model are for illustrative purposes only and may not be the particular topics a teacher would choose. Regardless of the topics selected, experiences in each core area can be developed that are relevant to the unit topic. Unless teachers consider the core areas when they are planning the unit, they will probably emphasize only the core area most logically related to the topic. For example, if they select the unit topic "measurement," the unit will probably be heavily oriented in arithmetic skills. At the same time, however, if they explore the topic's potential, they will find that there are many opportunities to build into the unit experiences in each of the other core areas. It becomes almost impossible to select a unit topic that does not allow for teaching experiences related to each core area.

Instructional areas such as art, music, and physical education are not considered core areas. In many programs, these areas are taught by the regular art, music, or physical education teacher; or exceptional children are grouped with children from regular classes for instruction. It may be that teachers will develop a unit around the topic of music, art, or physical education. In this situation, they could just apply the core concept as they would with any other unit topic. The limited reference to art, music, and physical education in this model does not imply relative importance. The areas are listed on a plane that permeates each core area as well as each unit topic. Teachers should incorporate experiences in art, music, and physical education into each unit when such activities are appropriate to the unit topic. In contrast to the core areas, these three areas represent experiences that are also technique-related. That is, art activities may be developed as a means of teaching a particular arithmetic skill. From this perspective, these areas are generic as applied to unit teaching.

Although learning experiences in the six core areas can be developed for each unit, the relative emphasis on the individual core areas will vary. For example, a unit on money lends itself more readily to the development of arithmetic skills than to skills in other core areas. But meaningful experiences in the other core areas can also be developed. The outcome is a unit with a major strength in one core area, with relevant content allowing for teaching of skills in other core areas. For purposes of clarification, each core area will be briefly discussed.

## Communication

The communication core area is probably the least difficult to integrate into an experience unit. Reading, writing, speaking, and listening are its major elements. Although reading and writing experiences cannot be overstressed, speaking or the use of conversational speech should not be neglected. Oral communication will probably be used much more by the retarded than reading or writing. The ultimate aim of this core is the teaching of a functional vocabulary for speaking, listening, and recognition. A secondary but important aim is the provision of opportunities for the retarded to apply their communication skills. Too often the emphasis on individual instruction detracts from encouraging spontaneous speech. The mentally retarded need opportunities to participate in discussions within a group setting. Through such experiences, they also develop their listening skills.

## Arithmetic Concepts

This core should be geared to the teaching of basic arithmetic skills including number facts and an understanding of their uses. Consideration should also be given to teaching concepts of measurement, time, money, comparisons, and so forth. When arithmetic is viewed in terms of its practical use in daily life, arithmetic experiences can be related to almost any unit topic.

## Social

This core warrants considerable emphasis. Regardless of the student's achievement in learning other skills, the success of some children, such as the retarded, in becoming socially and occupationally acceptable depends, to a large extent, on their possession of good attitudes and social traits. Most units offer unlimited opportunities for the introduction of this core. Children need to be taught how to get along with others, the social graces of having and being a guest, desirable social habits expected by employers, plus many more of sufficient importance to be included in curriculum for the mildly mentally retarded. It is the lack of acceptable social skills that often sets the retarded apart from their peer group. They become stereotyped because of social incompetencies. It is difficult to separate social performance from success on the job, family relations, or interpersonal interaction. Most unit topics involve subject matter of a social nature. However, particular attention must be given to developing socially acceptable attitudes and traits among the mentally retarded if their overall adjustment is to be fostered. This model calls for teachers to relate the teaching of social information and skills to every unit they teach.

## Health

There is obviously a strong tie between the core areas of health, safety, and social competencies. Because of the environmental conditions that surround a large proportion of the mildly mentally retarded, instruction in the area of health becomes crucial. This core area includes experiences involving cleanliness, good grooming, dental care, food, growth, preparation of meals, and overall self-concept. Relating the teaching of health to topics that have practical significance for the retarded makes the subject more meaningful than teaching health as a separate aspect of the program.

## Safety

The need for emphasis on safety can be observed through the student's mobility, participation in school, use of leisure time, and occupational pursuits. The acquisition of adequate safety consciousness necessitates continued emphasis on this core. In contrast to their normal peers, the retarded must be made especially aware of safety hazards at home, at school, and on the job. When selecting units applicable to a specific level, consideration must be given to those topics having potential for teaching safety habits consistent with students' present needs.

## Vocational Skills

At the primary level, vocational skills will take the form of such abilities as following directions, being punctual, and working cooperatively. At the junior-senior high level, they will be more directly related to work experience. As the pupil enters actual vocational training, the emphasis shifts to job acquisition, work habits, and personal responsibility.

In reviewing the model illustrated in Figure 4, it is obvious that some unit topics lend themselves to teaching one core area more readily than others. This means that any one unit will vary in the emphasis given to the core areas. If teachers are committing considerable time to unit teaching, they may teach fifteen to twenty units during the course of the school year. Under these circumstances, the variability of emphasis given to the core areas in individual units becomes an important consideration. It is possible to select unit topics over the school year to balance the emphasis in core areas. At the same time, teachers who feel that their pupils have a greater need for more experience in social development can select unit topics accordingly. Figure 5 illustrates the pattern of unit topics selected by an intermediate level teacher who felt that the students needed additional work on social development. Although experiences were included from the other five core areas in each unit taught, the teacher selected more units that were strong in social skills. Considering that the teacher plans to teach six units that are basically strong in social competencies and will also emphasize social competencies in all other units, he or she is giving considerable attention to this core in the instructional program.

It should be pointed out that teachers will differ on how they interpret a unit topic. One teacher may view a unit on the community at the primary

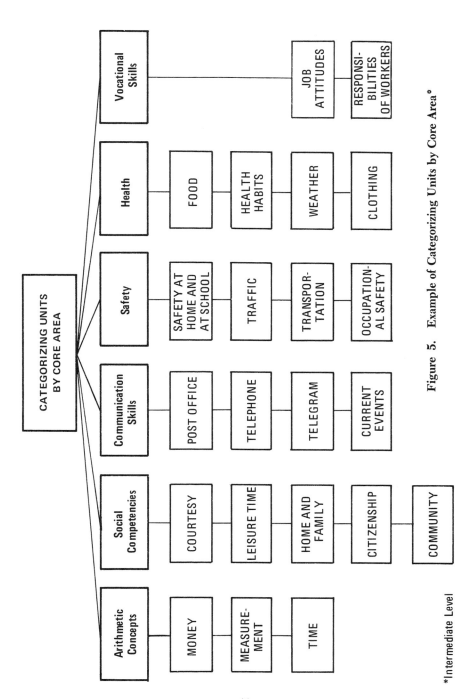

Figure 5. Example of Categorizing Units by Core Area [*]

*Intermediate Level

41

level as basically a social-oriented unit, while another may think in terms of an emphasis on safety. This presents no problem, since the individual teacher selects the unit topic and determines its relationship to the instructional program. Additional discussion on organizing units into a year's plan of work will appear in Chapter 9.

Utilizing the informational content of units as a means of integrating the teaching of academic skills with a practical frame of reference makes the teacher's knowledge of basic skills crucial. This is particularly true if considerable emphasis is given to unit teaching in the instructional program. The discussion on the core areas in general is offered from a descriptive perspective. If teachers are to implement this model, they must be familiar with the skills, concepts, and attitudes within each core area and strive to include these sequentially in the units they teach. This is not a new requirement, for teachers should be competent in basic skills regardless of the approach they take in their instructional program. But when teachers plan a unit, following the approach in this book, they must continue to place the emphasis on skill development, in contrast to using units primarily to teach information. In this model, the major concern is to maximize the benefits derived from unit teaching. Basically, it encourages making full use of the unit's potential rather than being content with the method as a dispenser of information.

The focus on skill development through units will not necessarily detract from the instruction offered in basic skills through other aspects of the program. Even teachers who devote a significant portion of the school day to units will probably structure separate periods for basic skills. This approach to unit teaching actually extends the opportunities for teaching skills. It also enhances opportunities for students to apply the skills they are learning.

## Summary

The model presented in this chapter was designed primarily for teachers who devote a substantial portion of their instructional time to unit teaching and who are oriented to a comprehensive experiential-type unit instead of a subject matter-related unit. Particular attention has been given to providing guidelines helpful to Special Education teachers who are assigned to groups of exceptional children. Because of this approach's direct application to programming for the mentally retarded, most examples have related to that student population.

Adherence to the model illustrated in Figure 4 and discussed in this chapter requires systematic planning by teachers. If they merely acknowledge the importance of stressing skills and proceed to write units in a global manner, the model is not being applied. To develop a unit as proposed in this book involves an investment in planning. Some teachers will feel that they haven't the time to plan their units methodically. Certainly, the task will be time-consuming. But, as is true of most tasks, once you become proficient the amount of time required is greatly reduced. Chapter 4 will deal with a systematic approach to writing units, emphasizing preliminary planning and the actual writing of teaching strategies or lesson plans.

The intent of the following procedures is to encourage teachers to explore fully the potential of the unit topic as a vehicle for teaching skills as well as information. Each step has an evaluative function and an exploratory function. The evaluative function is aimed at assessing the merits of both the unit topic and the specific activities being considered. The exploratory function is concerned with assisting teachers to expand their perspectives of what skills, concepts, and information might be included in the unit. The preliminary steps are designed to prepare teachers for the task of writing specific teaching strategies in the form of lesson plans. Throughout the preliminary steps, the emphasis is on extending the teacher's thinking about what should go into the unit and how the unit should relate to curriculum and other aspects of the instructional program.

### ADDITIONAL SELECTED REFERENCES TO THE UNIT APPROACH

CHAPPEL, B. M. "Are You Using Pupil-Made Charts?" *Grade Teacher,* April 1956.

GORTON, MALINDA DEAN. *Teaching the Educable Mentally Retarded. Practical Methods.* Springfield, Ill.: Charles C Thomas Publishers, 1964.

HERRICK, VIRGIL E., and NERBOVIG, MARCELLA. *Using Experience Charts With Children.* Columbus: Charles E. Merrill Publishers, 1964.

INGRAM, CHRISTINE P. *Education of the Slow-Learning Child.* 3rd ed. New York: Ronald Press, 1960.

LAMOREAUX, LILLIAN A., and LEE, DORRIS M. *Learning to Read Through Experience.* New York: Appleton-Century-Crofts, 1963.

LAZAR, MAY, et al. *Experience Charts: A Guide to Their Use in Grades 1-3,* Educational Research Bulletin No. 18. New York: Board of Education of the City of New York, May 1952.

LEE, DORRIS M., and ALLEN, R. V. *Learning to Read Through Experience.* New York: Appleton-Century-Crofts, 1963.

LIECHTI, A. O., and CHAPPEL, J. R. *Making and Using Charts.* Palo Alto: Fearon Publishers, 1957, 1960.

LYNCH, WILLIAM W., "Instructional Objectives and the Mentally Retarded Child." *Bulletin of Indiana University School of Education,* 43 no. 2 (March 1967).

MAGER, ROBERT F. *Preparing Instructional Objectives.* Palo Alto: Fearon Publishers, 1968.

STAUFFER, RUSSELL G. *The Language-Experience Approach to the Teaching of Reading.* New York: Harper and Row, Publishers, 1970.

# 4

# Developmental Steps
# for Writing
# Experience Units

This chapter is organized as a work exercise. Specific steps for writing units will be discussed and followed by an example. Work sheets are included after information or preliminary steps have been presented and again after the steps for preparing teaching strategies. The intent of the work exercises is to provide readers with an opportunity to test their understanding of the various steps. In the section on developing teaching strategies, the reader is referred to Chapter 6 on instructional objectives. A separate chapter has been devoted to this topic because of its importance to unit teaching and to the evaluation process. The reader will want to refer to this chapter before proceeding with the developmental tasks.

Many teachers approach the writing of units by briefly noting the major points to be covered. Others develop an outline of content and resources relevant to a particular topic. Although some teachers may teach a successful unit in spite of minimal planning, there is considerable room for error. It is also likely that the unit will be less comprehensive than if a major planning investment had been made. Coupled with these disadvantages, poorly planned units have little meaning for other teachers and contribute little to the development of a well-designed curriculum.

In view of the paucity of instructional materials designed for use with exceptional children by regular and special teachers, it is important that teacher-made materials be structured carefully so that they can be shared. This must be accomplished without adding to the teacher's burden. Units represent one of the most popular types of teacher-made material. If a conceptual framework for developing units can be agreed on, and if teachers are willing to write out their units, then the plans they teach from can also be exchanged with their colleagues. The cumulative effect of this approach will result in a resource of teaching units. If each unit is written in an organized format, units can be used as a reference by other teachers who will subsequently teach the same children. They also can serve as a means for accounting for subject matter covered over a period of time.

If experience units constitute a substantial portion of the instructional program, the teacher is obligated to plan them in detail. While the process

44

of systematically developing units may be time-consuming, it becomes less difficult as the teacher acquires skill in the development process. The approach proposed here is not unique; it does, however, require the teacher to complete prescribed steps. The process is divided into two areas: preliminary steps and lesson plans. The preliminary steps are designed to facilitate the writing of lesson plans, which become the body of the unit and represent the teaching strategies from which the teacher teaches.

### Preliminary Steps

Keep in mind that the purpose of the preliminary steps is to evaluate the unit's potential and, in the process, to generate a resource of ideas on content, materials, and techniques relative to the unit topic. To facilitate this effort, questions are used to introduce each step. It should also be noted that in the preliminary steps the teacher is not attempting to write in a final form. Rather, the steps are merely intended as an introductory planning process prior to the actual writing of lesson plans. The preliminary steps can be written in an informal style. The teacher does not teach from the preliminary steps, but rather goes through this process to prepare for the process of writing lesson plans. The body of the unit is comprised of lesson plans and will be discussed following this section. For purposes of clarification, examples are included from a unit developed for *junior high level mildly mentally retarded children*. The unit on "Likenesses and Differences" is viewed by the teacher who developed the unit as being strong in the social competency core. The examples included illustrate format and do not suggest content.

Step    I. RATIONALE.  Select the unit you plan to teach. (What are the reasons for teaching this particular unit at the present time?)

    A. When selecting a unit, you should consider the contributions that the unit can make to implementing your curriculum.

       1. Review the units that you have previously taught.

       2. Concern yourself with the needs of the class with respect to strengths and weaknesses in different core areas.

       3. Unless past experience with the class indicates a definite need for concentrated work in one core area, refrain from teaching more than one unit with major emphasis on the same core.

       4. Your personal interest in a unit topic is a poor criterion for teaching it.

    B. State your rationale in the form of a broad descriptive statement.

1.  It should reflect the basic reasons for teaching the unit.
2.  The statement should also suggest the major results expected from that unit.

---

## EXAMPLE

## STEP I.  RATIONALE

The junior high mentally retarded student in a regular class may be aware of likenesses and differences among people only in a gross sense. Because of an inability to understand and evaluate observed similarities and differences, the student may develop damaging stereotypes that will further limit adjustment to the environment. The purpose for including this topic in the instructional program is to help mentally retarded students recognize the roles of likenesses and differences in their lives and in the lives of others.

---

Step II.  SUB-UNITS.  A sub-unit as used in this approach is a fairly specific topic which is closely related to the basic theme. (What are the possible related themes on which lessons can be grouped within the context of the unit topic?)

    A.  At this stage the actual generation of ideas about the content and direction of your unit begins to take place. These sub-units will later represent collections of possible lessons. It is also quite probable that many sub-unit topics will be deleted as planning progresses.

        1.  This is the first test of the unit topic's potential as a teaching unit. If it is difficult to develop a list of more than five sub-unit topics, then the basic theme is probably too narrow.

        2.  This is the *key* step in reducing later efforts. Two or three lessons can easily be developed on each sub-unit. If the teacher does a good job of identifying sub-units relevant to the basic theme, then the lessons suggested by the sub-units will be interrelated.

    B.  Determining sub-units.

        1.  The sub-units should reinforce the basic unit.

        2.  Sub-units can be utilized to strengthen core areas in which the basic unit shows evidence of weakness.

        3.  Listing possible sub-units will facilitate the organization of learning experiences and activities pertaining to the unit.

4. What appear to be logical sub-units should first be listed in random order.

5. After listing possible sub-units in random order, organize them into what you consider a logical sequence.

---

## EXAMPLE

### STEP II.  SUB-UNITS

Unit Topic: Likenesses and Differences

| | |
|---|---|
| A.  Art | F.  Occupations |
| B.  Clothing | G.  Physical Fitness and Recreation |
| C.  Cleanliness | H.  Grooming |
| D.  Heredity | I.  Social Skills |
| E.  Interviewing | J.  Family |

---

Step III.  GENERAL OBJECTIVES. The general objectives should suggest areas in which lessons will be developed, but they should not be as specific as the instructional objectives that will appear in the lesson plans. The purpose of this step is to ascertain the comprehensiveness of the unit through the development of general objectives related to the unit topic. (What are the major goals of the unit?)

A.  Follow an outline form in stating objectives.

1. State the objectives in general terms. At this stage in your planning you are basically concerned with establishing broad expectations regarding what you anticipate your students to gain from the unit.

2. Following the objectives, you may find it helpful to list briefly information that helps convey the intent of the objectives.

B.  Keep the ability level of the class members in mind when writing the objectives.

C.  The objectives will later serve as a guide for lesson selection and development.

D.  Organize the objectives into a sequence that you feel represents the pattern in which the unit will be taught.

EXAMPLE

STEP III.  GENERAL OBJECTIVES

A. To provide students with a realistic understanding of likenesses and differences among people.

B. To develop students' ability to appraise the relative importance of differences observed in others.

C. To enhance students' feelings of self-worth by pointing out
advantageous differences they might possess.

D. To help students understand their own abilities and develop a
realistic perspective of themselves in society.

---

Step IV.  CORE ACTIVITIES. It is important that the core areas be well
represented in each unit. The intent of this step is to encourage
teachers to identify actual activities that can be utilized to teach
each of the core areas. In other words, they are asked to list specific
activities they might use to teach arithmetic, social, communication, safety, health, and vocational skills. Later, when writing lesson plans, they can refer to the list of core area activities in selecting activities for individual lessons. (What activities can be used to
teach the core area skills related to the unit topic?)

A. This is an important step in the development of a well-balanced
unit. If it is effectively done, the task of writing actual lessons
is easier.

B. This step is also a "test" to determine the unit's strength in the
different core areas. It may be easy to generate ideas on activities related to one or two core areas but difficult or impossible
to come up with many for the other areas.

C. Organizing activities.

1. Sometimes it is helpful to list at random activities that are
related to your basic unit and then categorize them according to basic core areas.

2. Arrange activities in a convenient order. Review each core
area and weed out duplications. Also, check to be sure they
are properly categorized by core areas. Compare the activities with the pattern of sub-units developed in Step II.
Again, the purpose is to generate ideas for activities and

techniques so that a resource is available to draw on when writing lesson plans.

3. The final point involves organizing activities by core areas. Be sure that they are listed as activities, not as concepts or ideas.

---

## EXAMPLE

### STEP IV.  CORE ACTIVITIES

A.  Arithmetic Activities
   1. Measure height, weight, and length.
   2. Compute changes in height and weight from student's own health record.
   3. Compare wages of different jobs requiring different skills and personal characteristics.
   4. Observe and compare money denominations.
   5. Compare prices when grocery shopping.

B.  Social Competence Activities
   1. Practice asking questions of a resource person.
   2. List proper behavior to exhibit on field trip.
   3. Role-play by dramatizing behavior desired during a job interview.
   4. Form a committee to plan a presentation to be given in front of the class.
   5. Develop a checklist to evaluate own behavior and appearance.

C.  Communicative Activities
   1. Retell stories that were used to teach.
   2. Use stories for practice of language skills (developing sentences, alphabetizing, spelling, punctuation).
   3. Participate in developing and writing experience charts.
   4. Use of tape-recorded lessons to develop listening.
   5. Use of tape recorder by students to evaluate speech.
   6. Present puppet shows reflecting understanding of likenesses and differences.
   7. Use telephone to request a visit by a resource person.

(Continued)

8. Write letters of thanks to resource persons or hosts for field trips.
9. Read newspapers to find jobs suited to specific types of people.
10. Read biographies or magazine articles about famous people who had physical differences yet managed to overcome them or use them to their advantage. Select books with high interest and low reading level.

D. Health Activities
1. Use a microscope to determine similar and/or different characteristics of small objects.
2. Discover how heredity determines our similarities to our parents. Complete a bulletin board with snapshots of students' families and try to match students with their families on the basis of physical similarities.
3. Show how nutrition affects our appearance and causes apparent differences (acne).
4. Discover how good grooming minimizes unwanted differences.
5. Read newspaper and magazine articles that explain the effects of some diseases (German measles, mumps) and stress the importance of immunization to prevent unwanted differences in babies.
6. Read newspaper articles about transplants of human organs.
7. Feed two rats on different diets and record physical differences that develop in appearance, disposition, weight, and so forth.

E. Safety Activities
1. Develop a bulletin board based on safety during field trips.
2. Develop bus safety rules for students.
3. Discuss pedestrian safety practices to employ on field trip.
4. Read pamphlets and books relating to home accidents.

F. Vocational Activities (The formation of attitudes conducive to realistic employment goals underlies much of this unit)
1. Study want ads to determine how differences apply to job seeking.

(Continued)

2. Have a resource person from the Employment Security Commission discuss the opportunities for people with individual differences.

3. Arrange a field trip to a business that hires handicapped people to see how they perform their jobs. (Do not discuss the people until after the trip.)

4. Visit Goodwill Industries or a job training school to discover avenues of employment.

---

Step V. RESOURCES. (What resource materials and/or people would be appropriate in teaching the unit?)

A. Compile a list of resource materials and people for possible utilization in teaching the unit.

B. There is generally an unlimited supply of materials for any given unit topic. These materials are available in many forms and from various sources.

1. Free and inexpensive materials from commercial companies, chambers of commerce, various civic departments, and the like are one source.

2. Field trips should be utilized to supplement units.

3. There is a wealth of material in the form of visual aids, films, records, magazines, newspapers, and disposable items that can also be used to advantage.

4. The construction of model stores, banks, and post offices may be used when these facilitate the understanding of a concept.

C. Resource people may be brought into the classroom for demonstration, discussion, evaluation, or stimulation purposes.

1. Resource people may be used to advantage prior to and immediately following a field trip.

2. This occasion provides an opportunity to evaluate the students' oral discussion, as well as their social attitudes toward having a guest in the classroom.

3. Use of resource people:

*a*) They should understand the nature of their audience.

*b*) The assignment should be clear to them. It may be helpful to provide them in advance with a list of questions that could be discussed with the students.

*c*) The students should be prepared for the visit.

*d*)  The students' evaluation of the activity should be elicited through a follow-up session.

---

### EXAMPLE

### STEP V.  RESOURCE MATERIALS

A.  Books for Pupils

Amram, Schienfeld. *Why You Are You.* New York: Abelard-Schuman, 1959 (*child and teacher resource*).

Benedict, Ruth, and Gelfish, Gene. *In Henry's Backyard: the Races of Mankind.* Henry Schuman, Inc. Also film: *Brotherhood of Man* (animated and in color).

Cohen, Robert and Heymoniken. *The Color of Man.* New York: Random House, 1968.

B.  Other Resources
1.  Newspaper want ads
2.  Driver's license forms
3.  Magazine and catalog pictures
4.  Cameras and color films
5.  Resource persons
    *a*)  police artist to demonstrate the method of developing a composite sketch
    *b*)  employment office personnel
6.  Trips by class members
    *a*)  police station where you may have to go to see the composite sketches
    *b*)  store or business with a handicapped worker
7.  Art supplies: butcher paper, colors or paints
8.  Film and filmstrip projector
9.  Microscope
10.  Overhead projector and transparencies
11.  Assorted objects for comparison (leaves, snowflakes, and so forth.)

---

Step VI.  VOCABULARY.  (What crucial words can most easily be taught in relation to this unit topic?)

A.  One of the principal contributions an experience unit should make to the retarded child's education is to help in developing a useful vocabulary. This vocabulary should include words that are relevant for speaking, writing, listening, and reading.

B.  Compile a basic list of words that are particularly relevant to the unit topic. Concern yourself with reading, speaking, and listening.

C.  You are in essence trying to identify the words that can best be taught in conjunction with the unit topic you have selected. The same words may also appear in other units.

D.  In listing the vocabulary words considered crucial to the unit topic, the teacher should keep in mind that the students will undoubtedly come up with additional words that should be included in the vocabulary list.

---

## EXAMPLE

### STEP VI.  VOCABULARY WORDS

| | | |
|---|---|---|
| abilities | | shape |
| advertise | features | shortest |
| alike | heaviest | silhouette |
| color | lightest | size |
| differences | likenesses | tallest |
| employers | prove | traits |
| expression | | transplant |

---

Although the preliminary steps are presented as an informal process, they are considered integral to the systematic procedures for developing units stressed in this book. The suggested informality pertains to the manner in which information is recorded at each step. Teachers are encouraged to adopt an efficient writing style for the preliminary steps. The suggested format will become much more structured in the subsequent discussion on preparing lesson plans.

Figure 6 (p. 54) illustrates the modified task analysis approach to the preliminary steps.

### Summary

If the preliminary steps have been well developed, the teacher will have a resource of ideas regarding the unit's content and scope from which to draw in writing lessons. The preliminary steps were designed to require the teacher to test the theme's potential while in the process of preparing the unit. At

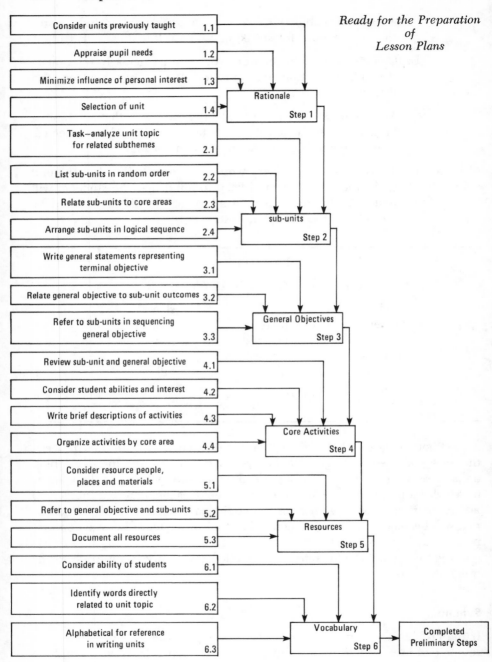

Figure 6.   Preliminary Steps Schemata

this point, each step should be reviewed in terms of its contribution to the lessons that need to be developed. The cumulative effect of completing the various steps should be kept in mind as each step is reviewed individually.

Having completed the preliminary steps, the next procedure is to review your notes for each step and to formulate an overall plan for the organization of the unit. This plan will then serve as a guide for developing individual lesson plans.

Steps II and III—sub-units and general objectives—are the major steps in terms of structuring your unit plan. The sub-units give you an indication of the potential scope of the unit, while the general objectives indicate the emphasis you plan to give to its different aspects. You will find that for each sub-unit, you will be likely to teach four or five lessons. Thus, by looking at your sub-units, you can estimate the approximate length of your unit. Most teachers find it is easiest to work from a sequential listing of sub-units in developing a plan to follow in writing lesson plans.

Step I.    Rationale—should have helped to bring into focus the overall purposes of the unit and its relationship to your instructional program.

Step II.   Sub-Units—will be helpful in determining the scope of the unit. If the list of sub-units contains six or fewer items, the unit theme may be too narrow.

Step III.  Objectives—will serve as a basis for organizing individual lessons. The listing of objectives compiled in this step will provide direction for the development of instructional objectives to be included in the lesson plans.

Step IV.   Core Activities—were designed to aid in generating ideas about activities and techniques for teaching core area skills.

Step V.    Resource Material—should have resulted in the selection of resources relevant to the unit theme. Some units may make considerable use of field trips and resource people while other units will rely more on resource materials. The more a teacher knows about the community the more meaningful this step will be.

Step VI.   Vocabulary—was placed last so that the teacher would have the general scope of the unit well in mind before attempting to build a vocabulary list. Teachers will want to make frequent additions to this list as the unit is taught.

An extended exercise is included at this point to help you in understanding the preliminary steps.

**Exercise 1.**  *Preliminary Steps.* Select a unit topic and complete the preliminary
steps. Don't be concerned with sentence structure, and so forth.

Unit Topic _____

*Step I.*  *Rationale*
See page 45.

*Step II.*  *Sub-Units*
See page 46.

*Step III.   General Objectives*
See page 47.

*Step IV.* *Core Activities*
          See page 48.

Arithmetic                                    Communication

Social                                        Health

Safety                                    Vocational

*Step V.   Resource Material*
See page 51.

*Step VI.    Vocabulary*
See page 52.

## Preparing Lesson Plans

When the preliminary steps have been completed, the task of writing the lessons should be greatly facilitated. Teachers now have a basic plan relative to the direction, scope, and general construct of the unit. They should also have a resource of ideas inherent in the preliminary steps from which to choose as they write the lessons. Teachers will want to make frequent reference to various preliminary steps as they enter the lesson-writing phase. The major purpose thus far has been to maximize their knowledge of the content and methodology most relevant to the unit topic selected.

The approach proposed for developing units places considerable emphasis on lesson design. Teachers are encouraged to write out the lessons carefully in advance. Each lesson does not need to be written exactly as the teacher anticipates teaching it, but the lessons should be sufficiently descriptive to be meaningful to other teachers. They should also be written so that a teacher can review a unit a year or more later and be able to determine the basic information, concepts, and skills emphasized. This is important for the development of other units as well as for communicating the instructional program to other staff members.

If the unit being planned is likely to require four to six weeks to teach, it may be advisable to write the first ten to fifteen lessons in detail and merely outline the remaining lessons. Once the unit is under way and it is possible to anticipate whether you have overlooked any major area of content in your preliminary planning, the remaining lessons can be developed. As they are developed, they should be completed in the same detail and format as the initial lessons. The composite of all lessons will represent the unit.

There is nothing sacred about a particular format for writing unit lesson plans. Certain risks prevail whenever a format is suggested. Some teachers prefer to use an outline form; others are less formal and merely record descriptive statements about the intent of the lessons and the activities they plan to use. If a teacher is part of a staff in which there is an interest in sharing units, then there will be considerable merit in adopting a uniform format. The suggested format, shown in Figure 7, differs from the typical outline format, since it is designed as a plan from which the teacher teaches. It allows the teacher to organize the lesson plan in a logical sequence that progresses from a statement of objectives to teaching activities and resources to be used. While teachers may prefer to develop their own format, it is vital to establish uniformity within a district. Through a uniform format, units become meaningful to other teachers. They are not dependent on the unit's author to explain the unit if they understand the format and if it has been carefully developed. An additional advantage of a uniform format is that as more teachers use a particular format, they become more proficient and are in a better position to refine its design.

Scope of Lesson Statement: _____

| Instructional Objective | Activities | Resource Materials | Experience Chart |
|---|---|---|---|
| | | | |

Figure 7.   Suggested Lesson Format

*Scope of Lesson Statement*

The purpose of stating the "Scope of Lesson" is to require the teacher to decide the lesson's general content prior to stating specific instructional objectives or selecting activities. Once the scope of the lesson has been decided, the alternatives relative to objectives, activities, and resources have been narrowed. In reviewing Steps II and III of the preliminary steps, pertaining to sub-units and general objectives, the teacher has an immediate resource of ideas from which to select meaningful lessons. When the general objectives from Step III have been organized into a logical sequence, the task becomes one of formulating a statement that reflects the intent of the lesson. It should be noted that you may need to develop a number of lessons that were not initially shown in the preliminary general objectives. Thus, in developing lessons, don't restrict yourself to the topics implied by the general objectives in Step III; situations will frequently occur that will cause your unit to move in a direction you had not anticipated.

In stating the scope of the lesson, you are actually writing a reminder to yourself as to its content. You will note in Figure 8 that the "scope of lesson" resembles an objective. It differs from an instructional objective in that it relates to the total lesson and does not focus on the individual student. Instead, it is placed in the context of teacher behavior.

Although the statements should be kept brief, they should cover the major content, concepts, and/or skills you anticipate teaching through the lesson. For many classes, a lesson will be brief and focus on only a single concept. With more advanced students, their attention span will be longer and their comprehension better. Thus, the scope of the lesson may comprise three or four major statements.

The advantage of identifying the scope of the lesson is that it helps you keep the lessons relevant to the unit theme. You can review the scope of lesson statements for ten or fifteen lessons and have an immediate check on whether or not you are keeping within the realm of your unit theme. This, of course, assumes that you teach what you imply in the scope of lesson statements.

In writing the scope of lesson statements, write them as notes to yourself. Say to yourself, "I am going to . . . teach, introduce, review, present, orient, establish, stimulate, and so forth," and then proceed to indicate the information, concept, or skill involved. Complete sentences are not necessary if you consistently begin with a verb. This type of phrasing implies you are referring to yourself, the teacher, as the subject. See Figure 8 for an example.

## Column I.  Instructional Objectives

Readers are advised to read first the following discussion on the use of instructional objectives in writing units. They should then refer to Chapter 6 for additional information and practice in writing instructional objectives.

In Step III of the preliminary steps, it was suggested that you identify the general or major objectives for the unit. While you were encouraged to focus on student behavior, the point was made that in the preliminary planning you were concerned primarily with the overall unit and not individual lessons; it was permissible to be general in stating the objectives. However, in stating instructional objectives for particular lessons, the circumstances change considerably. It now becomes necessary to be very specific.

The scope of lesson statements are a basis for setting the dimensions of the lessons. However, the major emphasis in instructional objectives is on student behavior rather than teacher behavior. They provide the basis for structuring activities and evaluating pupil performance, as well as for selecting resources. They also influence the content of the experience charts. Unless the objectives are well stated, the teacher will probably enter the teaching of a lesson with only a vague idea of what the students should gain as a result of the lesson. Well-designed objectives are necessary for every lesson. The cumulative effect of stating instructional objectives for each lesson throughout a unit has its greatest impact in the realm of evaluation. In essence, the instructional objectives serve as criteria for assessing pupil progress.

Instructional objectives have three main functions; namely, descriptive, conditional, and evaluative. The descriptive function pertains to the behavior you are attempting to influence; in other words, what you want the students to be able to do following instruction. The conditional refers to the condition under which you want the students to perform a task. Will they be asked to recall an example or will they be given a concrete situation in which to perform? The evaluative function relates to the kind of performance you will accept as successful. These three functions, specifically describing the process of developing instructional objectives, require the teacher to closely examine the pupils' strengths and weaknesses.

Teaching is aimed at changing the behavior of the student. Behavior means the student's performance. If you have been successful in teaching a

SCOPE OF LESSON: 1. To establish the concepts of likenesses and differences by comparing a variety of everyday objects.

| COLUMN I INSTRUCTIONAL OBJECTIVES | COLUMN II ACTIVITIES | COLUMN III RESOURCE MATERIALS | COLUMN IV EXPERIENCE CHART |
|---|---|---|---|
| 1. To be able to compare two or more objects provided by the teacher and: | 1. Initiate students' thinking by making a statement such as: "All these leaves came from the same tree, therefore, they are all exactly the same." Allow discussion and ask for proof of differing opinions. | Objects for comparison: 1. Leaves from the same tree. | Today we studied ways in which things are the same and different. We had to compare many things. The characteristics or traits we looked for were color, size, shape, length, width, and weight. Since our eyes did not always tell us likenesses and differences correctly, we had to be careful and prove them. |
| a. Identify at least two similarities. | | 2. Snowflakes | |
| b. Identify at least two differences. | 2. As a group, quantify the likenesses and differences: | 3. Printed letters from the same newspaper. | |
| c. Verbally state the trait compared (that is, color, shape, size, weight). | a. Compare color. | 4. Two hairs from one person's head. | |
| | b. Trace two leaves on separate transparency sheets and place one over the other to compare shape (or trace around two leaves on blackboard with different colors of chalk). | 5. Seeds from the same apple or two peach pits. | |
| | | 6. Flowers of the same kind. | |
| | c. Use ruler to measure length and width. | 7. Two stones or gems. | |
| | | 8. Two coins of same denomination. | |
| | 3. Formulate statements about the two leaves in the form the | Overhead projector | |

66

| | |
|---|---|
| pupils will be expected to use in Activities 4. "The leaves are the same color (green). They have the same number of points (5). They are different in shape and size."<br><br>4. Have the students form committees or groups to study the objects listed under resources. Each group is to use the necessary equipment to prove the likenesses and differences of the leaves and to formulate a summary sentence listing two likenesses and two differences.<br><br>5. After the reports, conclude by writing an experience chart of general findings.<br><br>6. Vocabulary: color, shape, size, compare, characteristics, traits, prove, likenesses, differences. | Transparencies<br>Chalk<br>Tape measure<br>Ruler<br>Microscope<br>Scale or balance |

Reprinted with permission from unit material prepared by the Special Education Curriculum Development Center, University of Iowa.

**Figure 8.   Sample Lesson**

particular concept, then there should be some change in what the student is now able to do. This change may be reflected in the performance of selected overt tasks, in verbal responses, or through some form of affective behavior. The objective may involve the ability to count five objects without error. You must, therefore, structure a situation in which the pupil is called upon to count five objects. Then you can determine whether or not the objective has been met.

Teachers have found the following suggestions helpful in writing instructional objectives for experience units:

1. Use the scope of lesson statements and the ability level of your students as a frame of reference. The objective should directly relate to the content suggested in the scope of lesson statement. Knowledge of student performance level is necessary if the objectives are to reflect reasonable expectations for your students.

2. Identify the specific behavior you wish to establish and determine the level of performance that you will accept as successful attainment of the objective. For example, if you are teaching the use of the telephone to a primary age group, the desired behavior may be to have the students successfully dial their home phone numbers.

3. The instructional objectives should suggest the conditions under which the desired behavior should occur. For example, if you write John's phone number on the chalkboard and then ask him to dial the number, this is a less difficult task than asking him to recall his phone number and dial it accurately. An additional task would be involved if you merely gave John someone's name and asked him to call that person. In this case the student must also be able to use a phone directory. The student who is capable of handling the latter situation is performing at a level higher than one who can only manage to complete the first example. Therefore, the teacher needs to make the instructional objective explicit so that the conditions under which the task is to be performed are also obvious.

4. In stating the instructional objectives, use phrases such as "to be able to ... write, recall, identify, contrast, solve, create, and so forth."

Examples of instructional objectives:

a. To be able to choose appropriate clothing, given an example of a social situation and weather conditions.

b. To be able to identify cities, towns, highways, and rivers on a specific road map.

c. To demonstrate competence in check writing and bankbook balancing by performing the assorted operations satisfactorily in a testing situation.

d. To be able to demonstrate understanding of the concepts of *tallest, shortest, middle-sized* by choosing appropriate objects.

e.  To be able to name a body part from its description.

f.  To be able to read and verbalize the correct time, given various positions on a demonstration clock.

5.  Keep in mind that if you are to ascertain whether the students have attained the objective, it will be necessary to evaluate their performance. See Chapter 7. Be alert for techniques you can employ in your evaluation. In many cases, the evaluation can take place through observation and other informal techniques. There will be times, however, when it will be necessary to develop test items, role-playing situations, or other formal means of evaluation. See Figure 8.

## *Column II.  Activities*

The instructional objectives specify the content of the lesson and identify the student behavior you hope will change as a result of the student's participating in the lesson. Thus, the direction of the lesson has been determined, and the task is now one of designing activities that can be used to carry out its objectives. In Step IV of the preliminary steps, activities were identified that both pertain to the unit theme and are applicable in teaching information and/or skills relative to the six core areas. Consequently, you have a resource of relevant activities from which to select in developing the experiences for each lesson in the unit.

Prior to deciding on activities for particular lessons, review Steps IV and V of the preliminary steps. These will remind you of the array of activities and resources relevant to the unit theme. The following conditions should be consulted when selecting activities.

1.  The selected activities must allow for the teaching of specified instructional objectives. This does not mean that additional information or skills cannot be taught. Rather, it is to reinforce the point that the objectives determine what is to be accomplished through the lesson, while the activities represent how the material is to be taught.

2.  The activities must be commensurate with the abilities of the pupils. Many activities are not successful with retarded pupils because they are too difficult or because the tasks involved are foreign to them. The teacher must know the ability level and experiential background of their pupils, as well as the subject matter of the unit theme, prior to selecting activities for a given lesson.

3.  As previously discussed, certain unit topics lend themselves to teaching information and skills in one core area, whereas they contribute fewer opportunities to present learning tasks related to other core areas. The teacher must take advantage of this situation. For example, if a unit on measurement is being planned, the teacher will want to select a number of arithmetic-type activities because the teaching of certain measurement

concepts relates closely to arithmetic. The selection of activities must also be geared to the needs of the pupils in the different core areas.

4. Keep the activities meaningful. It is particularly important for the mentally retarded to see some application of what you ask them to do. It is difficult for them to understand that they may later have a need for something you want to teach now. So, emphasis should be given to practical application.

5. Plan for evaluation. Since the activities column is used in this book for recording how the lesson is to be taught, reference should be made to evaluating what is taught. Some activities in a teaching sequence are evaluative in nature—for example, asking pupils to list specific information. In other cases, teachers may not record evaluation techniques for each lesson, but they should make a practice of noting appropriate means of assessing pupil performance.

6. Plan for use of experience charts. This book's approach to teaching units makes considerable use of them. A separate column is included for recording information to be developed on the experience chart. However, the content of the chart will relate directly to the activities you incorporate into the lesson.

*Guidelines to Describing Activities in the Lesson Plan Format*

1. Sufficient narrative information should be included so that another teacher reading the lesson plan will be able to relate the suggested activities to the instructional objectives.

2. List the activities in the order you anticipate using them in your teaching procedures. Of course, the sequence should remain flexible. However, ordering the activities in a logical sequence will add meaning for other persons who may read the lesson plans.

3. Resource materials or persons should be identified in Column III in close proximity to the activity in which they are to be used. Complete bibliographical data should be listed for books and other printed matter used.

4. If seatwork is to be used, it should be identified in the activities column but placed in the unit's appendix or attached to the page on which the activity is described. The important thing is to identify the exercise sufficiently so that there is no question about which particular seatwork exercise is being referred to. Seatwork can and should involve things in addition to work sheets and other duplicated materials—for example, copying an experience chart story to include in a student notebook, comparing prices used in newspaper advertisements, and so forth.

5. Plan for teaching the vocabulary words identified in Step VI of the preliminary steps.

## Column III:   Resource Materials

Column III should be used to identify the resources you plan to use in your lesson. The selection of resources will depend on the activities that have been planned. In Step V of the preliminary steps, an inventory of resource materials, persons, and field trips was developed. These suggestions should be reviewed when choosing resources for each lesson. In the lesson plan, it is important that the resources appear alongside the activity in which they are to be used. They should also be well documented. Documentation includes all necessary information for ordering a film, book, or other instructional material. In the case of field trips, the place, address, and key contact person should be specified. Resource people should be listed by name and address, or if you are mainly interested in using a representative of a particular occupation, merely listing the occupation would be sufficient. (See Figure 8.)

## Column IV.   Experience Charts

The use of experience charts has long been a popular tool for teachers of language arts, particularly in beginning reading. Although the technique has retained its popularity, its application in the classroom varies considerably from teacher to teacher. Some teachers use experience charts merely to record information, daily weather reports, student jobs for the week, and special events; others use them as the focal point in the development of teaching stories. However, the use of experience charts with the mildly mentally retarded can serve a more significant purpose. They can provide a means for teaching subject matter and are an effective tool for teaching academic skills. This expanded use of experience charts is central to the process of unit teaching presented in this book.

In regular classes, we find a wide array of printed material used to convey the subject matter of the curriculum. This is not the situation in special classes for exceptional children. Although there are some texts specifically written for the mentally retarded, the teacher is forced to modify regular material to their needs. Herein lies a major use of experience charts in teaching the mentally retarded—they can be effectively used in teaching subject matter. As discussed at the beginning of the book, experience charts should be used to teach content as well as to develop skills.

Experience charts typically take the form of a story or narrative statement developed by students and recorded on a large chart or chalkboard. They can also be used to present information or as an evaluation tool. While the use of 24-by-36-inch chart paper is recommended for unit teaching with elementary age children, the use of transparencies with an overhead projector is encouraged with older pupils. Both media serve the same purpose. However, the use of chart paper with older pupils is sometimes viewed as a little juvenile. It need not be perceived this way if presented appropriately by the teacher. Transparencies, on the other hand, can also be developed through class participation. The novelty aspects of the overhead projector help to hold attention. Because teachers face the class while writing on the transparencies, they are able to observe pupil interaction and give more attention to involving students in developing the content being recorded.

## Advantages of Experience Charts

1. They add continuity to your unit. If an experience chart is developed as part of each lesson, an accumulation of subject matter evolves through the series of experience charts. Charts from previous lessons can serve to stimulate student thinking about the unit's theme. At the completion of the unit, the experience chart represents the unit's text, with the order of experience charts representing the sequence in which the unit lessons were taught.

2. They provide a source for review. Experience charts can serve as the focal point for reviewing a particular lesson or the complete unit. As a permanent source of review, the charts can be used as much as a year later to review the basic content taught through the unit. Since the students contributed to building the charts and have read them numerous times during the teaching of the unit, the charts serve as a concrete and meaningful review technique. Without such a source, the review of units often falls into the realm of discussing scanty information on the unit topic, or reviewing student projects which, typically, are not inclusive of all the concepts or information originally covered in the unit.

3. They serve as an attention-holding device. Many teachers encounter difficulty in teaching units because they persist in "talking" rather than teaching. Even in a group with good listening skills, such an approach is not very appealing. Although student participation in activities can be encouraged and various audiovisual techniques employed, a need still exists for a center of attraction. The experience chart fulfills this need if used appropriately. It should be developed through the lesson and not merely as a culminating activity. As the children contribute to building the chart, it becomes the production of the lesson, and consequently, the focus of their attention.

Although the experience chart is placed last on the lesson plan format, teachers must begin to think about what they hope to record on the chart as they begin to specify the instructional objectives for a given lesson. When the scope of the lesson has been determined, the instructional objectives completed, and the activities described, you should have in mind the specific information you anticipate recording on the chart during the lesson. This is not to suggest that you should attempt to obtain from the students the exact wording included in your lesson plan. Rather, you should record in the experience chart column the major points you hope to gain from the students during the lesson. It then becomes the teacher's responsibility to stimulate discussion in order to obtain the desired response.

The content specified in the lesson plan, as well as the content resulting from the lesson, should reflect the scope of the lesson statements and the instructional objectives. The activities listed in the activities column may or may not be referred to on the experience chart. If a demonstration is provided or a field trip taken during the lesson, then the experience chart will probably contain information on the lesson activities. However, if the activities involve an exercise in making change or a task incidental to the theme of the unit, it may not be reflected in the experience chart. The following are some suggestions for planning experience charts in your lesson plans; they are applicable when using either chart paper or transparencies:

1. Plan at least one experience chart for each lesson.

2. In writing your experience chart as part of the lesson plan, write it as you would hope the children will develop it. Don't describe it. For example, don't say, "Identify safety rules." Instead, specify the rules in your plan. The process of writing the charts out in detail in your plan is excellent practice. It allows you an opportunity to evaluate the relevance of the content to the unit theme. It also affords you a chance to plan for the inclusion of specific vocabulary words on the experience chart.

3. Review the scope of the lesson statements and the instructional objectives prior to writing the experience chart in the lesson plan. Be sure the content of the chart relates to the scope and instructional objectives.

4. Review previous experience charts. Avoid redundant wording. Vary the beginning of each chart; for example, if a previous lesson begins, "Today we . . .," the following charts should be different.

5. Keep sentences short and avoid complicated punctuation. Sentence length should average about seven or eight words at the ten-to-twelve age level, and twelve words at the twelve-to-fourteen level. Pictures combined with words should be used on charts at the primary level.

6. Plan brief, explicit experience charts. If possible, keep them to one page, gearing the vocabulary to the reading level of the group. In planning the experience chart, keep in mind that their verbal responses during discussion will probably be beyond their reading ability.

If the teacher has planned the experience chart in advance, the task of stimulating appropriate discussion and obtaining the desired responses from the student will not be difficult. The strong emphasis on planning experience charts is due to their role in teaching unit subject matter. If experience charts were being used only in relation to teaching skills, less planning would be necessary, but this is not the case with the expanded use of experience charts.

Here are some suggested techniques in using experience charts developed on chart paper.

1. Use an easel large enough to hold 24-by-36-inch newsprint or other lined paper. The easel should be sturdy, and tall enough so that you can write on it comfortably, and the children can see it clearly from their desks. At the secondary level, many teachers find the use of the overhead projector as a more acceptable means of developing experience charts. (See Appendix for plans for constructing an easel.)

2. Experience chart paper can be purchased in a variety of sizes. However, 24-by-36-inch paper provides enough space for lengthy stories and is large enough to use for illustration purposes. Although experience chart tablets can be purchased, they are rather expensive. They are also restrictive in that they contain a standard number of pages. Lined newsprint can be purchased inexpensively by individual sheets. Teachers can bind in tablet form the number of sheets they anticipate using during the unit. Heavy tagboard can be used as a cover to protect the pages.

3. Use a black wax pencil. The type used to mark groceries works quite well. If you are using newsprint, marking pens will soak through. Crayons do not mark black enough to be easily read from a distance.

4. Use cursive or manuscript depending on the ability of your group. In a transitional group, manuscript printing may be used on the chart, but the advanced students may be required to copy in cursive.

5. When possible, record the chart in paragraph form. Occasionally, listing will be necessary; however, avoid frequent use of lists.

6. Prepare two or three leading questions in advance. The questions should be formulated to evoke responses relevant to the content you wish to develop on the experience chart.

7. While writing on the experience chart, you can hold the attention of the students by directing questions to specific students. For example, you might ask about the spelling of a particular word, ask about needed punctuation, or merely ask a student to relate the comment being recorded. Such questions help to keep the discussion going while you are involved in the writing process. It also helps to prevent management problems.

8. Have students read the experience chart aloud after it has been developed. Individual students may be called on to read the entire chart or a portion of it.

9. If it is necessary to copy a chart over after class, avoid changing the content. Sometimes the legibility can be improved if the chart is recopied under more favorable conditions. If grammar or misspellings are corrected,

they should be brought to the attention of the class during succeeding lessons.

The teaching of life experience units places considerable responsibility on the teacher in the development and use of experience charts. Many teachers will initially encounter difficulty in developing experience charts that present the content of the unit sequentially. The only shortcut is through good planning and practice. Students soon become acclimated to the technique and assume a major share of the responsibility for constructing the chart during the lesson.

The use of experience charts is not restricted to the recording of unit content. Charts can be designed to meet a number of uses. Once completed, they can also serve a number of purposes, such as (1) to record subject matter of a unit, (2) to develop academic skills, (3) to present seatwork activities, and (4) to administer short tests. They can also be put to a number of instructional uses, such as (1) reviewing a particular lesson or a completed unit, (2) reading, (3) writing experiences, and (4) source of discussion.

Experience charts serve as a means of developing skills and teaching unit subject matter. They also add continuity to the unit and provide a permanent review source. It should be kept in mind that the experience chart plan that the teacher includes in the lesson plan format is merely a guide. The wording of the experience chart developed during the lesson must come from the pupils. (See Figure 8.)

Figure 9 illustrates the relationship of the various steps in preparing lesson plans. After a teacher gains experience in following the procedures, the task becomes less time-consuming. It is important to keep in mind that although a teacher will focus on a sample lesson when writing a lesson plan, the total unit must be kept in mind. A frequent check on the sub-units and general objectives will be helpful.

## Numbering Lesson Plans

If a number of units are to be prepared and if it is likely that they will be used again, there are advantages to incorporating a numbering system into the lesson plan format. The system should be kept simple to avoid interfering with the lesson plan writing process. The value of a numbering system is primarily that specific lessons and/or activities can be located quickly. For example, as each unit is taught, an index of scope of lesson statements could be compiled. With a numbering system, it would be a comparatively easy task to locate a given lesson. Some teachers prefer to incorporate a numbering system into lesson preparation. Others find that, because of the many revisions made as a result of teaching a unit, it is less time-consuming to add the numbering system after the unit has been taught and revised. The basic

*Always Consider the Grouping of Lessons Around Sub-Units Prior to Preparing a Lesson.*

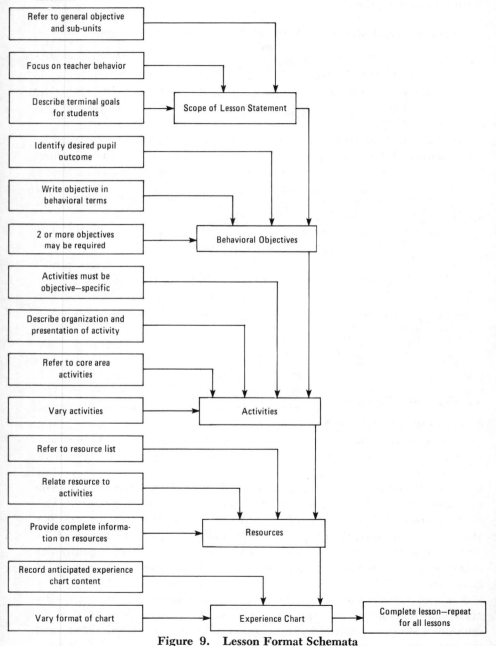

Figure 9.   Lesson Format Schemata

use of a numbering system in a lesson plan is for later reference, not necessarily for teaching the unit.

Sample numbering system:

1. Identifies the scope of lesson statement. Number the statements consecutively in the sequence in which the lessons are taught.
1.1. The second digit identifies the objectives. There may be more than one objective. For example, if there are three objectives for the first lesson, the third objective would be 1.3.
1.1.1. The third digit identifies the activity. Since several activities may be included, be careful to identify each activity with the appropriate objective. See Figure 10 for an example.

The three main parts of the lesson plan requiring identification are the scope of lesson statements, objectives, and activities. The only reason for retrieving resources or experience charts at a later time would be to relate to activities. Consequently, the numbering system need not be extended beyond the activity level. The identification number of the activity can be used to identify the resources and experience chart on the lesson plans. See Figure 10 for an example.

1. Scope of lesson statement (first lesson)
1.1. Behavioral objectives for first lesson
1.1.1. Activity one for objective 1 in lesson 1

**Requirements of a Good Unit**

Teachers who have taught units know that many changes are made in the unit plans during the process of teaching. Consequently, after you have taught a unit, your end product will differ from the unit plan you began with. The major changes that occur as a result of teaching a unit tend to pertain to the information aspect rather than to basic skills. This happens as a result of teachers' responding to current events and observed student interests that relate to the unit theme. Teachers should not resist making changes, but they should be certain that the changes are warranted. It may be that some of the cues the teacher interprets as reason to alter the unit are really suggesting the need for an additional unit(s) rather than modification of the one being taught.

This chapter has addressed an obvious requirement of a good unit—systematic development to assure good organization, appropriate content, and a sequential structure. Additional requirements have been implied and deserve mentioning.

SCOPE OF LESSON: 5. Acquaint students with different types of handsaws and techniques for using them efficiently.

| INSTRUCTIONAL OBJECTIVES | ACTIVITIES | RESOURCE MATERIALS | EXPERIENCE CHART |
|---|---|---|---|
| 5.1. To be able to measure and mark a line for sawing accurately to 1/8". | 5.1.1. Explain and demonstrate the uses of the various saws. Review measurement skills and give any remedial help needed in the use of a square in marking a straight line for cutting.<br><br>5.1.2. Have students work in pairs. Measure a scrap piece of lumber and mark off a predetermined length to be removed (each pair of students measures and cuts their own board). | 5.1.1. Handsaws (cross-cut, rip, coping, keyhole, hacksaw)<br>5.1.1. Measuring rules<br>5.1.1. Combination squares<br>5.1.2. Workbenches or sawhorses<br>5.1.2. Scrap lumber | 5.1.1. Almost every home maintenance project requires some use of basic tools. One of the most useful tools is the saw. There are many kinds of saws. The most common ones are the cross-cut saw, ripsaw, coping saw, hacksaw, and keyhole saw. Each of these is used for different jobs. Can you name these jobs?<br>Before sawing, one must first measure and mark the lumber to be cut. To do neat work, the measurements must be accurate. |
| 5.2. To be able to use handsaws properly as judged by the teacher. | 5.2.1. Before students begin sawing, point out some useful clues and aids:<br>a. Start by using the thumb knuckle to guide blade. Begin by drawing saw toward chest several times. | | |

78

b. Hold crosscut saw at 45° angle and the ripsaw at 60° angle.

c. To maintain square cuts, check blade often with square.

d. To prevent cutting the table or bench, allow plenty of clearance. Give individual help where needed. **Once students have demonstrated mastery, encourage them to help others. Cooperation is a valuable asset.**

5.2.2. Cover as many kinds of saws and techniques as time permits. However, the majority of students should master each saw before the class goes on to a different tool.

5.2.3. Point out the opportunities available for the skilled carpenter and encourage the students to think about possible employment in this field.

*Vocabulary:* measurement, ripsaw, crosscut saw, coping saw, keyhole saw, accurate, 45° angle, 60° angle.

**Figure 10. Example of Numbering System**

A good unit should:

... stand alone, that is, it should be sufficiently complete that it represents a complete teaching package in terms of teacher direction. To the degree possible, it should be designed so that a teacher other than the developer could implement the unit with the results approximating the intended outcome.

... be cumulative, in that the skills, concepts, and information are clearly integrated. The unit should also contribute to the cumulative nature of the overall curriculum of which it is part.

... provide instruction in academic skills and concepts, information, and social development. If only one content element is stressed, the potential of the unit is underutilized.

... allow for continuous evaluation of pupil progress. Inherent in the evaluation process should be an emphasis on feedback to participating students.

... represent an attainable goal for the students who will participate in the unit and for the teacher. In developing units, a frequent error is the construction of one that is too comprehensive for the time allotted to unit teaching. Teachers need to keep in mind the time-frame in which they will be teaching.

## Summary

The procedures for developing experience units discussed in this chapter have been used extensively by experienced teachers and teachers in training. Although use of the suggested steps is time-consuming at first, teachers soon become skilled in their use. The preliminary steps fall into a routine that the teacher follows with minimal effort while preparing for the actual writing of lesson plans.

The intent of these guidelines for developing units is to help teachers maximize the benefits of unit teaching. Particular attention has been given to building into units the opportunities for teaching specific academic and social skills. Attention has also been given to helping teachers avoid the pitfall of using units only for informational purposes. Reflected throughout has been a concern for planning units in terms of their relationship to the total curriculum. Units taught in isolation often fall short of their potential as a contribution to instructional programs.

**Exercise 2.** Develop a lesson representing selected content from Exercise 1 by completing each aspect of the lesson plan format.

Scope of Lesson Statement: _____

(See page 64)—

| Objective | Activities | Resource Materials | Experience Chart |
|-----------|------------|--------------------|------------------|
| (See page 65) | (See page 69) | (See page 71) | (See page 71) |

**Exercise 3.** Using the lesson plan format suggested in this chapter, have students prepare a unit. On the first three lessons, have them apply the suggested numbering system.

**Exercise 4.** Design a format different from that presented in Chapter 4. Include the same features. Provide an explanation of the advantage your design has over the one in the text.

ADDITIONAL SELECTED REFERENCES RELATED TO THE PROCESS OF
DEVELOPMENT OF UNITS

BLAKE, KATHRYN A. *Teaching the Retarded.* Englewood Cliffs, N.J.: Prentice-Hall, 1974.

KOLSTOE, OLIVER. *Teaching Educable Mentally Retarded Children.* New York: Holt, Rinehart and Winston, 1970.

*Life Experience Starter Units Set No. 1.* Special Education Curriculum Development Center. Iowa City: University of Iowa, 1968.

*Life Experience Starter Units Set No. 2.* Special Education Curriculum Development Center. Iowa City: University of Iowa, 1969.

*Management and Maintenance In the Home.* Special Education Curriculum Development Center. Iowa City: University of Iowa, 1970.

*The Newspaper: A Major Supplement to the Language Arts Program for the Educable Mentally Retarded.* Special Education Curriculum Development Center. Iowa City: University of Iowa, 1967.

*Science—A Guide for Teaching the Handicapped.* Special Education Curriculum Development Center. Iowa City: University of Iowa, 1971.

# 5

# Sample Units

The major problem in providing sample units is that some readers may view them as a standard. That is not the intent. Rather, they provide an illustration of units that have been written by classroom teachers in accordance with the procedures described in the previous chapters. The sample units do not represent highly sophisticated units which have been revised several times. These particular sample units were designed for use with mildly mentally retarded students. However, this should not lessen their value to regular class teachers, since the purpose of the sample units is to illustrate the application of the format procedure and not to suggest curriculum content. The sample units are not complete units, in that only selected lessons have been included. However, the lessons are representative of the content projected for each unit.

The first unit, entitled *Learning to Be Healthy,* was designed to be taught to mildly mentally retarded children at the primary level. The second unit, on *Time,* is intended for an intermediate level class of mildly mentally retarded children. Both units include complete preliminary steps and selected lesson plans. The major difference in the style of the two units is that the unit on *Learning to Be Healthy* incorporates descriptions of seatwork into the activity column of the lesson plans, whereas in the unit on *Time,* examples of seatwork are included in the units' appendix. This unit is also more skill-oriented than informational.

In reading the units, keep in mind that they represent the perspective of the teachers who wrote them. You might have selected different content and/or employed other instructional techniques.

**Unit Topic: Learning to Be Healthy**

Instructional Level—Primary[1]

I. RATIONALE

There is scarcely a topic more intimate and of more vital concern to children, of whatever age and intellectual capacity, than the human

1. Sample units from *Life Experience Starter Unit—Set No. 2,* Special Education Development Center, Project No. 6—2883, University of Iowa (Iowa City, 1969). Reprinted with permission of the publisher.

body. From earliest infancy we train them to exercise control over their bodies. However, there are two factors that work against retarded children.

1. Their retardation limits their ability to pick up the information, routines, habits, and attitudes necessary for proper care through informal practice in daily life.
2. Their cultural background and home environment may seriously interfere with opportunities for learning. The child's parents and relatives may be ignorant of, or unable to do, the things we attempt to teach. This results in improper examples and little reinforcement.

For these reasons, a unit on this topic should be taught as early as possible, and should be retaught, with expanded skills and information, as bodily needs and functions change.

## II. SUB-UNITS

| | |
|---|---|
| A. Health Routines | H. Courtesy |
| B. Food | I. Getting Along With Others |
| C. The Farm | J. Recreation |
| D. Stories and Supermarkets | K. Physical Fitness |
| E. Home and Family | L. First Aid |
| F. Clothing | M. Safety |
| G. Our Neighborhood | N. Cleanliness |

## III. GENERAL OBJECTIVES

1. To learn the names and basic functions of the parts of the body appropriate for the primary level.
2. To develop and practice daily routines and habits necessary for keeping healthy and clean.
3. To understand the importance of proper nourishment for the body.
4. To practice health habits related to food and eating.
5. To learn about and become familiar with people who help keep our bodies well.
6. To become aware that people have similarities and differences—size, shape, color of skin, hair and eyes, likes and dislikes.
7. To become aware that children grow and change as they increase in age and that the things they can and can't do also change.

8. To learn how the human body employs the senses to get information about the world around it.
9. To realize that being healthy entails feeling good physically and mentally.
10. To learn to recognize symptoms of common childhood illnesses.
11. To become aware of some human emotions.
12. To learn and practice safety rules along with elementary first aid.

IV. CORE AREA ACTIVITIES

A. *Arithmetic Activities*

1. Prepare various foods for snacks—measure amounts of ingredients.
2. Set table for snack—one place setting for each person. Use relational terms such as *next to, on top of, behind.*
3. Mark off heights of children and teacher on a long sheet of paper on wall. Compare height concepts: tall, short; taller, shorter; and tallest, shortest. Repeat with other dimensions.
4. Make handprints of children and teacher—concepts of big and little.
5. Set up a store with empty food cartons and plastic foods. Children can use play money to make purchases.
6. Prepare a chart with pictures of various parts of the body. Count how many of each part (each child can do this on his or her own body) and indicate the number next to the picture on the chart.
7. Develop rudimentary concepts of time: have children turn the hands on the Judy Clock around ten or eleven times to indicate how much sleep they need at night. Mark real clock with masking tape to indicate when the children are to get off their mats at the end of rest time and have the children note when this happens.
8. Using toy telephones, play a game where children call other people and invite them over to play. Be sure they include their name, address, and phone number. Discuss reason for knowing this information.

B. *Communication Activities*

1. Use toy telephones to invite other children and teachers to a party. Prepare snacks beforehand.
2. Write to school nurse (experience chart approach, to be re-

copied by teacher) asking her if the class can visit her office. This may be repeated with other field trips and resource people.

3. Prepare a scrapbook on foods by having children cut out and paste magazine pictures on construction paper. Show meals of appropriate quality and quantity for proper nutrition.

4. Listen to, observe, and follow directions of resource people, both in classroom and on field trips. Discuss possible questions to ask (in advance). Ask these questions.

5. Review visits and field trips by having children draw a picture of what they remember most or liked best.

6. Display a chart with pictures of people eating each of the three meals and a snack. Show the children magazine pictures of various foods and have them categorize according to proper meal. Paste pictures on chart in the appropriate section.

7. Prepare get-well cards for children who are absent from class because of illness.

8. Use 35 mm. camera to document field trips and recap with slide show and discussion.

C. *Social Competencies Activities*

1. Invite other school personnel (principal, nurse, secretary) to the class party. Have the class decide on the appropriate way to treat guests in the classroom and put this into effect.

2. Cooperatively develop simple rules of behavior for field trips. Review class behavior after each trip—how did we act; did we break the rules; how can we be sure to remember the rules next time.

3. Learn to set the table according to what will be eaten. Practice this during snack. Additional practice may be gained utilizing doll dishes and silverware.

4. Using flannel-board figures, have students assist in making up little stories about children who know how to share and those who don't. Concepts such as waiting for one's turn, sharing when there isn't enough of a particular item, and so forth, should be worked in wherever possible.

5. Have children help one another with shoes (lacing, buckling), clothing (zippers, buttons, snaps).

D. *Health Activities*

1. Practice daily routines in class, verbalizing about what the class is doing (such as: "It's lunch time, time to wash our hands.")

2. Talk about and have children demonstrate the various ways we can move our bodies—stretch, jump, roll, wiggle, slide, bend, and so forth.

3. Reinforce the names of the parts of the body by singing songs in which the children must move a portion of their bodies: "One Finger, One Thumb, Keep Moving," "Head, Shoulders, Knees and Toes," "Where is Thumpkin?" "Put Your Finger on Your Nose," and others.

4. Play a circle game in which one child is blindfolded and moves to the center. Another child is chosen to clap. The child in the center must indicate the direction from which the sound is coming. Vary this by picking one child to move about the room in some way (walk, run, jump) and having the others close their eyes and guess how the child is moving.

5. Demonstrate and develop the sense of touch by placing objects with distinctive textures and shapes (fur, feather, sandpaper, wood, bark, stone, and so forth) under a piece of cloth. The children take turns reaching under and, without looking, try to identify the object.

6. Have children taste several common fruits, vegetables. Discuss the procedures necessary to render food edible. Warn against eating unknown fruits or plants.

7. Have a sensory contest. Blindfold the children and let them try to guess what they are touching, tasting, smelling, hearing. Discuss the implications of the loss of these senses, emphasizing ways of protecting them from damage.

8. Dramatize various emotions—give examples such as anger, friendship, or sadness. Discuss how they feel and how to handle such feelings.

9. Visit the school nurse, dentist, optometrist, and other health workers to become acquainted with their role in the children's healthy growth.

10. Note individual differences among children in the class. Make a chart that displays some obvious characteristics (hair and eye color, for instance) and under each category list the names of people in the class who display that particular characteristic.

11. Discuss and dramatize how a sick body feels and what we do about it—go to bed, check our temperature, take medicine.

12. Arrange for an infant to visit the class. Have the children note the general level of development and compare with their own.

Talk about how the baby must be cared for and fed by the mother.

E. *Safety Activities*
1. View films on safety in classroom and on the playground.
2. Prepare flannel-board figures from Leaf's *Safety Can Be Fun*. Read the story and have children tell what is happening to the flannel-board figures, manipulating them if necessary, to indicate falling, and so forth.
3. Play a sentence completion game. Teacher provides the beginning: If I ran into the street without looking . . . ; if I used a sharp knife . . . ; if I put my hand on a hot stove . . . . The children should supply a logical ending.
4. Take a walk in the vicinity of the school, crossing streets, etc. While on the walk, have children verbalize about the safety rules they are practicing.
5. Set up "streets" with chalk or masking tape on the floor of the classroom. Two children can hold up red and green signs, a third can direct the rest of the children across the streets. Dramatize other common traffic problems using standard street and traffic signs.
6. Prior to food preparation, show children a pictorial chart of safety procedures in this area. Discuss those related to using sharp instruments, walking carefully while carrying breakables, hot stoves, wiping up spills immediately, and so on. Implement them in the actual preparation of food.
7. Discuss safety hazards of tasting or touching unknown substances (such as medicine, contents of bottles, and so forth).
8. Discuss hazards of fire, explosives, electric shock, firearms, and pointed objects.
9. Take field trip to local industrial complex. Have management discuss and demonstrate safety practices to be observed by children.

F. *Vocational Activities*
1. Prepare a helper's chart in which each child is made responsible for a simple room task. These jobs should be rotated periodically.
2. Care for pets in the classroom: compare the things we must do for pets to what we do for ourselves.
3. Provide many opportunities for children to listen, follow direc-

tions, and complete a sequence of activities both in games and in the course of daily activity.

## V. RESOURCE MATERIAL

### A. *Books*

Benedick, Jeanne. *The Emerging Book.* Rand McNally, 1967.

Boyer, Richard L. *Lucky Bus.* Oddo, 1974.

————. *Safety on Wheels.* Oddo, 1974.

Cobb, Vicki. *How the Doctor Knows You're Fine.* J. B. Lippincott, 1973.

Kessler, Leonard P. *Who Tossed That Bat? Safety on the Ballfield and Playground.* Lothrop, Lee and Shepard, 1972.

Klein, Lenore. *Just Like You.* Harvey House, Inc., 1968.

Paulet, Virginia. *Blue Bug's Safety Book.* Children's Press, 1973.

Rinkoff, Barbara. *No Pushing No Ducking.* Lothrop, Lee and Shepard, 1974.

Smaridge, Norah. *What a Silly Thing to Do.* Abingdon, 1967.

Wise, William. *Fresh as a Daisy—Neat as a Pin.* Parent's Magazine Press, 1970.

### B. *Picture sets and posters*

*Teaching Pictures* (David C. Cook Publishing Co., 1966)

1. Social Development
2. A Trip to the Farm
3. Health and Cleanliness; Food and Nutrition

*SVE Picture-Story Study Print Set* (Society for Visual Education, Inc., 1966)

1. Neighborhood Friends and Helpers
2. Hospital Helpers

*Songs for the Flannel Board* (David C. Cook, Publishers, 1966)

*Trend Bulletin Board Teaching Sets* (Trend Enterprises)

1. Health Day-By-Day

### C. *Miscellaneous*

plastic fruits and vegetables

food cartons and cans; play money; cash register

doctor kit

Teaching Clock; Judy Co.

resource people and places to visit—doctor, nurse, dentist, supermarket, school cafeteria, infant

magazine pictures

Peabody Language Development Kit—Level 1

cards for activity, clothing, fruits and vegetables, food, people

Instructo Activity Kit—The Classification Game
familiar objects of various shapes, textures, and so forth
real fruits and vegetables
cooking equipment and supplies (pudding, applesauce)
soap, towels, toothbrushes and paste, cups
art supplies
classroom pets
flannel-board materials and figures

D. *Films* (from University of Iowa *Catalog of Educational Films,*
Audiovisual Center)

Ordering address:  Audiovisual Center
Division of Extension and University Services
University of Iowa, Iowa City, Iowa 52240

Films:

*Beginning Responsibility: Doing Things for Ourselves in School;*
U-6096
*Growing Up Day by Day;* U-5055
*Patty Learns to Stop, Look, and Listen;* U-3462
*Choosing Clothes for Health;* U-3622
*Cleanliness and Health;* U-2695
*Primary Safety: In the School Building;* U-3518
*Primary Safety: On the School Playground;* U-4317
*Tommy's Healthy Teeth;* U-4224
*Your Friend, the Doctor;* U-3154
*How Billy Keeps Clean;* U-3355
*Eat Well, Grow Well;* U-6155
*I Never Catch a Cold;* U-2196

## VI.  VOCABULARY

| | | | |
|---|---|---|---|
| body | hair | stop | different |
| legs | nails | careful | color |
| arms | clothes | hurry | grow |
| nose | home | doctor | change |
| mouth | family | nurse | baby |
| ears | together | office | grownup |
| head | food | hospital | medicine |
| skin | fruits | shot | druggist |
| fingers | vegetables | dentist | drugstore |
| toes | meat | teeth | pets |
| move | farmer | toothbrush | animals |
| run | cook | eye doctor | homes |

| | | | |
|---|---|---|---|
| jump | breakfast | eyes | warm |
| bend | lunch | checkup | cold |
| stretch | supper | sick | hot |
| exercise | snack | thermometer | wet |
| wash | healthy | angry | rain |
| bath | manners | sad | snow |
| shower | polite | happy | sunny |
| store | please | laughing | small |
| flush | thank you | hurt | smaller |
| soap | taste | wait your turn | poison |
| water | big | see | ice |
| dirt | little | hear | fog |
| warm | middle-size | small | milk |
| sleep | safe | touch | hamburger |
| hours | hurt | taste | Band-Aid |
| minutes | danger | tongue | handkerchief |

# Lesson 1

SCOPE OF LESSON:  1.  Introduce the unit topic on Health.

2. Develop the concepts of good and poor health practices by presenting situations for comparison.

3. Emphasize the need for good health practices in the personal lives of the children.

| INSTRUCTIONAL OBJECTIVES | ACTIVITIES | RESOURCE MATERIALS | EXPERIENCE CHART |
|---|---|---|---|
| 1. Is able to demonstrate interest in health practices by participating in class discussion. <br><br> 2. Is able to verbalize the importance of good health practices in becoming strong and healthy. | 1. Tell, via flannel-board figures, the story of "A Very Bad Day." Introduce Tom, a young boy with a sad face. Ask class if he looks happy or sad. Establish that he is sad and have them speculate about what would make him feel sad. Move him through the events of his day as the teacher depicts them in story form: <br><br> a. Went to bed late and woke up tired. <br><br> b. Wouldn't eat breakfast and was hungry all day. <br><br> c. Dawdled with dressing and missed the school bus. <br><br> d. Wore a thin sweater on a cold, rainy day and sat in school wet and chilled. <br><br> e. Didn't like school lunch and ate dessert only. <br><br> f. Wouldn't let sister or friends share his toys and was left to play by himself. <br><br> g. In taking a walk, he ignored red light and didn't look before crossing; a car nearly hit him. | Flannel-board figures and scenes—Tom, bed, table, Mother, school bus, children at lunch, children and toys, sweater, rain and clouds, car and traffic light, Father. <br><br> Oaktag, marker <br><br> Magazine pictures <br><br> Paste | *BAD DAY* |

96

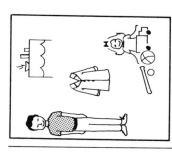

GOOD DAY

h. Wouldn't come to dinner when his mother called and refused to wash hands when he did come; was spanked for this behavior.

i. Was so tired by the end of the day that he had to go to bed right after dinner.

2. Have children review the story, retelling the various events in their own words. Discuss what happened to Tom to make it such a bad day for him.

3. Have children relate their own experience with such events. Prompt, if necessary, by general references to occurrences in the classroom and expand from there.

4. Ask children how Tom could have avoided that bad day. Develop idea that by learning how to take care of ourselves we are able to have better days and are happier and healthier.

5. Develop experience chart by showing magazine pictures of good and bad events. Have children describe what is happening and decide which is the appropriate column of the chart for each picture. Paste it on chart. Seatwork: Children draw pictures depicting their own bad days.

Vocabulary: unhappy, hungry, share, accident, healthy.

**Lesson 2**

SCOPE OF LESSON: 1. To present opportunities for the children to name and manipulate appropriate body parts.

2. To aid the children in developing an integrated concept of self.

| INSTRUCTIONAL OBJECTIVES | ACTIVITIES | RESOURCE MATERIALS | EXPERIENCE CHART |
|---|---|---|---|
| 1. Is able to name parts of the body given appropriate pictures. | 1. Using a large poster of a child, ask individual children to come up and point to various parts of the body—head, hands, legs, feet, hair, eyes, mouth, nose, ears, and fingers. As each part is shown, children find this part on their own bodies. In unison, say the name of the part. | Poster of a child<br><br>Magazine pictures of body parts | 2 FEET |
| 2. Can follow verbal directions given by the teacher. | 2. Teacher names a part of the body and calls on one child to demonstrate how to move that part of his or her body. If possible, get child to verbalize what he or she is doing (i.e., I'm blinking my eyes). | Work sheets<br><br>Paste | 2 EYES |
| 3. Able to demonstrate movements of body parts. | 3. Play a riddle game where children supply answers to teacher's incomplete statements:<br>I see with my____.<br>I put food into my____.<br>I walk on my____.<br>The barber cuts my____.<br>The dentist fixes my____. | Aliki, *My Hands* (T. Y. Crowell, 1962) | 1 MOUTH |
| 4. Is able to name a body part from a description of it. | 4. Sing, with motions, "One Finger, One Thumb, Keep Moving" and "Head, Shoulders, Knees, and Toes." | | 10 FINGERS |
| 5. Can develop one-to-one correspondence between the counting numbers 1, 2, and 10 and body parts. | 5. Develop experience chart. Using magazine pictures of body parts, have children determine how many of each we have. Record this on chart next to the pictures. | | 1 HEAD |

**Lesson 3**

SCOPE OF LESSON:
1. To emphasize that individual differences in physical size and abilities are normal among children.
2. To promote the concept of self by comparing oneself to other children.
3. To develop an awareness of health factors that help children reach their growth potential.

| INSTRUCTIONAL OBJECTIVES | ACTIVITIES | RESOURCE MATERIALS | EXPERIENCE CHART |
|---|---|---|---|
| 1. Is able to name several factors that contribute to growth.<br>2. Recognizes that children in the class are of different sizes.<br>3. Is able to demonstrate understanding of concepts of tallest, shortest, and middle-sized by choosing appropriate objects. | 1. Prior to film on growth, have children guess who is the largest and smallest in the room. Explain that these differences are normal and that the largest may not always remain largest because growth is not consistent through childhood. Make a special effort to point this out to the smaller children.<br>2. Show film, *"Growing Up Day by Day."*<br>3. Discuss factors that help children to grow—rest, exercise, diet. Stimulate this discussion by referring to the film and by showing appropriate Hayes Posters.<br>4. Point out that children in the class are alike as far as some of these factors—same age, eat same lunch, exercise and play at school. Ask them if all children in class are the same size. Is one person the tallest, shortest? Develop the idea that measuring is a way to find out. | Film: *Growing Up Day by Day* U-5055 (Audiovisual Center, University of Iowa)<br><br>*Hayes Health Posters*, Set One (Hayes School Publishing, Inc., 1957)<br><br>Sheet of paper<br><br>Tape<br><br>Marker<br><br>Magazine pictures | *GROWING UP*<br><br><br><br>SLEEP<br><br><br><br>FOOD |

**Lesson 3** (continued)

| Instructional Objectives | Activities | Resource Materials | Experience Chart |
|---|---|---|---|
| | 5. Mark off heights of all children and teacher along a long sheet of paper on the wall. Children should measure each other and the teacher label each mark. Decide who is the tallest of the children and who is the shortest. (Keep this sheet for comparison later in the year.)<br><br>6. Develop experience chart. Show and discuss magazine pictures which depict things mentioned in the film, and some which do not. Decide which show things we learned were important for growth. Have children help paste these on a chart and label them.<br><br>Seatwork: Each child receives a work sheet that shows 9 figures of various heights in 3 rows. As the teacher directs, children circle a particular picture in each row—tallest, shortest, middle-sized. Teacher discusses each picture, emphasizing the size concepts.<br>Vocabulary: growing, strong, healthy, size, tall, short, middle-sized.<br><br>7. At story time, read *The Growing Story.* | Oaktag<br><br>Paste<br><br>Work sheets<br><br>Pencils<br><br>Krauss, *The Growing Story* (Harper & Row, 1947) | <br><br>PLAY |

100

# Lesson 4

**Scope of Lesson:** 1. To introduce food representative of a healthy diet.

2. To develop an understanding of the differences between edible and nonedible items.

| Instructional Objectives | Activities | Resource Materials | Experience Chart |
|---|---|---|---|
| 1. Is able to identify and name ten common foods.<br><br>2. Speaks in simple but complete sentences.<br><br>3. Is able to recognize edible and non-edible items, given appropriate pictures. | 1. Show 10 pictures of common foods. As each picture card is held up, ask, "What is the name of this food?" Call on one child to identify it and then have the class repeat the name in unison. Use sentence format: "This is a(n) _____." Put each picture up on the corkboard after it is identified.<br><br>2. When all pictures are put up, randomly name food items and have children find the pictures, again using a complete sentence to identify.<br><br>3. Have each child come up and indicate the food he or she likes best, saying "I like _____."<br><br>4. Point to each picture and ask, "Is _____ food?" Wait for response. Then ask, "Do we eat _____?" Wait for response. Reinforce by saying, "Yes, we eat _____." After doing this for all pictures, ask, "What do we do with all these kinds of food?" Develop idea that food is something we eat.<br><br>5. Develop experience chart by having each child choose picture of food displayed on board. Label each picture simply.<br>Seatwork: Each child receives a work sheet with pictures of food and non-food items. Review meaning of *food* and have children identify each picture, crossing out the ones that are not food.<br>Vocabulary: food, eat, eggs, bread, milk, hamburger, tomato, lettuce, carrot, cake, apple, pear. | Peabody Language Development Kit–Level 1; 10 food cards.<br><br>Magazine pictures of foods<br><br>Oaktag<br><br>Marker pen<br><br>Work sheets<br><br>Pencils<br><br>Paste | WE EAT FOOD<br><br><br>APPLE<br><br>MILK<br><br>MEAT<br><br>BREAD<br><br>EGGS |

101

**Lesson 5**

SCOPE OF LESSONS
1. To develop an understanding of the democratic process of voting.
2. To orient the class to the process of cooperative planning to gain a common goal.
3. To develop the ability to carry through plans agreed on cooperatively.

| INSTRUCTIONAL OBJECTIVES | ACTIVITIES | RESOURCE MATERIALS | EXPERIENCE CHART |
|---|---|---|---|
| 1. Participates in group decision making and exercises the right to vote in the class-room on certain issues.<br><br>2. Is able to write a letter of invitation.<br><br>3. Can plan a table setting according to the event and the type of food served. | 1. Class members plan together to have a party. Vote upon whom to invite (principal, nurse, or someone familiar to all children) and what to serve. Teacher must guide choice of food to something easy to prepare, nutritious, and amenable to preparation by many hands (i.e., pudding, applesauce, sandwiches).<br><br>2. Develop experience chart—a letter inviting the guest to the party. Begin by discussing with class the various ways to ask someone to a party—telephone, send an invitation, speak to the person. Decide on sending a letter and discuss what must be included in such a letter. Teacher is to recopy and send out.<br><br>3. Display and discuss magazine pictures which show parties. Call attention to the table settings—placemats, decorations, napkins, silverware, etc. As children name table items needed for their party, make a picture list on the board. Decide what must be made (decorations, placemats) and what we have in class (dishes, spoons, napkins).<br>Seatwork: In preparation for the party, each child will make a placemat by painting with watercolor on manilla paper. Faster workers can make mats for the teacher and guest.<br>Vocabulary: party, guest, invite, invitation, setting the table, placemat, decorations, napkin, silverware. | Lined oaktag<br><br>Marker<br><br>Magazine pictures of parties<br><br>Chalk<br><br>Manila paper<br><br>Watercolors<br><br>Paint smocks | Dear ................,<br><br>We are having a *party* in our class. We would like you to be our *guest*.<br><br>It will be on Wednesday at 2:00 p.m.<br><br>Sincerely,<br><br>The Primary Class |

# Lesson 6

SCOPE OF LESSON: 1. To provide an understanding of the division of labor by assigning classroom tasks to members of the class.
2. To encourage individual responsibility in choosing a desired job.
3. To discuss the jobs in the class in relation to health concerns.

| INSTRUCTIONAL OBJECTIVES | ACTIVITIES | RESOURCE MATERIALS | EXPERIENCE CHART |
|---|---|---|---|
| 1. Is able to develop a list of classroom jobs.<br>2. Can verbally state the purpose of a film along with the basic idea or information conveyed by the film.<br>3. Recognizes own name in printed form.<br>4. Can make a choice regarding a desirable classroom job. | 1. Discuss the jobs that have to be done in the school room—feeding pets, helping with snack, watering plants, etc. Relate these to health issues.<br>2. Show film. Suggest that class look for other jobs not yet mentioned.<br>3. Decide on a number of tasks equal to the number of children. As each task is named, hold up a sketch to represent that task and have the children discuss what each job entails. Which jobs have health implications?<br>4. Develop an experience chart. Prompt class to decide that they can keep track of who is to do which task by making a chart. Read and discuss the title, explaining that each student will have one job to do for a week and that jobs will rotate. Review tasks by fastening the pictures to the chart while a child names the task. Write a word description next to each picture and read the word to the children.<br>5. Hold up name cards. As children recognize their names, they place their card in the slit next to the job they would like. Review job each child will have.<br>6. Put these jobs into effect in class immediately.<br>7. Seatwork: Each child gets a work sheet and is to cross out the activities that are not on the Helpers Chart. It should be plainly visible.<br>8. Vocabulary: job, helper, chart. | Film:<br>*Beginning Responsibility: Doing Things For Ourselves in School*, U-6096 (Audiovisual Center, University of Iowa)<br><br>Sketches<br><br>Oaktag<br><br>Marking pen<br><br>Name cards<br><br>Work sheets<br><br>Paste<br><br>Pencils | *HELPERS*<br><br>CUPS<br><br>LIGHTS<br><br>PLANTS<br><br>FISH |

**Lesson 7**

SCOPE OF LESSON: 1. To introduce the class to procedures to be followed in preparing food.
      2. To provide opportunities for discussion of these procedures and their relation to health.

| INSTRUCTIONAL OBJECTIVES | ACTIVITIES | RESOURCE MATERIALS | EXPERIENCE CHART |
|---|---|---|---|
| 1. Is able to prepare a snack for an upcoming party. | 1. Prepare for making pudding by reading aloud the directions on the box. Explain that directions tell us how to make the food and we must follow them carefully so that it comes out tasting good. Place sketches illustrating the various steps along the chalk ledge in random order. Reread the directions, one step at a time, and call on children to come up and find the appropriate sketch. As each one is located, place it in sequence. Include sketches of washing hands, putting on aprons and cleaning up. Cite these along with directions. When all are in order, have class review the steps by "reading" the cards. | Sketches of directions<br><br>Instant pudding<br><br>Milk<br><br>Bowls, spoons, beaters, measuring cups, dishes, aprons | *WE COOK*<br><br> WASH HANDS<br><br>APRONS PUDDING<br><br>MILK MIX<br><br>PUT IN DISHES CLEAN UP |
| | 2. Get children to verbalize about the importance of washing hands before cooking and of wearing aprons. Then have entire class do these two things before beginning. | | |
| | 3. Prepare the instant pudding. Have children determine what to do by referring to the remaining sketches. Make sure every child has a chance to help with the tasks. Spoon the pudding into dishes and refrigerate for the next day. | Oaktag, paste, marker pen, magazines, paper, scissors | |
| | 4. Using the sketches from Activity 1, develop an experience chart. Have the children recount the steps in cooking and find and fasten the picture for each step to the chart. Label the pictures with simple words. | | |
| | 5. Seatwork: Look through magazines for pictures of food. Cut these out and paste on a sheet of paper. | | |
| | 6. Vocabulary: directions, add, mix, egg beater, apron. | | |

# Lesson 8

SCOPE OF LESSON:
1. To stimulate consideration for others by preparing guidelines for proper treatment of guests.
2. To review previous lessons on food preparation, party plans, and guest treatment.
3. To provide a meaningful social experience by carrying through a class party with invited guests.

| INSTRUCTIONAL OBJECTIVES | ACTIVITIES | RESOURCE MATERIALS | EXPERIENCE CHART |
|---|---|---|---|
| 1. Is able to describe the appropriate way to treat a guest. | 1. Begin discussion of how to treat a guest by reminding children that the visitor doesn't know how we do things in our room. How can we help? Discuss such things as greeting and letting the guest see the room, showing him or her a place at the table, serving, displaying good manners at the table, etc. | Pudding napkins, spoons, placemats | OUR PARTY |
| 2. Can plan jobs necessary for the party. | 2. Discuss the jobs that must be done for the party —setting the table, preparing decorations, greeting the guest (who has been forewarned to knock rather than walk in), serving the pudding, clearing the table, washing, drying and putting dishes away. Assign these tasks to various children. | Flowers, vase | |
| 3. Is able to demonstrate the behavior decided upon in Objective 1. | 3. As a class, prepare table decorations. In fall or spring, leaves or flowers can be gathered and put in vases. Other times, paper chains can be made and taped to the table. | Paper  Crayons | |
|  | 4. Have party. Before beginning, remind children about their various jobs. Do this again, if necessary, as the party proceeds. Clean up and wash dishes. | Oaktag  Paste |  |
|  | 5. Seatwork: Each child will draw a picture of the class preparing for, having, or cleaning up after the party. Ask each child to tell what the picture shows and indicate this on it. | Marking pen |  |
|  | 6. These pictures will be used for the experience chart. When all are in place on the chart, review by having each child tell what his or her picture is about. |  |  |
|  | 7. Vocabulary: visitor, serve, clear away. |  |  |

105

**Lesson 9**

SCOPE OF LESSON:  1. To provide the class an acquaintance with a community health service.
2. To review correct procedures for brushing teeth.

| INSTRUCTIONAL OBJECTIVES | ACTIVITIES | RESOURCE MATERIALS | EXPERIENCE CHART |
|---|---|---|---|
| 1. Willingly participates in first-hand experience with a dentist, the office and equipment in the non-threatening context of a class visit.<br><br>2. Is able to demonstrate brushing teeth correctly. | 1. Show the dentist picture from the Health and Cleanliness set. Have children discuss who the dentist is and what the dentist does.<br><br>2. Before the lesson, the teacher should thoroughly prepare the dentist for the visit, explaining the purpose and expectation of the visit as well as the level of student understanding. If necessary, the teacher may guide the dentist in choosing vocabulary and concepts.<br><br>3. Visit the school dentist (or a children's dentist near the school). Arrange for the dentist to show and demonstrate some equipment, allow children to sit in the chair, show X rays and models of teeth, explain the importance of brushing the teeth, and demonstrate the correct way of doing so. Emphasize the idea of the dentist as a friend who helps us.<br><br>4. When back in class, review the correct way of brushing teeth. Practice using actual toothbrushes and toothpaste.<br><br>5. Seatwork: Children draw a picture of what they liked best at the dentist's office. Teacher labels these according to what children say they represent.<br><br>6. Experience Chart: Using pictures the children drew, review what the class saw at the dentist's office. Paste these pictures on oaktag.<br><br>7. Vocabulary: dentist, office, teeth, toothbrush, toothpaste. | Teaching Pictures: *"Health and Cleanliness"* (David C. Cook Publishing Co., 1966)<br><br>Dentist<br><br>Toothbrushes<br><br>Toothpaste<br><br>Cups<br><br>Paper, crayons<br><br>Oaktag, felt marker<br><br>Pen<br><br>Paste | *THE DENTIST*<br><br> |

106

**Lesson 10**

SCOPE OF LESSON: 1. To stimulate concern related to common health dangers.
2. To provide a "real" opportunity to practice proper safety procedures.

| INSTRUCTIONAL OBJECTIVES | ACTIVITIES | RESOURCE MATERIALS | EXPERIENCE CHART |
|---|---|---|---|
| 1. Is able to verbalize common safety principles:<br>a. Don't play in the street.<br>b. Don't play with fire.<br>c. Look up when running.<br>d. Don't play with sharp things, and so forth. | 1. Prior to lesson, prepare a safety bulletin board using the Hayes Posters. Review previous lessons on safety by discussing what is happening in each picture and stating the safety rule that follows.<br>2. Show film *Patty Learns to Stop, Look, and Listen.* In preparation for Activity 3, review what was mentioned in the film about safety in crossing the streets. Use a hand puppet to stimulate conversation with the children. Have the puppet draw out and reinforce certain rules:<br>    Always cross at the corner.<br>    Never run into the street.<br>    Always cross with a green light.<br>    Always look both ways before crossing.<br>    If a ball or other toy rolls into the street, always ask an adult to get it for you.<br>3. Take a "safety" walk in the vicinity of the school. Cross | *Hayes Posters,* set I, "Health" (Hayes School Publishing Inc., 1957)<br><br>*Patty Learns to Stop, Look, and Listen,* U-3462 (Audiovisual Center, University of Iowa)<br><br>Hand puppet<br><br>Sketches from Leaf, *Safety Can Be Fun* (J. B. Lippincott Co., 1938)<br><br>Oaktag<br>paste | *SAFETY CAN BE FUN*<br><br><br><br> |

107

**Lesson 10** (continued)

| Instructional Objectives | Activities | Resource Materials | Experience Chart |
|---|---|---|---|
| | streets that have traffic lights and those that don't, always emphasizing the proper way to cross. Have various children assume responsibility for telling the class when it is okay to cross. | | |
| 2. Can explain rules for crossing the street safely and to put these into effect on a walk. | 4. Develop experience chart using stick figure sketches from *Safety Can Be Fun*, which has been read to the class as part of a previous lesson. Each child picks one sketch to tell about and then puts it on the chart. | Work sheets<br>Pencils | |
| | 5. Seatwork: Each child receives a work sheet that depicts several scenes of a child trying to cross the street—with a green light, with a red light, with no light and no cars, with no light and a car coming, etc. They are to draw a line from the figure to the other side of the street on the scenes where it's safe to cross. For each scene, verbalize about the decision reached and explain why. | | |
| | 6. Vocabulary: traffic, red light, green light, crossing the street, corner. | | |

**Unit Topic: Time**

Written for Intermediate Mildly Mentally Retarded Children[2]

This unit on time was selected for illustrative purposes primarily because of the extensive use made of sequential seatwork. The sample lessons represent only the portion of the unit pertaining to telling time. Lessons regarding the social and vocational implications of time would also be included if the unit were developed in detail. The reader will note that the lessons in this unit differ considerably from those in the unit on "Learning to Be Healthy." One reason is the skill orientation of the time unit; the other is that it is designed for an older group of children. This unit was written for use with mildly mentally retarded children in intermediate grades.

I. RATIONALE

The ability to handle the concept of time is crucial to the adjustment of all children, whether normal or retarded. The affairs of the individual and of all members of a community are organized and to some degree controlled by various aspects of time. Most of us are awakened by the clamor of an alarm clock, and the activities of the ensuing day are governed by whether it is a workday, a Saturday, or a Sunday. The changes of the seasons and the ticking away of seconds are extremes that are separated by many aspects and applications of time-related concepts.

Because retarded children usually lack the ability to grasp spontaneously the abstract aspect of time, they often meet with difficulties at home, at school, and in the community. Therefore, a unit of instruction designed to teach time in a concrete and meaningful manner should be indispensable in contributing to the overall adjustment of these children.

The following pages will provide some guidelines and ideas for presenting a portion of the subject of time over a fifteen-day period.

II. SUB-UNITS

| | | |
|---|---|---|
| A. Recreation | D. Measurement | G. Holidays |
| B. Seasons | E. Jobs | H. Newspaper |
| C. Science | F. Money | |

III. OBJECTIVES

The following concepts and skills should be accomplished as a result of the teacher's work in this area.

2. Modified and reprinted by permission of Corydon Crooks, who developed this unit while a graduate student at the University of Iowa.

1. To develop the different concepts of time through knowledge of the seasons, the calendar, and daily time (clock usage).

2. To develop the ability to tell time in hour, half-hour, quarter-hour, and five-minute units and to be able to relate this ability to everyday usage. Note: It is reasonable to expect that some pupils will be able to work in smaller time units. When this is the case, these pupils should be encouraged and reinforced. The exercises should be altered to make use of and to give practice in their refined ability to use the clock.

3. To develop time concepts in general terms, that is, early, late, now, then, morning, afternoon, day, night, yesterday, tomorrow, A.M., P.M., and so forth.

4. To identify various consequences related to time. For example:
   a. What might happen if you are late for school?
   b. Will going to bed early give me more energy for working and playing? Why?
   c. Would a two-hour walk make me tired?
   d. Would a half-hour run make me tired?
   e. What happens if we are late for the school bus?
   f. Why do you need to turn on the TV at a certain time for your favorite program?

IV. ACTIVITIES

The following list of activities has been arranged according to various competencies. This list is not intended to be complete but should be used as a guide and a suggestion for the general level of competency that may be expected. We recognize that individual differences will determine the level of achievement to a considerable degree and that though teacher expectations should be optimistic, not all children will reach the same level. Some will go beyond our expectations, some will fall short of them. Adjustments will have to be made to modify the activities appropriately for various individuals in the class.

A. *Arithmetic Activities*
   1. Make a calendar for this month. This can be both a group project and an individual one.
   2. Construct a demonstration clock for the bulletin board.
   3. Make a season wheel.
   4. Tell the time given various locations of the hands on a demonstration clock using whole-hour, half-hour, fifteen-minute, and five-minute intervals.

5. Count the number of days, weeks, months before or after an important date such as a birthday, Christmas, or Thanksgiving.

B. *Social Competency Activities*[3]

1. List some problems resulting from being late for school, work, and so forth.
2. Role-play a situation that might occur when tardy for a class, work, or a date.
3. Work as a group to construct bulletin boards to illustrate holidays.
4. Clap hands to keep time with a metronome.
5. Do simple rhythm steps in time with a metronome.
6. Participate in elementary group dances that require some sense of rhythm to execute.

C. *Communication Skills Activities*[3]

1. Read the day, month, and year on newspapers, magazines, books, and so forth.
2. Obtain schedules of the departure and arrival of postal pickups at the post office.
3. Obtain timetables from the bus depots.
4. Make out time schedules for daily activities.
5. Write invitations to another class to attend a class function at a certain time and date.
6. Write friendly letters indicating the date and time of the letter as well as the date and time of certain events that have occurred.
7. Role-play making arrangements with a friend to go to a movie— time, date, place, and so forth.

D. *Safety Activities*[3]

1. Call the local hospital to determine the times that doctors are on duty.
2. Demonstrate safety precautions to be taken related to seasonal sports.
3. Figure starting times for trips so that destinations may be reached without careless hurrying.
4. Role-play possible accidents that might occur as the result of hurrying because of tardiness.

---

3. These particular activities were selected from sample lessons included in *Planning an Arithmetic Curriculum*, Special Education Curriculum Development Center, University of Iowa (Iowa City, 1968). Reprinted with permission.

5. Call hospital to determine the regular hours as well as emergency hours that are followed.

E. *Health Activities*

1. Plan different menus to correspond to the various holidays and seasons.
2. Read to determine the amount of sleep needed each night.
3. List the detrimental effects of eating too rapidly.
4. Construct and discuss a bulletin board showing pictures of appropriate clothing for various occasions, time of day, and season of the year.
5. Demonstrate the length of time to leave thermometer in the mouth.
6. Take the pulse and respiration of a classmate using a stopwatch.
7. Watch a film related to the timing of artificial respiration.

F. *Vocational Competency Activities*

1. Interview personnel from local businesses and factories to determine the working hours.
2. Visit a larger business that utilizes a time clock—have the manager demonstrate and explain its function.
3. Investigate the number of hours various community workers spend on the job (police officers, grocer, teacher, truck driver, doctor, and so forth.)
4. Compute a simple hypothetical wage for a worker who works a set number of hours for a certain rate. Emphasize that time may indeed be equivalent to money.

## V. RESOURCES

It is desirable to identify and plan how you will use the resources for your lessons. Be certain that all resource materials for any particular lesson have been assembled beforehand and that you are thoroughly familiar with them. Audiovisual equipment should be set up and ready for only the flick of a switch to become operative. Threading film or tape, focusing, screen placement, and so on should be done before the class begins. It is often helpful to have one or more of the class members "certified" as an A-V "technician." This leaves the teacher free to utilize the movie, filmstrip, or whatever to greater advantage. This is also reinforcing to the pupils who have been qualified to assume this responsibility.

A list of resources that may assist in teaching this unit follows. The teacher should use any available films and books that will serve to enrich the presentations, whether they are listed here or not.

A. *Materials*

| | |
|---|---|
| Newspapers | TV schedules in newspapers |
| Books and magazines | *TV Guide* |
| Calendars | Clock and watches |
| Demonstration clock | Pictures of sundials and clocks |
| Hourglass | Projector (slide, movie, overhead) |
| Films | Bulletin board and materials |

B. *Films*

The following films are listed in the *Catalog of Educational Films* published by the Audiovisual Center at The University of Iowa.
Mail orders for films may be sent to:

Audiovisual Center
Division of Extension and University Services
The University of Iowa
Iowa City, Iowa 52240

1. *The Calendar: Story of its Development;* (U-5066)
2. *The Story of Measuring Time: Hours, Minutes, Seconds;* (U-6037)
3. *The Calendar: Days, Weeks, Months;* (U-4024)
4. *Children of Switzerland;* (U-776)
5. *How to Measure Time;* (U-5684)
6. *What Time Is It?;* (U-3346)

C. *Books*

Abisch, Roz. *Do You Know What Time It Is?* Prentice-Hall, Inc., 1968.

Borland, Kathryn K. *Clocks, From Shadow to Atom.* Follet, 1969.
Jupo, Frank. *A Day Around the World.* Abelard Schuman, 1968.
Mendoza, George. *The Scarecrow Clock.* Holt, Rinehart and Winston, 1971.
Piltz, Albert. *Time Without Clocks; How Nature Tells Time.* Grosset and Dunlap, 1970.
Roy, Cal. *Time Is Day.* Astor-Honor, 1968.
Waller, L. *A Book To Begin on Time.* Henry Holt and Co., 1969.

## VI. VOCABULARY

A working vocabulary relevant to the subject of time is necessary. The following list should be in the repertoire of intermediate level children.

These should be familiar as sight words, although many pupils will be able to write and spell some of these words.

| day | : (colon) | late | alarm | May |
|-----|-----------|------|-------|-----|
| week | channel | A.M. | set | June |
| month | program | season | wind | July |
| year | television | spring | decade | August |
| calendar | TV | summer | P.M. | September |
| second | holiday | fall | morning | October |
| minute | sun | autumn | night | November |
| today | moon | winter | afternoon | December |
| tomorrow | stars | Sunday | evening | timetable |
| tonight | time | Monday | noon | motel |
| yesterday | hour | Tuesday | now | clock |
| past | hand | Wednesday | January | leap year |
| present | face | Thursday | February | century |
| future | clock | Friday | March | half-hour |
| o'clock | early | Saturday | April | quarter-hour |

**Lesson 1**

SCOPE OF THE LESSON: To introduce the subject of months and seasons and to relate them to our lives.

| INSTRUCTIONAL OBJECTIVES | ACTIVITIES | RESOURCE MATERIALS | EXPERIENCE CHART |
|---|---|---|---|
| 1. Each child shall be able to tell his or her birthdate and either write it on paper or point to the proper date on a yearly calendar when asked to do so. | 1.1* Have each pupil draw a birthday cake on heavy, white paper. Children should draw on the cake the number of candles that would represent their age. Under the cake each child shall letter name, present age, and birthdate (month, day, year). | White drawing paper | Our date of birth is important to remember. We need to know the day, month, and year of our birth. |
| | 1.2. Let each child cut out a candle from colored paper and then put name and the numerical date of birthday on it. These candles should then be attached to a cake with his or her birth month lettered on it. These birth month cakes will be prepared by the teacher and put on a bulletin board or as decoration in the room. | Colored drawing paper<br><br>Pencils<br><br>Felt pens<br><br>Crayons<br><br>Rulers<br><br>Cake cut-outs (the teacher should prepare these before class)<br><br>Stapler, thumbtacks, cellulose tape or paste | List each child's name and birthdate. |
| | TOM 9 | | |
| | 1.3. Use an existing large yearly calendar (or make one) and have each child place a small name disc over the correct day and on the right month for his or her birthday. This can serve as a reminder for parties to the class. | Large calendar for the year | |

*1.1 indicates first activity with objective number 1.

115

**Lesson 2**

Scope of the Lesson: To continue activities related to the seasons and months.

| Instructional Objectives | Activities | Resource Materials | Experience Chart |
|---|---|---|---|
| 1. The child shall demonstrate a knowledge of the months and seasons by being able to read and/or write the name of each month (with reasonable spelling), know its numerical place in the yearly sequence, and arrange the months into seasonal groups when asked to do so. | 1.1. Construct a season wheel similar to the one on page 133. <br><br> 1.2. Discuss the seasons by having the children consider: <br> a. weather characteristics <br> b. tree foliage and plants <br> c. animals' seasonal habits <br> d. changes in animals' coats <br> e. seasonal activities <br>　(1) school <br>　(2) sports <br>　(3) farm <br>　(4) recreational <br><br> 1.3. Relate the seasons to the months using the season wheel and a large calendar. Show the relationship between the succession of the months and the passage of the year through the seasons. <br><br> 1.4. Each child can make a seasonal scrapbook with the seasons and months lettered at the top of each page. Paste appropriate pictures on the pages. | Season wheel (see page 133) made of stiff cardboard. <br><br> Magazines for pictures <br><br> Paste <br><br> Scissors <br><br> Crayons <br><br> Notebook paper <br><br> Construction paper for notebook covers <br><br> Stapler | We have four seasons during the year. The weather changes during each season. <br><br> Winter (cold) <br> December <br> January <br> February <br><br> Spring (cool and rainy) <br> March <br> April <br> May <br><br> Summer (hot and sunny) <br> June <br> July <br> August <br><br> Fall or Autumn (cool) <br> September <br> October <br> November |

**Lesson 3**

SCOPE OF THE LESSON: To introduce seasonal holidays to further knowledge about seasons and months.

| INSTRUCTIONAL OBJECTIVES | ACTIVITIES | RESOURCE MATERIALS | EXPERIENCE CHART |
|---|---|---|---|
| 1. Each child shall participate in a discussion of seasonal holidays by making at least one appropriate verbal contribution. | 1.1. Introduce the subject of seasonal holidays by talking about each of the four major holidays observed during the winter, spring, fall, and summer (Christmas, Easter, Thanksgiving, Fourth of July). | Ditto copies of the exercise Season Fun for each pupil (page 136)<br><br>Crayons<br><br>Transparency of Season Fun for projection on a screen or the chalkboard | We celebrate many holidays during the year. Some holidays are winter holidays and some are summer, spring, and fall holidays.<br><br>Christmas comes in the winter. Easter comes in the spring. The Fourth of July comes in the summer. Thanksgiving comes in the fall. |
| 2. Each pupil shall complete the Season Fun Exercise (page 136) by coloring the pictures and by writing (or verbalizing) the proper responses to fill in the blanks. | 2.1. The children shall be encouraged to color the sketches accompanying Season Fun.<br><br>2.2. Finish the exercise by having each pupil complete the sentences by writing the appropriate words in the blanks. | Note: A transparency of the lesson being worked on will help the teacher and pupils during group discussion of a lesson.<br><br>Overhead projector | |

117

**Lesson 4**

Scope of the Lesson:    To provide for a review of the seasons and the months.

| Instructional Objectives | Activities | Resource Materials | Experience Chart |
|---|---|---|---|
| 1. Each pupil shall complete the Review of the Seasons exercise on page 137 to the teacher's satisfaction. | 1.1. This exercise can be done as a joint project with the whole class participating and answering the questions. Those children who have the ability can do the exercise as seatwork. | Ditto copies of the review exercise on page 137. <br><br> Thermal transparency of the exercise <br><br> Wax pencil for use on the transparency | Use a copy of the exercise on page 137 as the experience chart. After each child has completed it, the exercise can be done on the chart and the pupils can correct their own papers. |
| | 1.2. Using the exercise as a group review, project the exercise using a transparency of page 137 for group discussion and deciding the correct answers. | Overhead projector | |
| | 1.3. Either as the result of group discussion, or of individual seatwork, individual children can copy or provide the answers on their own initiative and complete the exercise on dittoed copies of this review. | | |

**Lesson 5**

SCOPE OF THE LESSON:   To introduce and to provide learning experiences in the use of the calendar.

| INSTRUCTIONAL OBJECTIVES | ACTIVITIES | RESOURCE MATERIALS | EXPERIENCE CHART |
|---|---|---|---|
| 1. The pupil shall complete Calendar Exercise 1 on page 138 according to the instructions. The pupil may use a current calendar as an aid. | 1.1. The teacher shall read the instructions to the first calendar exercise and demonstrate how to do the exercise either on the chalkboard or by using the overhead projector and a transparency of the lesson. A calendar of the current month should be prominently displayed. | Large calendar for the current month<br><br>Ditto copies of Calendar Exercise 1 for each member of the class—see page 138.<br><br>Thermal transparency of the exercise<br><br>Wax pencil<br><br>Overhead projector | The Calendar<br>The calendar helps us keep track of the days, months, and years. Some calendars sit on the desk and some hang on a wall. We have four calendars in our classroom. This is the month of March. March has 31 days. |

# Lesson 6

SCOPE OF THE LESSON: To provide for continuing exercises to strengthen knowledge about the calendar.

| INSTRUCTIONAL OBJECTIVES | ACTIVITIES | RESOURCE MATERIALS | EXPERIENCE CHART |
|---|---|---|---|
| 1. In a class discussion each child shall demonstrate by accurate statements, and to the teacher's satisfaction, that he or she has sufficient knowledge about the calendar to answer the questions on pages 138-39. | 1.1. The pupils can take turns reading the questions on pages 138-39, either from their own copies of the exercises or from projected transparencies. | Copies of pages 138-39 <br><br> Thermal transparency of each page | We can tell what is today by looking at the calendar. <br><br> March 1976 <br><br> S M T W Th F S <br>    1  2  3  4  5  6 <br> 7  8  9 10 11 12 13 <br> 14 15 16 17 18 19 20 <br> 21 22 23 24 25 26 27 <br> 28 29 30 (31) <br><br> Today is Wednesday, March 31, 1976. |
| 2. Each pupil shall complete the supplements to Calendar Exercise 1 on page 138-39 by writing the correct answer on the dittoed copies of the exercises. The pupils who are unable to meet writing skills needed may supply the answers verbally. | 2.1. After a discussion of the question has elicited a correct answer, the teacher should write the answer on the transparency with wax pencil. Pupils can then write the answers on their individual copies. <br> Note: The use of an overhead projector with this exercise can reinforce reading skills and provide a model for writing the answers. <br> The exercises on pages 138-39 have been presented in small groups so that the pupils will not be overwhelmed by a full page of questions. The teacher shall use discretion concerning the number of questions that the class can tolerate during one class session on Time. | Overhead projector <br><br> Wax pencil | |

120

**Lesson 7**

SCOPE OF THE LESSON:  To strengthen skills in using the calendar.

| INSTRUCTIONAL OBJECTIVES | ACTIVITIES | RESOURCE MATERIALS | EXPERIENCE CHART |
|---|---|---|---|
| 1. Each child shall complete Calendar Exercise 2 to the teacher's satisfaction and within the time allotted by the teacher. | 1.1. Calendar Exercise 2 (page 140) can be done as a class activity using individual copies as well as a projected transparency. The teacher may administer this lesson in a manner similar to the previous one. | Copies of Calendar Exercise 2 for each pupil. See page 140.<br><br>Thermal transparency of the exercise<br><br>Overhead projector<br><br>Wax pencil<br><br>Calendar for the current year | Record Calendar Exercise 2 from page 140 on the chart and complete as a group activity. |

121

## Lesson 8

SCOPE OF THE LESSON: To continue to provide exercises and activities that utilize the calendar.

| INSTRUCTIONAL OBJECTIVES | ACTIVITIES | RESOURCE MATERIALS | EXPERIENCE CHART |
|---|---|---|---|
| 1. Each child shall make at least three appropriate contributions to a discussion concerning the exercise on pages 140-41. | 1.1. With the help of individual copies of Calendar Fun and a projected image of the work sheets, discuss and verbalize the answers to all of the questions on the three sheets. | Individual copies of Calendar Fun<br><br>Thermal transparency of the exercises<br><br>Wax pencil | Dates to Remember<br><br>My birthdate is _____.<br>Today's date is _____.<br>My teacher's birthdate is _____.<br><br>The last day of school is _____. |
| 2. Each pupil shall complete the three parts of Calendar Fun either by writing the answers in the spaces provided, or by verbalizing the answers to the teacher. | 2.1. Each child shall write the correct answers to the seat-work activity in the spaces provided. Those who cannot write sufficiently well may verbalize the answers.<br><br>2.2. Utilize the questions on the work sheets to stimulate a time-related discussion that goes beyond the scope of the work sheet.<br>Note: As with the questions following Calendar Exercise 1, the number of questions per page has been kept to a nonthreatening number. | Overhead projector<br><br>Calendar for the current month | |

122

# Lesson 9

SCOPE OF THE LESSON:   To introduce and provide a variety of experiences for teaching and strengthening knowledge and skills associated with using a clock or watch.

| INSTRUCTIONAL OBJECTIVES | ACTIVITIES | RESOURCE MATERIALS | EXPERIENCE CHART |
|---|---|---|---|
| 1. Each child shall demonstrate that he or she can correctly and with little hesitation tell time by full-hours, half-hours, quarter-hours, and five-minute intervals by reading aloud the correct time from a demonstration clock, a projection of a clock face, a wall clock, or a watch when asked to do so. Note: The limitations and abilities of individuals must be recognized and the goals set must be individually realistic. Not every child will be capable of reading a clock or watch at five-minute intervals, for example. | | Transparency of a clock face<br><br>Overhead projector<br><br>Assortment of clock faces—enough so each child can have one at his or her desk. Use small demonstration clocks, old watches or alarm clocks with the hands intact and movable. | Clocks<br>Clocks help us in telling time. We have a clock in our classroom.<br>Some of us have wristwatches.<br>Clocks have *hands.*<br>  The long hand tells the minute.<br>  The short hand tells the hour.<br>Some clocks have second hands which move fast. |
| 2. Each pupil shall participate in the discussion of clocks and watches and their function by making at least one appropriate contribution during the discussion. | 2.1. The teacher will introduce the clock to the class using a projection of a clock face from an overhead projector or by using a *large* demonstration clock. It is recommended that each child have a small clock face with movable hands, a watch, or an alarm clock to use at the desk during these exercises. | | |

123

# Lesson 9 (continued)

| Instructional Objectives | Activities | Resource Materials | Experience Chart |
|---|---|---|---|
| | Old, nonfunctioning clocks with the faces and hands intact would be adequate. These can be procured from parents, friends, Goodwill or Salvation Army stores, etc. | | |
| | 2.2. As a part of the previous activity the teacher should evaluate the ability of the members of the class to use a clock by showing a variety of settings on the demonstration clock using full-hour, half-hour, quarter-hour, and five-minute graduations. | | |
| 3. Each child shall demonstrate the ability to discriminate between the minute and hour hands by indicating (pointing or touching) the correct one when asked to do so. | 3.1. Involve the class in a discussion of the length of the hands on the clocks and watches. Ask them to discriminate between the long one and the short one on clock faces and watches of different sorts and sizes. | | |
| 4. Each child shall provide at least one correct answer to a time-related situation that requires reading time from a clock or watch. | 4.1. Provide for practice in reading time by discussing time-related situations and by having pupils take turns in showing their ability to set the hands to a variety of discussed times and/or to read | | |

124

the clock set to different readings.
Examples: "How does the clock look when we watch a TV program at 6 o'clock?" "When the clock is like this (set the hands to 12 o'clock) and it is daytime, it is time for (*lunch*)."

## Lesson 10

SCOPE OF THE LESSON:   To provide for more activities in using the clock.

| INSTRUCTIONAL OBJECTIVES | ACTIVITIES | RESOURCE MATERIALS | EXPERIENCE CHART |
|---|---|---|---|
| 1. Each pupil shall complete Clock-Face Exercises 1 and 2 in a manner commensurate with assessed ability and to the teacher's satisfaction.<br>Note: This exercise calls for writing the correct time in numerals and words. If writing the words is too advanced for any of the pupils, that part of the exercise may be modified. Always keep in mind, however, that we are concerned with gains in learning as well as strengthening what has been previously learned. | 1.1. Use the overhead projector to help moderate a discussion of the exercises in the project. The class may decide collectively or individuals may take turns suggesting what times are shown on each of the six faces. With each decision, have each child write first in numerals (on the top line) then in words, on the bottom line) the time represented on each clock face. This shall be done on the individual copies by each pupil.<br>Note: Instructions for Exercises 1 and 2 appear on page 142. | Ditto copies of the exercises on page 142 for each pupil<br><br>Thermal transparency of the exercise<br><br>Overhead projector<br><br>Wax pencil | Record exercises 1 and 2 from page 142 on the experience chart. After the pupils have been given the opportunity to work independently on the exercise, work then as a group exercise. Have the pupils explain how they completed each example. |

125

**Lesson 11**

SCOPE OF THE LESSON: Continue to provide experiences that will develop clock-reading skills.

| INSTRUCTIONAL OBJECTIVES | ACTIVITIES | RESOURCE MATERIALS | EXPERIENCE CHART |
|---|---|---|---|
| 1. Each child shall draw the hour and minute hands in the proper relative positions according to the times given under each clock face in Exercises 3 and 4. Attention must be given to the difference in the lengths of the hour and minute hands. The teacher should expect at least 5/6 of each exercise to be correct. | 1.1. Distribute copies of Clock-Face Exercise 3 to each pupil and explain the exercise. Use the overhead projector to demonstrate how to draw lines in their relative positions and of the correct lengths. Use a ruler or straightedge and wax pencil on the acetate transparency. | Ditto copies of Clock-Face Exercises 3 and 4 for each child<br><br>Rulers or straightedges for drawing lines to represent hands<br><br>Demonstration clock<br><br>Clock transparency | Record Exercises 3 and 4 from pages 143-44 and repeat the process suggested in Lesson 10. |
| | 1.2. Use the same techniques with Clock-Face Exercise 4. Note: As in other exercises, it may be of advantage to the pupils to instigate the exercise as a group project. However, the individual pupil should be encouraged to strike out independently as quickly as possible.<br><br>Exercise 3 is on page 143.<br><br>Exercise 4 is on page 144. | Assortment of clocks as in Lesson 9<br><br>Transparency of the lessons<br><br>Wax pencil | |

# Lesson 12

SCOPE OF THE LESSON: Provide for further activities to strengthen clock use.

| INSTRUCTIONAL OBJECTIVES | ACTIVITIES | RESOURCE MATERIALS | EXPERIENCE CHART |
|---|---|---|---|
| 1. Each child shall complete Clock-Face Exercise 5 by numbering the dots correctly on the clock faces and by drawing the hands in the correct positions. The difference between the hour and the minute hand should be easily recognized. Accuracy should be at least five correct out of six.<br><br>Note: The pupils may write the numbers around the perimeter of the clock faces if this is easier for any of them. They should, however, attempt to keep the numbers small and directly relative to each face. | 1.1. Distribute copies of Clock-Face Exercise 5 (page 145) to each pupil.<br><br>1.2. Project a transparency of the exercise to help explain it to the pupils and to demonstrate how to do the exercise.<br><br>1.3. Discuss and do, as a group, one or two parts of the exercise using the projected copy. The teacher may want to make additional practice examples for group work by using an acetate sheet and a wax pencil to construct similar problems. | Ditto copies of the exercise (page 145)<br><br>Transparency for use with the overhead projector<br><br>Plain acetate sheet<br><br>Wax pencil<br><br>Rulers or straightedges for drawing hands | In telling time, we must be careful to read the correct time. We must look closely at the hour hand and the minute hand. Some clock faces do not have numbers. We need to know where the numbers are supposed to be. This will help us tell time.<br><br>The time is the same. |

127

**Lesson 13**

SCOPE OF THE LESSON: Improve clock skills.

| INSTRUCTIONAL OBJECTIVES | ACTIVITIES | RESOURCE MATERIALS | EXPERIENCE CHART |
|---|---|---|---|
| 1. Each child shall participate in a discussion of the Clock-Face Exercises 6 and 7 and shall correctly (five out of six accuracy expected) write the numbers on the faces, write the time in numbers on the top line and the time in words on the bottom line under each face. | 1.1. By now the children should be fairly competent in reading time correctly and should be able to fill in the numbers on the faces, write the time in numbers and in words as directed.<br><br>1.2. As in other exercises, the overhead projector may be an asset.<br><br>Exercises 6 and 7 are on page 146. | Ditto copies of the exercise for each pupil<br><br>Transparency of the exercise | Record Exercises 6 and 7 from page 146 on a chart as a means of correcting students' work. |

**Lesson 14**

SCOPE OF THE LESSON: Introduce the use of the clock as a means of timing and scheduling activities.

| INSTRUCTIONAL OBJECTIVES | ACTIVITIES | RESOURCE MATERIALS | EXPERIENCE CHART |
|---|---|---|---|
| 1. Each child shall be engaged in activities 1.2 and 1.3 and shall supply at least three correct answers to each set of questions. | 1.1. Use the demonstration clock or the overhead projector and/or individual clocks, and so forth in the following ways. | Transparency demonstration clock. | No experience chart is necessary for this lesson. |
| | | Large demonstration clock | |
| | | Wax pencil | |
| | 1.2. Set a demonstration clock to a time (example: 3 o'clock) then ask the pupils what time it will be in 5 minutes, 15 minutes, 30 minutes, an hour, and so on. Do this as a group exercise and give each child an opportunity to respond. Use a variety of clock settings. | Individual clocks as in Lesson 9 | |
| | 1.3. Do as in 1.2 but ask the pupils what time it was 15 minutes ago, an hour ago, and so on. | | |

# Lesson 15

SCOPE OF THE LESSON: To provide a continuation of clock-related activities.

| INSTRUCTIONAL OBJECTIVES | ACTIVITIES | RESOURCE MATERIALS | EXPERIENCE CHART |
|---|---|---|---|
| 1. Each pupil shall complete Exercise 8 by writing, in numerals, the correct answers to the questions in the exercise. Expected accuracy should be at least 80%. | 1.1. Distribute copies of the exercise and read each of the five questions from a projection of the exercise. Pupils may be asked to do the reading whenever possible. <br><br> 2.1. The pupils shall determine individually the correct answers and write them in the spaces provided. Exercise 8 is on page 147. | Ditto copies of the exercise (page 147) <br><br> Transparency of the exercise | Half an hour equals 30 minutes. One hour equals 60 minutes. A quarter of an hour equals 15 minutes. <br><br> Half past means 30 minutes after the hour. For example, half past ten is the same as 10:30. <br><br> Before assigning Exercise 8 on page 147 to the class, complete the following as a group activity. Ask volunteers to draw hands on the clock faces indicating the appropriate time. <br><br> 2:40  1:30  7:00 <br><br> 12:15  5:20 |

130

# Lesson 16

SCOPE OF THE LESSON: To further skills in clock-related time situations.

| INSTRUCTIONAL OBJECTIVES | ACTIVITIES | RESOURCE MATERIALS | EXPERIENCE CHART |
|---|---|---|---|
| 1. Each pupil shall complete Exercise 9 by either writing the numerals (except for part one of the fourth question) in the blank spaces or by giving the correct answer verbally. | 1.1. Using the projection of the transparency of the exercise, discuss how to do these clock-related problems. <br><br> 1.2. Encourage the children to make contributions by asking the whole class similar questions. This could develop into a game similar to a spelldown, with the person who gets the correct answer having the privilege of asking a child on the other "side" a question from a bank of problems or an original problem. Exercise 9 is on page 148. | Ditto copies of the exercise (see page 148) <br><br> Transparency of the exercise | Have the class participate in developing a daily schedule. The following is an example. <br> School starts at 8:30 <br> We have arithmetic at 9:00 <br> Reading begins at 9:30 <br> Recess 10:00 <br> Units 10:15 <br> Lunch 11:30 <br> School begins 12:15 <br> Language 12:15 <br> P.E. 1:15 <br> Music 1:45 <br> Study time 2:15 <br> We go home at 3:00 |

131

**Birthday Cake Exercise**

Have each child draw a birthday cake on the order of the one shown. Have the children letter their own names, ages, and birth dates including the month, day, and year under the drawing. The correct number of candles should be drawn on the cake to represent the child's present age. The whole drawing can be colored and used as a bulletin board decoration to remind the class to prepare for birthday celebrations.

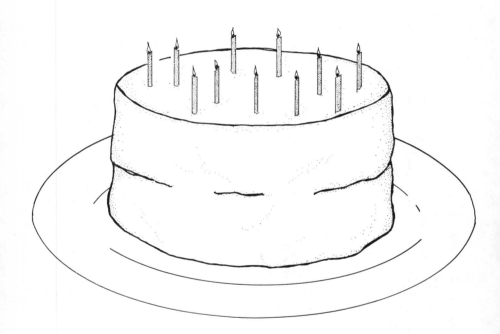

# JACOB PETERS-11 YEARS
# MARCH 17, 1965

## Season Wheel

This season wheel can be made of stiff paper or tagboard and should be large enough so that the whole class can see it (at least 24″ diameter). If the inner wheel is a separate disc, one exercise could be to turn the discs until the seasons line up with the proper months. The wheel can also be colored, and pictures cut from magazines showing seasonal activities can be grouped in clusters around the appropriate season.

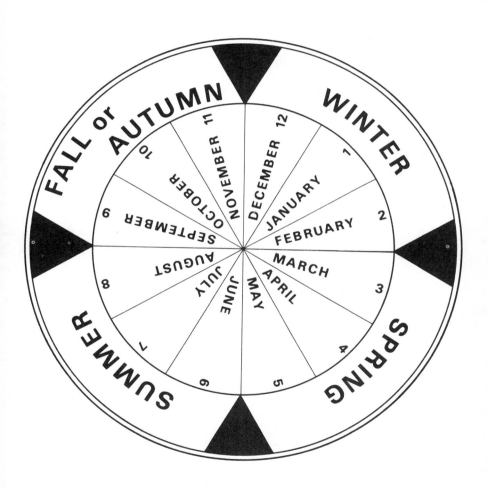

## Month Flower

Fill in the missing letters to complete the names of the months. Also, give each month its proper number, starting with January as month number 1.

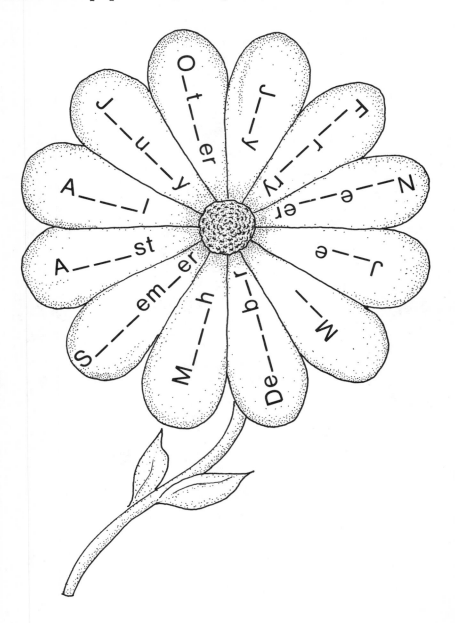

**Facts About the Seasons**

1. Fill in the missing letters to complete the names of the months.
2. Fill in the blanks from the list of words below so that the sentences make true statements.


1. In J .... .... y it is usually ........................ but in J .... .... u .... .... y it is the ........................ season so it is snowy and ........................

2. M .... .... .... h, A .... .... .... l, and M .... .... are all in the ........................ of the year. They are the ....rd, ....th, and the ....th months.

3. The Thanksgiving month is N .... .... .... m .... .... r. It is the month that comes in the ........................ and is the ...........th month of the year.

4. The last month of winter is F .... .... r .... .... .... y and the first month of summer is J .... .... .... .

5. Christmas comes during the month of D .... .... .... m .... .... r. It is in the ........................ and is the ........................ month of the year. The next year begins with J .... .... .... .... ry.

6. We start school in S .... .... t .... .... b .... r. This month begins the ........................ season.

7. The 8th month is A .... .... u .... .... .

8. A summer month that comes after July that is usually a very hot month is A .... .... u .... t.

9. O .... .... .... b .... r is the middle month of the ........................ season.

10. The winter months are ........................ but in the ........................ it is warm.


| spring | fall | cold | warm | 3 | 5 |
|--------|------|------|------|---|----|
| summer | winter | hot | last | 4 | 11 |

**Season Fun**

We celebrate Thanksgiving in the .................. during the month of ........................ .

Our nation's birthday is in the ........................... on the ........th of ........................ .

Christmas comes in the ................ during the month of .................. .

A religious celebration in the ........................ is Easter.

## Review of the Seasons and Months

Write the correct answer in each blank.
1. School begins in the ............................ .
2. Christmas comes in the ............................ .
3. Easter is in the ............................ .
4. You play in the snow in the ............................ .
5. In the ............................ it is usually very hot.

Draw a line between opposites.

Example:  Fast ──────── Far
          Hot ──╳── Slow
          Near ──────── Cold

Winter                      First
Past                        Tomorrow
Yesterday                   Spring
Autumn                      Summer
Last                        Future

Write in the months in the spaces under the correct season.

| | | | |
|---|---|---|---|
| | | | |
| | | | |
| | | | |
| | | | |

**Calendar Exercise 1**

*The Calendar*

| | | | | | | |
|---|---|---|---|---|---|---|
| | | | | | | |
| | | | | | | |
| | | | | | | |
| | | | | | | |
| | | | | | | |
| | | | | | | |

1. Letter in the name of this month in the top space of the calendar form.
2. Letter in the names of the days of the week in the seven spaces on the second line.
3. Complete this month's calendar by filling in the numbers of the month, being sure to start the first (number 1) on the right day of the week.

*Names and Dates*

1. What day of the week is the last day of this month? ...................................

2. Write the numbers (dates) of the days of this month that are all on a Sunday. ............, ............, ............, ............, ............

3. Write the days of the month that are all on a Tuesday. ............, ............, ............, ............, ............

4. What day of the week did the first fall on this month?

5. What is today's date (number of the day)? ............

6. What was yesterday's date? ............

*Names of Days and Months*

1. What was yesterday's day-name? ........................

2. What will be tomorrow's date? ............

3. What will be tomorrow's day-name? ........................

4. What was the day-name of the first of this month? ........................

5. What day is today? ........................

6. Write the names of the following:

    This month ...........................

    Next month ...........................

    Last month ...........................

*Counting the Days*

1. There are ............ days in this month.

2. There are ............ days in a week.

3. Next month will have ............ days. (consult a calendar for the year)

4. Last month had ............ days.

5. What day did last month begin on? ...........................

6. What day will next month begin on? ........................

**Calendar Exercise 2**

*Days of the Month*

| | | | | | | |
|---|---|---|---|---|---|---|
| | | | | | | |
| | | | | | | |
| | | | | | | |
| | | | | | | |
| | | | | | | |

1. Write in the days of the week on the second line in the form above.
2. Make Sunday the first day of this month; write the number 1 under Sunday in the third line.
3. Make Tuesday the last day of this month; number all the days up to and including the space under Tuesday on the last line.
4. How many days are there in this month you have made? ............
5. How many months have the same number of days as your month? ............ Suggestion: Get a calendar for this year to help you.
6. What is the least number of days there can be in a month? ............
7. In this month you have made what is the date of:
   The second Tuesday? ............         The third Sunday? ............

*Birthday Days*

Note:  You will need to use this year's calendar for help in answering these questions.

1. What is today's date? ............
2. My birthday is the ............ of ............................ .
                    (date)         (month)

3. This year my birthday falls on the ............ day of the week. This is .............................................. .

4. I will have to wait ............ months, ............ weeks, and ............ days until my birthday is here.

5. There are ............ days in a week.

*School Days*

Note: You will need to use this year's calendar for help in answering these questions.

1. But, there are only ............ days to a school week.

2. This year school began on the ............ of ............................. .

3. This year school is over on the ............ of ............................. .

4. The days of the week are:    (1) .........................................

(2) ...................................... (3) .........................................

(4) ...................................... (5) .........................................

(6) ...................................... (7) .........................................

5. Christmas is the ............ of ............................. and falls on the ............ day of the week which is ........................... .

*Vacation Days*

Note: You will need to use this year's calendar for help in answering these questions.

1. January 1st this year was on what day of the week? .................................

2. This year Christmas vacation begins on the ............ of ............................. and we go back to school on the ............ of ....................... .

3. There are ............ days to the Christmas vacation.

4. How many days was the Thanksgiving vacation? ............

5. What other vacations are there during the school year and what are they? .................................................................................................

**Clock-Face Exercise**

Exercises 1 and 2

On the top line under each clock face write the correct time in numerals. On the second line under each clock write in words the time shown by the position of the hands.

Exercise 3

7 o'clock

5 o'clock

3 o'clock

11 o'clock

12 o'clock

9 o'clock

Draw the hands in the proper positions to show the times given under each clock face. Be certain the hands are drawn to show a difference in length between the minute hand and the hour hand.

**Exercise 4**

10:55

6:00

11:25

1:15

8:05

3:20

Draw the hands in the proper positions to show the times given under each clock face. Be certain the hands are drawn to show a difference in length between the minute hand and the hour hand.

**Exercise 5**

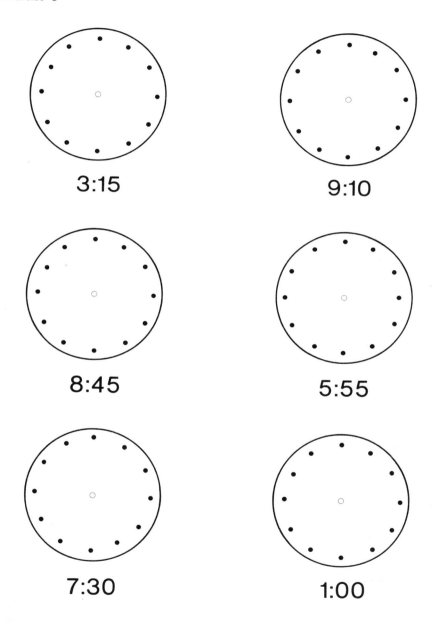

3:15                    9:10

8:45                    5:55

7:30                    1:00

Write the numerals on each clock face, and then draw the hands in the proper position (and lengths) to show the times given under each clock.

**Exercises 6 and 7**

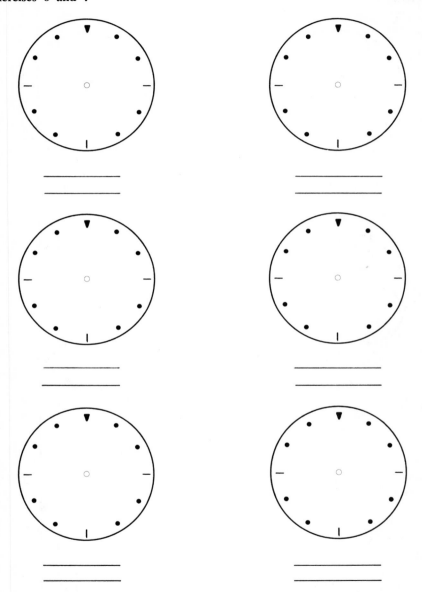

Write the numerals on the clock faces and then:
1. On the top line under each clock face write in numerals the time indicated by the position of the hands.
2. On the second line under each clock face write the time in words.

**Exercise 8**

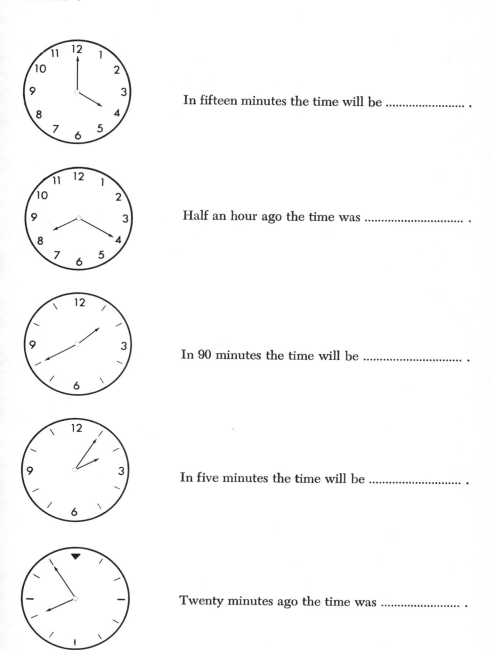

In fifteen minutes the time will be ..................... .

Half an hour ago the time was ..................... .

In 90 minutes the time will be ..................... .

In five minutes the time will be ..................... .

Twenty minutes ago the time was ..................... .

**Exercise 9**

How many minutes is it before 4:30? ....................

If the TV program we wanted to watch was at 8:00 o'clock, how late are we? .............................

If the bus leaves at 2:45, how much time is left?
.........................

The football game begins at 1:30. Are we late or not? ................................. If we are late, how many minutes late? ...........................

New Year's begins at 12:00 midnight. How long do we have to stay up to see the New Year in?
.........................

BIBLIOGRAPHY

CROOKS, CORYDON. "Time." Unpublished doctoral dissertation, University of Iowa, 1971.

*Life Experience Starter Units Set No. 2.* Special Education Curriculum Development Center. Iowa City: University of Iowa, 1969.

*Planning An Arithmetic Curriculum.* Special Education Curriculum Development Center. Iowa City: University of Iowa, 1968.

# 6

# Instructional Objectives

The skill of writing instructional objectives in behavioral terms is basic to the unit development approach suggested in this book. The developmental steps for writing units require the teacher to prepare instructional objectives for each lesson; the use of objectives is recommended in preparing a year's plan of unit work; the evaluation techniques suggested in Chapter 7 rely on instructional objectives as a frame of reference. Although the reader is referred to this chapter from various sections, specific information on instructional objectives has also been incorporated into other chapters when appropriate.

The intent of this chapter is to orient the reader to the use of instructional objectives in the process of individualizing instruction through unit teaching and to provide experience in writing objectives. Exercises are included at the end of the chapter. The terms *instructional* and *behavioral* will be used interchangeably in describing objectives.

The development of objectives has a long history in education. Terms such as *aims, goals,* and *outcomes* have frequently been used along with *objectives* to indicate a desired level of achievement or the direction for a particular curriculum area. For the most part, these terms have been used to reflect different levels of specificity. Although they have been used to establish expectancy levels for pupil performance, the more typical application has been to use them within the context of general statements which are somewhat philosophical in nature. Used in this context, they offer little direction to teachers responsible for structuring learning experiences specific to the needs of individual pupils. Nor do they provide much guidance for persons responsible for the selection, modification, and/or development of instructional materials. Consequently, teachers have tended not to perceive objectives or the process of writing them as contributing to their teaching effectiveness in the classroom.

Objectives need not take the form of vague statements. They can be structured to serve as an effective tool in the process of individualizing instruction and in the assessment of pupil performance. Both of these areas are major responsibilities of a classroom teacher. The teacher must be able to analyze learning tasks based on a knowledge of learner characteristics and organize teaching strategies commensurate with pupil ability. At the same time, it is essential that the teacher assess pupil performance to determine the level of competency attained on prescribed tasks. Teachers willing to invest the effort required to become skillful in writing behaviorally stated instructional objectives will find that the skill as well as the objectives will contribute significantly to their efforts at individualizing instruction.

The increased attention given to the development and use of behaviorally stated instructional objectives in recent years has resulted in the appearance of various definitions in the literature as well as the generation of a number of schemes for specifying them. A review of selected definitions and schemes should be of help to teachers as they develop their own style. Mager defines objectives as follows:

> . . . an objective is an intent communicated by a statement describing a proposed change in a learner—a statement of what the learner is to be like when he has successfully completed a learning experience. It is a description of a pattern of behavior (performance) we want the learner to be able to demonstrate.[1]

According to Mager, you have been successful in stating an objective if your statement communicates to the reader your instructional intent. For example, if you have written an instructional objective for a unit lesson, the degree to which your objective communicates your intent can be tested by having another teacher teach the lesson. If students are taught to perform according to the expectations you had in mind when structuring your instructional objective, then it communicates your intent. The scheme that Mager suggests for the specification of instructional objectives includes the following features:

1. Identify a terminal behavior by name; you can specify the kind of behavior that will be accepted as evidence that the learner has achieved the objective.
2. Try to define the desired behavior further by describing the important conditions under which the behavior will be expected to occur.
3. Specify the criteria of acceptable performance by describing how well the performer must perform to be considered acceptable.[2]

General Programmed Teaching defines behavioral objectives in this way:

> Description of the form of the behavior that instruction is to produce, stated in terms of what the student is to be able to do, the conditions

1. Robert F. Mager, *Preparing Instructional Objectives* (Belmont, Calif.: Fearon Publishers, 1962), p. 3. Reprinted with permission of the publisher.
2. Ibid., p. 12.

requiring the action, and where appropriate, a standard of accuracy or speed.[3]

They distinguish affective objectives from behavioral objectives by defining affective objectives as "an objective dealing with emotions or feelings indicated by words such as interest, appreciation, enthusiasm, motivation, and attitudes." For purposes of clarification and consistency, their scheme also includes three classifications of objectives, namely:

1. Discrimination Objectives—involves the ability to describe or select two or more similar alternates.
2. Verbal Objectives—involves the ability to write or describe orally.
3. Motor Performance—involves the ability to demonstrate a motor skill.[4]

McAshan presents a comprehensive performance objective approach that differs somewhat from those previously mentioned. He proposes a construct of performance objectives, broken down into specific noninstructional objectives and behavioral objectives. He uses the term behavioral objectives

> . . . to identify a particular type of performance objective. It is interpreted as meaning a performance objective having an identifiable goal which identifies the learner, the program variable, and implies some type of learner behavioral change that can be evaluated as a direct outcome of the goal. This type of objective is a two component statement written in exact terms which includes the first component, the goal, and the second component, the outcome or evaluation of the goal. Its key characteristic is that it not only states the goal but also identifies the instrumentation, performance, activity, or behavior the learner will become involved with as a means of evaluating the success he has achieved as an outcome of the intended goal of the particular objective.[5]

Esbensen, in describing the individualized instruction program developed by the Duluth (Minnesota) public schools, places considerable emphasis on the role of performance objectives. He indicates that

> Objectives are precise descriptions of the behavior that instruction is to produce stated in terms of what the student is to be able to do, the conditions requiring the action, and where appropriate, the standards of accuracy or speed.[6]

---

3. General Programmed Teaching, *Designing Effective Instruction* (Palo Alto, 1971). Reprinted with permission of the publisher.
4. *Ibid.*
5. H. H. McAshan, *Writing Behavioral Objectives* (New York: Harper and Row, Publishers, 1970), p. 17. Reprinted with permission of the publisher.
6. Thorwald Esbensen, *Working With Individualized Instruction: the Duluth Experience* (Belmont, Calif.: Fearon Publishers, 1968), p. 3. Reprinted with permission of the publisher.

The model proposed by Armstrong, Cornell, Kraner, and Roberson for writing objectives classifies them according to the three behavioral domains of cognitive, affective, and psychomotor.[7] These authors also introduce a new procedure centered on descriptive variables, behavioral variables, and instructional variables. For example, a well-stated objective might focus on a student's demonstrating the use of a ruler in measuring the dimensions of a desk within an accuracy of one-fourth of an inch. In this example, the student is the instructional variable, and the behavior variable is in the cognitive domain. These authors' comprehensive approach to specifying behavioral objectives also extends the use of objectives to program evaluation techniques.

### Criticisms of Using Behaviorally Stated Objectives

The practice of developing behaviorally stated objectives has been criticized for two major reasons. First, there is the feeling by some that strict adherence to precisely stated objectives makes learning somewhat of a mechanical process. In the same vein, it is implied that the student is not required to use cognitive abilities in order to accomplish the narrowly defined and sequenced tasks. The second criticism centers on the time-consuming job of stating objectives in behavioral terms. Both criticisms are legitimate under certain circumstances and serve to remind teachers of their responsibility to their pupils and themselves. Task analysis does not have to be so detailed that the teaching strategy does not challenge the child's thought processes.

In reality the teacher who is effectively using instructional objectives as a basis in teaching is using them as a means of individualizing instruction. This approach includes the teaching of cognitive as well as social and motor skills. The formulation of an instructional objective by the teacher may well be aimed at requiring the child to use higher cognitive processes. A major advantage of specifying instructional objectives as a result of task analysis is that the teacher is able to determine what level of cognitive processes the pupil is capable of using and can then maintain instruction for the pupil at that level. Unless a teacher employs a system similar to specifying instructional objectives, the teaching of skills and concepts is likely to be less than sequential.

The second criticism pertaining to the time involved in writing instructional objectives must be viewed in terms of the results derived by the teacher. Most teachers become proficient at writing behavioral objectives after a minimum of training. The determining factor regarding the amount of time required to become skilled in writing behaviorally stated objectives is closely

---

7. Robert J. Armstrong, et al., *The Development and Evaluation of Behavioral Objectives* (Worthington, Ohio: Charles A. Jones Publishing Company, 1970).

related to the complexness of the model followed. If the teacher is primarily concerned with writing objectives for his or her own teaching strategies, the model need not be complicated. The model suggested later in this chapter is very basic but sufficient for the type of objectives required in writing units. These same persons may also find that the process makes them more effective teachers. The question of time is most applicable in situations where teachers are required to write detailed objectives for everything they teach. Regardless of how efficient they are at the process, it can become very time-consuming if they proceed to write detailed objectives for every skill or concept taught to each child. For purposes of unit teaching, such objectives should be specific; however, they need not cover everything taught through a lesson. Rather, they should focus on the major skills and concepts the lesson has been designed to teach. Once teachers have become skilled at writing objectives in behavioral terms, they can determine for themselves how specific they must be in order to present the skill or concept sequentially and obtain evaluation feedback on the child's performance.

Some writers suggest that a teacher should strive for as much specificity as possible. The approach taken in this book supports the point of view that teachers vary in their skill at stating objectives; content varies in the degree of specificity required; and teachers vary in their knowledge of curriculum content, pupil behavior, and teaching techniques. Consequently, it is suggested that teachers strive for specificity through the preparation of behavioral objectives but that the number of objectives developed per lesson be decided upon after they have gained some experience in writing them for unit lessons. For example, if the teacher finds that representative objectives for selected skills rather than a detailed number of objectives are sufficient for planning and evaluating lessons, then little is gained by developing additional and more precise objectives for the same skill or concept.

If teachers find, after writing several unit lessons using behavioral objectives, that they are devoting a disproportionate amount of time to writing behavioral objectives, then they are well advised to develop a model of their own that can be used efficiently and enhances their efforts at individualizing instruction.

The schema or format that you choose to use should be the one that works best for you. *Above all, don't let the task of writing objectives become your end product. The goal is to change the behavior of kids.* Don't invest all of your effort in writing your objectives.

## Advantages of Using Behaviorally Stated Objectives in Writing Units

The advantages for teachers and students resulting from the use of behaviorally stated instructional objectives in unit teaching do not differ significantly from those derived in other instructional approaches. However, the advantages become particularly important in unit teaching because of the teachers' responsibility for determining what is to be taught. In unit teaching, teachers not only design their teaching activities but also make major decisions on the curriculum content and when it is taught. Under these circumstances, the use of behavioral objectives forces them into more precision in planning than they might otherwise attain. The following advantages are oriented toward unit teaching, but they are also applicable to other approaches.

1. The process of stating objectives in behavioral terms places teachers in a situation where they are called on to examine what they intend to teach as well as their motivation for teaching the content.
   a. Objectives representing different levels of competency in a general skill area can be developed. This allows the teacher an opportunity to check for sequence.
   b. Having developed a series of behavioral objectives for unit lessons and subsequently carried out the objectives, the teacher now has a ready-made checklist for assessing the content covered through the lessons.
2. Behaviorally stated objectives serve as criteria for teachers to determine whether they have actually taught what they intended to teach.
   a. Objectives include criteria for successful performance.
   b. Teachers need only to evaluate the child's performance against the specified criteria to ascertain if they have accomplished their intent.
3. The use of behaviorally stated objectives contributes to an evaluative set on the part of the teacher. If a teacher consistently evaluates a child's performance, he or she is in a better position to individualize instruction.
   a. Evaluation is a built-in feature of behaviorally stated objectives.
   b. As a result of routinely using behaviorally stated objectives, teachers increase their knowledge of each pupil's capabilities and consequently should less frequently ask pupils to perform tasks above or below their competency level.
   c. They facilitate feedback to students, who can be informed of the performance level expected of them. They now know when they are successful.
4. Having specified objectives for a specific task, teachers are free to select the activity for teaching the task they feel will work best with the class. The objective merely specifies what the child is expected to attain; it does not indicate the methodology. However, having narrowly defined the task, a teacher is in a good position to consider alternate approaches.
5. Instructional objectives are helpful in translating test findings into teaching strategies. Given the results of formal or informal tests, objectives can be used as a means of planning an instructional program.

6. The use of behavioral objectives increases the opportunity for decision making on the part of students. They can participate in establishing objectives for themselves.

7. A major advantage of building units based on behaviorally stated objectives is that the cumulative effect produces a descriptive definition of what is to be covered through units. They serve the same purpose in terms of providing a frame of reference for explaining your curriculum.
   a. Objectives in sequential form can be used in explaining the curriculum to teachers at other levels and to the administration.
   b. They can serve the same purpose in communicating the curriculum to parents.

8. Having developed the skill of writing behavioral objectives, teachers should be able to critically review commercial materials to determine which material is most applicable to their pupils and the content they intend to teach.

## Prerequisites to Writing Objectives

If a teacher plans to use behaviorally stated objectives as a means of improving classroom instruction, the goal must be more than merely learning the task of writing a well-stated objective. The teacher must be concerned with how to analyze a task so that the objectives help to identify prerequisite skills and to delineate the specific skill that will be taught. The teacher's thinking also must be oriented toward pupil behavior. Too often, as teachers, we think in terms of what *we* are going to teach or what *we* want to accomplish with our pupils. This type of thinking is in reference to teacher behavior rather than pupil behavior. A thorough discussion of what is meant by pupil behavior and task analysis is not possible within the scope of this book, but some clarification relative to behavioral objectives is required.

### Pupil Behavior

The two major characteristics of behaviorally stated instructional objectives involve (1) emphasizing pupil rather than teacher behavior and (2) specifying precisely what the child is expected to be able to do following instruction. Some teachers encounter as much difficulty with the emphasis on pupil behavior as they do with the precision. This is partially due to procedures often followed in writing lesson plans where teachers write a reminder to themselves to use certain materials, help specific children, and assign certain tasks. Teachers often have a set that focuses on their association with the learner rather than on the behavior of the learner which they are attempting to change.

An understanding of what is meant by the term *behavior* is important if a teacher is to state instructional objectives in behavioral terms. The learning of an arithmetic skill, the development of an attitude, the understanding of a concept, as well as a reduction in the occurrence of disruptive behaviors are examples of changes in behavior. A child is now able to do something he or she previously could not do. For example, a child who has been taught the meaning of the term *reverse* is now able to define it. As the child gains experience with the concept of *reverse*, he or she will be able to apply the term appropriately and respond to directions involving the concept. In essence, the child has learned a concept that is reflected in behavior.

Obviously some behaviors are more easily observed than others. Children who have learned to write their names can easily demonstrate this newly learned behavior. On the other hand, children who have improved in their respect for others are dependent on a situation to arise where they can demonstrate that they respect the rights of peers. Under the latter circumstances, teachers can create a situation that will allow them to observe the child interacting with classmates. In both behaviors, the child is called on to do something that is observable. The child writes his or her name in one case and in the other, shares, takes turns, and is cooperative in a group activity.

Much of what is taught in school involves the acquisition of knowledge that may not necessarily be routinely reflected in the child's overt behavior. For example, we cannot observe thinking, just as we cannot observe the process of learning. We can, however, engage children in activities that require them to perform selected tasks. As they perform, their behaviors expose what they do or do not understand. Thus, as teachers we must plan our teaching strategies so that our pupils are allowed to demonstrate what they have learned. Rather than approaching a lesson with the perspective that you are going to teach Janie the use of the ruler, it is more helpful to approach the situation from the perspective of her being able to use the ruler accurately in measurement tasks. The latter stresses the pupil's behavior as well as the skill.

## Task Analysis

A major requirement of making efficient use of behaviorally stated objectives is the capability to break down a general skill or concept into specific tasks. In unit teaching particularly, we find that the skill or concept around which a lesson is planned includes a hierarchy of skills or understandings. For example, in teaching making change, the child must first understand the concept of money, be able to recognize coins, and know their value. In analyzing the global skill, we can determine the prerequisite skills the child must possess as readiness for the specific skill we want to teach. Having done this, we can ascertain the present level of competence and direct our attention to building on this competence in the process of teaching toward the higher level skill. The developmental steps for writing units suggested in Chapter 4 represent a point of departure for task analysis within the construct of unit teaching. If you follow these procedures in writing your unit, you will already have made many content decisions prior to planning a selected lesson. As you approach the specification of objectives for a particular skill, it becomes essential that you examine the skill, concept, or information you plan to teach for indications of how it can be broken down into teachable steps. The specificity of these steps will be dependent on the capabilities of your pupils. As you gain experience in applying this procedure, it becomes less difficult to anticipate pupil needs.

Obviously, the more knowledgeable a teacher is of the sequential development of skills and curriculum content being implemented the easier the job of analyzing tasks will be. The approach to developing units presented in this book is designed to assist teachers in extending their knowledge of the curriculum content to be taught through units. However, a teacher may find a need to review the sequential development of academic skills.

In summary, the teacher's prerequisites for writing behavioral objectives include:

1. An orientation toward pupil behavior.
2. Good observation skills which result in being aware of *what* is happening *when* it is happening.
3. A knowledge of curriculum requirements and content.
4. The ability to analyze tasks and content.
5. The ability to identify the specific behavior that is to be influenced.

## A Suggested Model for Writing Instructional Objectives in Behavioral Terms

The primary value of developing objectives in behavioral terms is the precision it brings to the teaching process. If teachers have considered both the nature of the content to be taught and the characteristics of the learner in the process of stating objectives, they should be able to structure a task that will lead to attainment of the objective. Under these circumstances, the chances that the task will be excessively difficult or easy are greatly reduced.

As noted earlier in the chapter, schemes for writing objectives vary in complexness. Some make use of sub-objectives and some do not. Some consider the dimensions of cognitive, adaptive, and psychomotor. Others recommend that the process incorporate consideration of situational variables. For purposes of developing units, a less involved approach is adequate.

In writing units, many teachers have found that a simple format that requires them to be specific but does not involve having to cope with different kinds of objectives or varying levels of specificity is sufficient. This does not lessen the demand for a consistent format. But it does free the teachers to focus primarily on writing objectives for the pupil behavior they desire to influence rather than on the process of writing objectives. The situation would be different if a school system were attempting to develop a comprehensive curriculum based on behaviorally stated objectives. Under these circumstances, they would be well advised to develop a model that assesses representativeness of kinds of learning as well as sequential coverage of content.

The model recommended in this book for writing behaviorally stated objectives for use in developing units includes three major requirements. The objectives must:

1. *Describe* the behavior you want the student to be able to perform. Use specific terms such as to name, to list, to count, to write, to compare, to complete, and so on.
2. Indicate the *conditions* under which the student will be expected to perform.
3. Specify the level of performance you will accept as *successful attainment* of the objective.

If teachers are able to write objectives in behavioral terms that include the three major functions of a good objective—namely, descriptive, condition, and evaluative—then they should be able to write statements that clearly reflect what they intend to teach. For example, if a teacher at the primary level is planning to teach a lesson on color identification, he or she might write an objective as follows:

The student will be able to identify red, blue, yellow, and green colors given four appropriately colored objects and verbally instructed to name the color of each one.
Descriptive—to identify colors
Condition—given colored objects
Evaluative—name color of each object

Some teachers find it helpful to think in terms of questions when they consider the three basic requirements of an objective:

Descriptive:  What do I want the student to do?
Condition:    What will be given as a means of demonstrating his or her performance?
Evaluative:   What will I accept as evidence of successful performance?

In the case of our objectives for identifying colors, the answers to the above questions would be:

1. I want the student to be able to identify red, blue, yellow, and green.
2. I will give him or her four objects colored red, blue, yellow and green.
3. I will expect him or her to correctly tell me the color of each object.

In addition to meeting the descriptive, condition, and evaluative requirements, you must be concerned with clarity of wording and the appropriateness of the objective to your students. Figure 11 illustrates a simple model that can be used to evaluate the basic qualities of objectives as you write them. The model is used merely as a check on whether or not the objective meets the basic requirements. It also helps the teacher to determine which aspects of the objective need to be revised. As one becomes accustomed to writing objectives in behavioral terms, there is less need to use the model as an evaluative device.

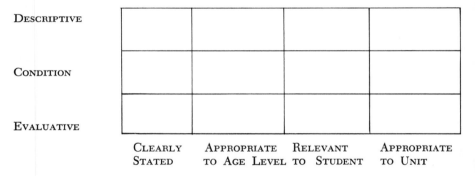

Figure 11.   Model for Evaluating Objectives.

*Clearly stated.* The major emphasis is on being certain the objective clearly conveys your intent. Some people suggest that each objective begin with statements such as "will be able to . . ." or "Given . . . student will be able to . . . ." Although for purposes of convenience a teacher may wish to adapt a uniform pattern, it is not essential. The concern should be for clarity, not necessarily uniformity or grammatical structure.

*Appropriate to Age Level.* The age or ability level of your class should be your frame of reference. You may find that you have developed a well-stated objective, but it is not appropriate for the age level of your group.

*Relevant to Student.* This feature is somewhat related to age level but it incorporates your knowledge of the interests of your students. In some cases, the objective is important in spite of little perceived interest on the part of students if it is important to their academic or social development. Thus, relevance must also include the importance you place on the objectives for the students.

*Appropriate to Unit.* This factor is an additional check to be sure you are teaching the skill or concept in relationship to the most appropriate unit. It may be more logically taught as part of another unit.

## Work Exercises

The following exercises are designed to provide practice in writing behavioral objectives as previously described in this chapter. Most teachers will find that additional practice is necessary. Once you feel reasonably comfortable in writing objectives, you are encouraged to proceed with writing objectives as part of lesson plans for actual units you plan to teach. Your skill will improve as you write objectives for lessons, teach activities, and assess pupil performance.

Exercise 5. Global and Instructional Objectives. Differentiating between global and behaviorally stated instructional objectives. Check the appropriate column. Disregard the style in which the statement is written. Focus on the implications of the statement. Some statements, while not meeting all the requirements of a good objective, are definitely more instructional than global.

| GLOBAL | INSTRUCTIONAL | |
|--------|---------------|---|
| ____ | ____ | 1. Understands the basic principles of budgeting. |
| ____ | ____ | 2. Is able to locate a phone number in a phone book, given a person's first and last names. |
| ____ | ____ | 3. Given information on quantity and price, is able to determine the best buy. |
| ____ | ____ | 4. To develop respect for the property rights of others. |
| ____ | ____ | 5. Is knowledgeable of job opportunities. |
| ____ | ____ | 6. Provided a local street map, the student is able to locate home, school, and a specified business. |
| ____ | ____ | 7. Knows the reasoning behind traffic laws. |
| ____ | ____ | 8. To develop the concept of credit. |

**Exercise 6.**   Basic Requirements. Analyze the following objectives by identifying the three basic requirements of a good objective. Underline the words reflecting the three functions, using *d* to indicate *descriptive*, *c* for *conditional*, and *e* for *evaluative*. In some cases, two requirements may be in the same phrase.

$$d \qquad\qquad\qquad e$$

1. The student will be able to (write his or her name)(legibly in the appropriate space)(given a job application form.)

$$c$$

2. Given a newspaper, the student will be able to locate the section reporting weather conditions.

3. Will be able to tell time verbally within an accuracy of five minutes using a clock that includes only the numerals of 12, 3, and 9.

4. Given five objects of varying sizes, the student is able to place them in order from small to large.

5. Given a list of fruits and vegetables, the student will distinguish between them with 100 percent accuracy.

**Exercise 7.** Use of Evaluative Model. Using your own class or a hypothetical class you can define and rate the following objectives using the Evaluative Model. Revise objectives as necessary. Select your unit topic before rating the objectives.

a.  Will be able to demonstrate making change, given a 23¢ purchase and a dollar bill for payment. Four quarters, three nickels, four dimes, and five pennies will be provided.

b.  Given a yardstick with quarter-inch markings, will be able to measure a desk top.

c.  Student will be able to find a number in a phone book, given a person's name in written form.

## EVALUATIVE MODEL

| | | | | |
|---|---|---|---|---|
| DESCRIPTIVE | | | | |
| CONDITION | | | | |
| EVALUATIVE | | | | |
| | CLEARLY STATED | APPROPRIATE TO AGE LEVEL | RELEVANT TO STUDENT | APPROPRIATE TO UNIT |

Revise objective if necessary:

_____

_____

_____

**Exercise 8.**   Writing Behavioral Objectives.

1. Unit Topic:  Measurement
2. Behavior:  Correct use of the ruler
3. Write each aspect separately.

Descriptive _____

_____

_____

Condition _____

_____

_____

Evaluative _____

_____

_____

4. Write your final objective in one statement.
   Final Objective: _____

_____

_____

5. Rate your objective against the Evaluative Model in Figure 11.

**Exercise 9.**    Writing Behavioral Objectives. (Practice Sheet)

1. **Unit Topic:**  Traffic Safety
2. **Behavior:**  Reading crucial safety signs
3. Write each aspect separately.

    Descriptive  _____

    _____

    _____

    Condition  _____

    _____

    _____

    Evaluative  _____

    _____

    _____

4. Write your final objective in one statement.
    **Final Objective:** _____

    _____

    _____

5. Rate your objective against the Evaluative Model in Figure 11.

**Exercise 10.**   Writing Behavioral Objectives. (Practice Sheet)

1. Unit Topic:
2. Behavior:
3. Write each aspect separately.

    Descriptive  _____

    _____

    _____

    Condition   _____

    _____

    _____

    Evaluative  _____

    _____

    _____

4. Write your final objective in one statement.
    Final Objective: _____

    _____

    _____

5. Rate your objective against the Evaluative Model in Figure 11.

1. Read the activities and write one or more instructional objective for your own class.
2. Rate your objective(s) against the Evaluative Model in Figure 11.

SCOPE OF THE LESSON: Involve the pupils in activities and situations which will result in an awareness of their home address as an identifying number.

| INSTRUCTIONAL OBJECTIVES | ACTIVITIES | RESOURCE MATERIALS | EXPERIENCE CHART |
|---|---|---|---|
| | 1. Introduce the lesson by involving the class in a general discussion of homes and where we live.<br>a. City or country<br>b. Farm, house, apartment, duplex<br>c. One- or two-story house<br>d. On a corner or in the middle of a block<br>e. Color of house<br>f. Big or small house<br>g. Home near other children in the class<br>h. Walk to school or take bus<br>2. Direct each child to bring to class his or her correct home address (house number, street, town, apartment number if applicable). Note: This should be checked against school records as there may be changes or errors that would need verification.<br>3. Initiate a project in which each child will make a drawing of his or her dwelling place. Encourage the children to add the family members, pets, etc., to the drawing. | Drawing paper<br><br>Pencils | We live in a building called home.<br><br>Our home is our own. It is in a special place called an address.<br><br>We should know our address. |

Sample lesson reprinted by permission from material developed by the Special Education Curriculum Development Center, University of Iowa.

**Exercise 12.** Writing Behavioral Objectives.

1. Read the activities and write one or more instructional objective for your own class.
2. Rate your objective(s) against the Evaluative Model in Figure 11.

SCOPE OF THE LESSON:   Establish an awareness of weight differences and how they are used.

| INSTRUCTIONAL OBJECTIVES | ACTIVITIES | RESOURCE MATERIALS | EXPERIENCE CHART |
|---|---|---|---|
| | 1. Offer an assortment of objects for examination that have obvious weight differences such as a brick, an empty milk carton, a sheet of paper, etc. Encourage the children to handle them and describe them as being heavy and light. | Block of balsa<br><br>Block of lignum vitae (or lead) | We know things can be long or short. They can also be big or small. Now we know about heavy and light. |
| | 2. Use the projector to show pictures of paired objects and have the pupils determine the relative weight differences. | Empty milk carton<br><br>Empty coffee can | Sometimes big things are heavier than little things.<br><br>Sometimes little things are heavier. |
| | 3. Demonstrate that small objects may be heavy and large ones light by using a large block of balsa and small block of lignum vitae (or lead) and a small sack of lead shot and a feather pillow. | Quantity of dry corn kernels (or wood beads)<br><br>Overhead projector or opaque projector. | A scale helps us to know what is heavy and what is light. |
| | 4. Put a weight equal to the average weight of pupils in the class on one end of a seesaw. Note: This weight can be adjusted by using small sandbags often available from the P.E. Dept. Let children in turn sit on the other end of the seesaw to see if they are lighter, equal to, or less than the weight. | | |

Sample lesson reprinted by permission from material developed by the Special Education Curriculum Development Center, University of Iowa.

**Exercise 13.** Writing Behavioral Objectives.

1. Select a Unit Topic _____

2. Write a scope of lesson statement _____

3. Write a lesson including behavioral objectives.

4. Check your objective against the Evaluative Model in Figure 11.

| Instructional Objectives | Activities | Resource Materials | Experience Chart |
|---|---|---|---|
| | | | |

## BIBLIOGRAPHY

ARMSTRONG, ROBERT J. et al. *The Development and Evaluation of Behavioral Objectives.* Worthington, Ohio: Charles A. Jones Publishing Company, 1970.
*Designing Effective Instruction.* Palo Alto: General Programmed Teaching, A Division of Commerce Clearing House, 1971.
EBENSEN, THORWALD. *Working with Individualized Instruction: The Duluth Experience.* Belmont, Calif.: Fearon Publishers, 1968.
MAGER, ROBERT F. *Preparing Instructional Objectives.* Belmont, Calif.: Fearon Publishers, 1968.
MCASHAN, H. H. *Writing Behavioral Objectives: A New Approach.* New York: Harper and Row, 1970.

### ADDITIONAL SELECTED REFERENCES RELATED TO BEHAVIORAL OBJECTIVES

BLOCK, JAMES H., ed. *Mastery Learning Theory and Practice.* With selected papers by Peter W. Airasian, Benjamin S. Bloom, John B. Carroll. New York: Holt, Rinehart and Winston, 1971.
BLOOM, BENJAMIN E., ed. *Taxonomy of Educational Objectives, Handbook I.* New York: David McKay Company, 1969.
BOSTON, ROBERT E. *How to Write and Use Performance Objectives to Individualize Instruction. Vol. 2. How to Write Performance Objectives.* Englewood Cliffs, N.J.: Educational Technology Publications, 1972.
*Instructional Objectives: Developing Teaching Strategies for the Mentally Retarded.* Iowa City: Special Education Curriculum Development Center, University of Iowa, 1970.
KAPFER, MIRIAM B. *Behavioral Objectives in Curriculum Development.* Englewood Cliffs, N.J.: Educational Technology Publications, 1971.
KRATHWOHL, D. R.; BLOOM, B. S.; and MASIA, B. B. *Taxonomy of Educational Objectives, Handbook II.* New York: David McKay Company, 1969.
LYNCH, WILLIAM W. "Instructional Objectives and the Mentally Retarded Child." *Bulletin of Indiana University School of Education* 43 (March 1967):2.
MAGER, ROBERT F. *Analyzing Performance Problems or "Your Really Oughta Wanna."* Belmont, Calif.: Fearon Publishers, 1970.
NOAR, GERTRUDE. *Individualized Instruction for the Mentally Retarded: They, too, Can Be Winners.* Glen Ridge, N.J.: Exceptional Press, 1974.
PADZENSKY, HERBERT R., and GIBSON, JANE. *Goalguide: A Minicourse in Writing Goal and Behavioral Objectives for Special Education.* Participant Manual, Participant Workbook. Belmont, Calif.: Fearon Publishers, 1975.
PLOWMAN, PAUL D. *Behavioral Objectives.* Chicago: Science Research Associates, 1971.

# 7

# Evaluation Techniques

How do you know whether or not the unit you just finished teaching on "the community" added to your students' knowledge of the community in which they live? Do you know which students gained the most information? Which concepts were the most difficult for your students? Which were the least difficult? Answers to questions like these are essential if you are to improve your instructional program and ultimately to have a more significant influence on the lives of children for whose education you are responsible. Such answers are not easily derived. While the evaluative data may be obtained in an arbitrary fashion, if evaluation results are to be meaningful to teachers and contribute to better curriculum decisions, the evaluation process must be carefully planned and ongoing. Obviously, there are problems inherent in evaluating the educational progress of children as a result of unit teaching. Most standardized achievement tests are designed to assess pupil progress in the skill area of the regular curriculum and are not entirely applicable for assessing pupil performance based on unit instruction. Many formal assessment instruments are too global and do not provide teachers with the specific information they need relative to planning teaching strategies. These problems dictate the need for designing evaluation procedures as part of each unit.

When teachers commit themselves to individualizing instruction to pupil needs, they become dependent on feedback on the child's performance. To make accurate decisions about the level of difficulty at which a skill should be presented as well as the type of activity that will best engage the student, a teacher must look to the student for the needed information. Students also need feedback; they need to know if they have been successful or if they have failed. If they have failed a particular task, they need to know the nature of the failure so that they can utilize this information in approaching the task from a different perspective. Feedback can also be a source of reinforcement. A teacher's lack of evaluation techniques often results in the postponement of meaningful feedback for the student. The reinforcement that might be forthcoming is delayed and consequently is less meaningful for

179

the learner. Evaluation requires that the teacher closely observe the performance of individual students as well as the group. This practice in itself can
have a positive influence on teaching effectiveness.

The benefits to be derived by teachers and pupils from the evaluation
process should be sufficient to motivate teachers to apply evaluation techniques in the classroom. The current emphasis on accountability serves to
accent this need for evaluation. Barro, in discussing the application of accountability to public schools, states that

> although the term "accountability" is too new in the educational vocab-
> ulary to have acquired a standard usage, there is little doubt about its
> general meaning and import for the schools. The basic idea it conveys
> is that school systems and schools, or, more precisely, the professional
> educators who operate them, should be held responsible for education-
> al outcomes—for what children learn. If this can be done, it is main-
> tained, favorable changes in professional performance will occur, and
> these will be reflected in higher academic achievement, improvement
> in public attitudes, and generally better education results.[1]

Before procedures for assessing accountability are applied, decisions must be
made on what is to be assessed and, in turn, what is to be considered accountability evidence. Once this has been accomplished, a determination must
be made relative to teacher contribution to the result of accountability. Barro proposes the following principle:

> Each participant in the educational process should be held respon-
> sible only for those educational outcomes that he can affect by his ac-
> tions or decisions and only to the extent that he can affect them.[2]

He goes on to suggest that teachers should not be held accountable for
shortcomings in the curriculum. However, if one examines the role of the
teacher in the instructional program, it becomes apparent that he or she
serves as a quality control agent and assumes considerable responsibility for
the structuring of learning experiences as well as for decisions relative to
what is taught and the context in which it is taught. Although there are many
constraints placed on teachers who have instructional responsibility for exceptional children in the form of insufficient materials and lack of curriculum
direction, the necessity of evaluation is no less than for other teachers.

Guba has indicated that "the primary task in evaluation today is the
provision of sensible alternatives to the evaluator."[3] The intent of this chapter is to offer teachers alternatives in the evaluation of their unit instruction.

1. Stephen M. Barro, "An Approach to Developing Accountability Measures for the
Public Schools," *Phi Delta Kappan* 52:4 (December 1970), p. 190. Reprinted by permission of Phi Delta Kappan, Inc.
2. Ibid.
3. Egon G. Guba, "An Overview of the Evaluation Problem." A paper read at the
symposium on "The World of Evaluation Needs Reshaping," AERA Convention, February 1969.

Although the degree of responsibility varies, the breadth of the teacher's responsibility for evaluation ranges from the assessment of pupil performance on specific learning tasks to the contribution of the instructional program to the total curriculum. The emphasis in this chapter will be restricted to assessing instruction via unit teaching. Three aspects of evaluation will be considered: (1) the collective contribution of unit teaching to the instructional program, (2) the effectiveness of individual units, and (3) pupil performance on specific learning tasks.

Evaluation, assessment, and appraisal are often viewed by teachers as synonymous. The meanings given to these terms usually are oriented to measurement, research, or personal judgments. For purposes of clarification, the definition of assessment by Stephens will be considered as a frame of reference for this chapter.

> Assessment, as used here, is a survey of student functioning. Its purpose is to determine those responses and skills which are adequate and those which need to be taught or improved. The term assessment is used to convey a meaning more specific than "testing." It is distinct from diagnosis which means to identify a disease or abnormality after studying its origin.[4]

Responses will be considered within the context of responding to instruction units as well as to specific learning tasks. This definition places responsibility on the teacher for observing behavioral changes in the students. This means that the teacher must also be concerned with environmental characteristics which produce changes in student behavior as well as with the appraisal of changes themselves. Knowledge of the learning environment necessitates an awareness of pupil-pupil interaction, pupil-material interaction, pupil-classroom interaction, and pupil-teacher interaction. Added to this is a sensitivity to the child's school history and family background. It is not enough to merely assess a child's performance on a particular task without also being cognizant of those variables that contribute to success or failure on the respective tasks. This dimension of evaluation obviously broadens the teacher's responsibility. The learning characteristics of a mentally retarded child combined with a history of poor performance make the evaluation process a complicated but necessary task.

### Prerequisites to Evaluation

Prior to engaging pupils in evaluation tasks, teachers must decide what they plan to evaluate and why, as well as how, they anticipate using the results. These decisions will facilitate the selection of appropriate techniques. They

---

4. Thomas M. Stephens, *Directive Teaching of Children With Learning and Behavioral Handicaps* (Columbus: Charles E. Merrill Publishing Company, 1970), p. 63. Used by permission of Charles E. Merrill Publishing Company.

will also minimize the time commitment of students to the evaluation process. The following are examples of reasons why teachers evaluate instruction. They are presented in an objective format merely for illustrative purposes:

To assess competence in a particular skill that is being taught.

To determine baseline behavior as a basis for planning a unit or a particular lesson.

To obtain information that can be used in revising a unit.

To gain meaningful data for purposes of reporting pupil progress.

To substantiate or refute implications reflected in a pupil's school history.

To appraise the effectiveness of selected activities.

To determine the reaction of pupils to instructional materials.

Each reason requires a different evaluation approach. Certainly you can obtain data during the process of evaluating the performance of a pupil on a selected learning task that may also contribute to the assessment of an instructional unit. However, the evaluation of the pupil's performance should be the major target, and the evaluation process should focus on the child's behavior relative to the selected task.

In addition to circumscribing why an evaluation technique will be applied and specifying the target of evaluation, teachers must allow the behavior to occur. If they are evaluating unit effectiveness, then the unit must be taught and the student allowed to participate in the activities that it includes. If the evaluation target is the performance of an individual child on a task, a situation must be structured that allows the child to perform the task. It may take the form of a test item, a structured situation, or merely observation of the child in a real-life situation that requires performance of the tasks. In order to evaluate the pupil's performance, the teacher must decide on a criterion level for successful performance against which to measure performance. The results then become part of a pool of information on individual pupils and on pupils as a group. The teacher draws on this information when planning the child's program, when making decisions on curriculum content, and when planning units.

In the remainder of this chapter we will discuss evaluation procedures and ways in which the evaluation results can be used in the improvement of classroom instruction through unit teaching.

### Evaluating Pupil Performance on Selected Tasks

Individualization of instruction necessitates that teachers be knowledgeable of pupil capabilities and the manner in which they respond to learning tasks. If a teacher approaches teaching with a commitment to enhancing the growth and development of each child, he or she finds that the child is not only the target of teaching, but also the primary resource in determining the best approach. The cues to the learners' needs are reflected in behavior. Their behavior takes many forms. It may be in the realm of performance on structured tasks, in their response to the classroom environment and to others around them, or it may be in the form of nonverbal cues. However, children do express their needs in a variety of forms. The degree to which these expressions communicate is dependent on the awareness of teachers and their capabilities to interpret the implications of observed behavior.

Closely related to the tasks inherent in interpreting behavior is the skill of structuring situations that allow teachers to obtain information on behavior related to specific tasks. This requires an evaluation-type set. Teachers need to be oriented towards assessing student performance. It is not enough to know that Johnny reads at the fourth-grade level or that he has difficulty with the process of division. Teachers must pursue a more analytical approach to evaluation.

The selection of evaluation techniques should be an integral aspect of the planning process teachers engage in when developing their instructional program. Until decisions have been made regarding what is to be taught, there is no basis for evaluation of pupil progress. However, once teachers have decided what is to be taught, they are in a position to develop alternative procedures for assessing pupil performance in the respective area of instruction. Although the evaluation process is dependent on a curricular frame of reference, the curriculum should not be viewed as independent of evaluation. Unless teachers assess pupil performance, they do not know to what extent their instructional program is successful in teaching the curriculum. Without the feedback derived from evaluating pupil performance on specific tasks, they are at a disadvantage in attempting to individualize instruction.

Generally speaking, teachers have two major resources available to them as they integrate evaluation techniques into their instructional program. These include formal and informal procedures. The first is primarily in the form of standardized instruments such as achievement tests, developmental tests, aptitude tests, etc. The latter tests involve evaluation techniques that the teacher can become skilled at devising and administering.

The formal procedures are a resource accessible to most teachers. To use these instruments, the teacher needs to be familiar with their purpose, when they can be effectively used, and what can be gained through their use. For informal techniques to materialize as a resource, the teacher must invest in acquiring assessment skill through informal techniques as well as a knowledge of the various types of informal techniques which can be applied to assessing the behavior he or she is attempting to influence through the instructional program. The advantage of the latter is that once the skill is developed, the teacher has a resource that is always accessible. The informal approach has an added advantage in that the teacher is not bound by predetermined strategies and can be much more specific in assessing pupil performance relative to his or her own instructional program.

Formal evaluation procedures tend to be normative in nature while informal procedures have more of a criterion-reference base. Since normative and criterion measures yield different kinds of information, both will be discussed relative to their application in assessing pupil performance within the context of classroom instruction. Popham and Husek define criterion-referenced and norm-referenced measures as follows:

> Criterion-referred measures are those which are used to ascertain an individual's status with respect to some criterion, i.e., performance standard. It is because the individual is compared with some established criterion, rather than other individuals, that these measures are described as criterion referenced. The meaningfulness of an individual score is not dependent on comparison to others.
>
> Norm-referenced measures are those which are used to ascertain an individual's performance in relationship to the performance of other individuals on the same measuring device. The meaningfulness of the individual score emerges from the comparison. It is because the individual is compared with some normative group that such measures are described as norm referenced. Most standardized tests of achievement or intellectual ability can be classified as norm-referenced measures.[5]

When a teacher applies a criterion-reference approach in assessing pupil progress, a child's performance is compared only to the level of performance you as a teacher establish as a criterion of success. For example, if your objective is to teach a child to identify coins by indicating their value, you can show him or her a quarter, penny, dime, and nickel and ask the student to label the coins and tell you their value. The criteria for success might be all correct or three out of four correct. The child's performance is being assessed in terms of your criterion. Success or failure is not dependent on how well classmates perform on the item. You obtain information on how well he or she performs the task as well as on how he or she approaches the task and responds to having succeeded or failed. If necessary, you can collect normative-type information by administering the same item to other children. However, normative information in most situations is not necessary if your major goal is to provide experience which allows a child to progress at his or her own rate. What is needed is information on how the student approaches performing a task as a basis for your structuring subsequent tasks. Criterion-ref-

5. W. James Popham and T. R. Husek, "Implications of Criterion-Referenced Measurement," *Journal of Educational Measurement,* Spring 1969, p. 1-9. Used by permission of the publisher.

erence measures in the form of informal techniques provide the needed information.

Normative-type measurement instruments such as achievement tests certainly contribute information which is helpful in planning instructional programs. However, the criterion-reference approach is more appropriate for assessing the results of unit teaching. There are several reasons for this. First of all, the content covered through unit teaching is not uniform to the extent that standardized achievement tests sufficiently sample what is taught through units as differentiated from the total instructional program. Normative measures are generally designed to be global in nature and are not as usable in assessing performance on specific skills. The major advantage of the criterion-reference approach is that it focuses the teacher's attention on the child and the task rather than the child, several tasks, and peers.

## Teacher Preparation for Assessing Pupil Performance

Evaluation of pupil performance should be a conscious effort on the part of teachers. It should be carried out in accordance with prescribed purposes. The evaluation tasks in which students are engaged should reflect an awareness of their capabilities and their emotional response to having their skills appraised. To accommodate these conditions requires that teachers examine their own motives for evaluation. Questions such as the following must be answered.

> Are you truly interested in gathering data as a reference for making decisions on the respective pupil's instructional program or are you more interested in obtaining a grade for each student?
>
> Do you plan to make maximum use of the results in terms of improving your overall instructional program? For example, when you find that several students perform unsuccessfully on a variety of tasks are you prepared to re-examine your teaching style and the content of your units?
>
> How do you view feedback to students regarding their performance? Should they receive immediate feedback?
>
> Are you willing to make the investment required to specify instructional objectives to the degree that the performance to be evaluated is explicitly stated?

For the most part these questions fall into the realm of the evaluation set that teachers need as a frame of reference. If teachers feel strongly that they need to measure their own effectiveness, and if they perceive the students as capable of providing information on their own needs as well as demonstrating their competencies, then the teachers have already made considerable progress toward establishing an evaluation program. The remaining requirement is for them to develop evaluation skills.

Basic to the process of evaluation is the specification of what is to be evaluated. The stating of instructional objectives in behavioral terms is discussed in Chapter 6. The reader is encouraged to review this chapter. A well-written instructional objective should include a description of:

1. the desired behavior in terms of the task to be performed
2. the condition under which the behavior will occur
3. what you will accept as successful performance

It should be noted that the above requirements for a good objective are designed to encourage specificity, but they should not be taken literally to the extent that the process of writing objectives becomes an end in itself. Some teachers lose sight of the purpose of writing objectives and become wrapped up in the task of wording them. The more precise you can make the objectives, the easier will be the task of evaluating pupil performance. *However, if a teacher devotes a disproportionate amount of time to writing objectives, the amount of time devoted to evaluation is reduced. The important factor is that teachers attempt to define what they want to measure, formulate an expectancy level for the pupil, and structure a situation that allows the desired performance to occur.*

The expectancy or criterion level may vary with each child. As the teacher gains experience in assessing the behavior of particular children, fewer errors should occur relative to establishing inappropriate criterion levels. While teachers should be able to evaluate most of what they teach, given sufficient time and opportunity, it is not reasonable to expect this to occur. They will find it necessary to evaluate a sample of representative behaviors. It is important, however, that they establish a sequential pattern for the behaviors they select to evaluate. For example, if they are carrying out a plan of pacing pupils through instructional tasks, it is important to evaluate pupil performance at varying points in the sequence of skills so that a determination can be made on whether or not the pupil possesses the necessary prerequisite skills to proceed with subsequent tasks.

As teachers, we need to be reminded that we must share some of the responsibility whenever a child fails at a task we have structured. This is true regardless of the child's intellectual ability. If we have examined the task to determine what skills are required to perform it and if we know the child's capabilities, we can alter the task or the criterion level to increase the child's chances of success. This is not to say that children should be asked only to perform tasks at which they can succeed. The point is that if you are asking children to perform a task far below or above their ability, you learn nothing about them and they gain little in the form of feedback. You also run the risk of discouraging them or, in the case of an exceedingly easy task, you may be misleading them in terms of what they think you expect.

## Examples of Informal Evaluation Techniques

When informal evaluation techniques are applied within the context of criterion-reference evaluation, teachers use their judgment in establishing the difficulty of the item. The difficulty level is determined by the criterion set for successful performance. Since this may vary for each child, we find a situation in which a particular evaluation technique can be used in assessing the performance of students with varying abilities merely by raising or lowering the criterion set for success on the task. Consequently, the examples to be presented are not categorized by age or ability levels. Rather, samples of informal evaluation techniques are listed under general topical headings without regard to ability or age levels.

Teachers will find that with minor modifications the techniques are applicable for a wide range of ability levels. Although the examples offered are in the areas of communication skills, arithmetic, and social competencies, the techniques are not mutually exclusive. Some techniques suggested for assessing arithmetic skills can be applied in assessing communication skills. The suggestions are also not exhaustive but are intended to provide assistance to teachers in developing a criterion-reference orientation to evaluation, particularly in assessing the effectiveness of unit teaching.

## Communication Skills

### LISTENING

Tell or read a story and then ask specific questions regarding the sequence of events and major characters.

Ask a student to summarize a lesson by identifying the main theme of the lesson. You might also ask the student to review previous lessons on the same topic.

Give directions to a child that require two, three, four, or more tasks to be completed. For example, "Pick up the red book on my desk and put it on the shelf where we keep the dictionaries."

Present an audio tape of sounds routinely heard in the home and have the students identify them.

Record a group discussion conducted by students and have pupils identify the speakers. You could also ask them to respond to what was being discussed.

Play a record and have the students respond to the rhythm of the music.

Read aloud words having similar beginnings and/or endings and have pupils record those that sound alike.

Have students "brainstorm" the sounds they hear on the way to school.

Read aloud sentences and have students identify those that are incorrect. They can also be asked to restate them correctly.

Record radio and TV commercials and ask students to identify the kind of store that would be likely to sell the product—a grocery, drug, or clothing store.

Read the beginning of a story and have the students complete it. The amount of information from the story provided for the students can be varied.

Give the students three categories such as vegetable, fruit, and meat. Then verbally present them with a list that can be sorted into these three categories.

VISUAL

Using a projection device such as an overhead, slide, or opaque projector, project a picture on the screen and have students describe what they see. Specific questions regarding inference can be posed.

Present students with a series of illustrations on cards. Ask them to place the cards in an order that makes a story.

Read a story aloud and ask students to select from a series of pictures those that best illustrate the story.

Present in work sheet form a series of pictures and related words. Have pupils match the words with the appropriate labels.

Use pantomime as a means for presenting nonverbal cues. Ask pupils to indicate what you are attempting to tell them through your gestures and facial expressions.

Project a picture on a screen for a specified period of time and then ask the pupils to reproduce it from memory.

Present a sequential series of pictures illustrating a situation and ask pupils to anticipate what will occur following the last picture.

Give pupils a stack of word cards randomly ordered and have them place the cards in alphabetical order.

Have students locate specific names in the phone book.

Provide the students with a list of familiar words and have them identify those correctly spelled.

VERBAL EXPRESSION

Identify a task and have a student describe verbally how the task should be performed.

Have a child demonstrate proper use of the telephone.

Direct specific questions to students and observe their speech fluency.

Use dramatic play to create situations that require verbal expressions. Be alert for relevance of comments and use of language.

Give children a topic such as "going shopping" and have them state verbally as many things as they can think of that they might shop for during the trip.

Have a child give directions to another on the shortest route to his or her home from school.

Ask a pupil to describe a recent television program.

Use puppets as a means of encouraging verbal expression. Specific instructions can be given to generate the kind of expression you want to assess.

Ask pupils to imitate sounds.

## Arithmetic Skills

Have students select a specified number of objects from a large group of objects.

Place several sticks of varying lengths on a desk and have students select the largest, shortest, and so forth.

Present a student with a container and ask him or her to estimate how many cups of water it will hold. Have the child complete the task and determine to what degree the estimate was larger or smaller than what the solution required.

Give a student a story problem that requires him or her to select the appropriate process and derive the answer. This type of problem can be varied to require the student to overlook irrelevant information.

A wide variety of performance tasks can be developed using money. These can include identification and computational tasks as well as tasks requiring the student to anticipate the amount required for a particular expenditure.

Provide pupils with a map and ask them to calculate the distance between two points. The difficulty of the maps can vary from a simplified teacher-made map to a highway map.

Use puzzles as a means of requiring students to discriminate shapes and sizes.

Structure tasks that require pupils to count objects and record the appropriate numerals.

Assign pupils the task of measuring the dimensions of their desks. The proper use of a ruler as well as the accuracy of their measurements can be determined.

Time-telling experiences can be used to assess accuracy. They can also be used to assess time estimation. Students can be asked to estimate how long they think it will take them to perform a particular task, such as going to the office and returning.

Problems using newspaper ads can be developed to assess their understanding of the "best buy." The same exercise can be used to evaluate their understanding of value.

Specific problems involving the reading of a thermometer can be designed to evaluate their ability to read the thermometer, interpret the significance of temperature, and use computational skills.

Computational items involving use of multiplication, addition, subtraction, and/or division skills can be devised and presented individually or collectively in test form. This procedure is more meaningful for the teacher if he or she can observe the pupils' performance and attempt to identify systematic errors.

Create situations that require pupils to utilize arithmetic terms, such as add, larger than, take away, divide, and so forth.

## Social Competencies

Develop a brief checklist to assess behavior while on a field trip. For example, did the pupils observe good safety practices or were they courteous to others?

Simulation activities requiring individuals to portray different roles can be used to assess the understanding of behavior appropriate for given situations.

Committee assignments can be used to evaluate the ability of pupils to work together.

Provide verbal description or illustration of appropriate and inappropriate behavior. Pupils can be asked to discriminate between behaviors.

Structure situations that call for specific kinds of behavior and observe the performance of individuals. For example, have a pupil ask for information from another teacher, make an introduction, or lead a group activity.

Assess the frequency with which a child displays a disruptive behavior. Talk with the child about behavior and help the child monitor his or her own efforts in altering the behavior.

Use films involving children at their peer level engaging in social activities. Have the students analyze what is taking place in the film and why.

Have adults purposely engage students in conversation. Obtain feedback from the adult and the student regarding the interaction.

Have students write a script for a play. Ask them questions about the roles they develop for different characters. As the play is cast and presented, observe the interpretation given to the various roles.

## OBSERVATION SKILLS

Skill in observation is important to the process of employing informal evaluation techniques. All the evaluation activities previously discussed require the teacher to observe the behavior of pupils and to make inferences from what is observed. If the observation is focused on the child performing a particular task, the job of drawing an inference is enhanced by the circumscribed nature of the task and the anticipated type of response. However, throughout the school day, pupils are performing in less structured situations. They respond to each other in the process of preparing for lunch, they react to assignments, they exhibit a wide array of behaviors that may or may not be observed by the teacher. If a teacher happens to notice a child engaged in an activity, the teacher may or may not make a mental note of what the child is doing. On the other hand, a teacher may watch a child fail at what appears to be a routine activity and infer that the child is unable to perform the task. Whether teachers are observing routine behavior or employing a specific evaluation technique, they must keep in mind that children vary in their behavior. They may be observing the child at a low ebb. For this reason, it is important that teachers not make judgments on a single observation. They should obtain behavior samples over a period of time and under different circumstances. As they observe the child, attention should be given to the surroundings in which the child is performing the activity as well as to preceding events. The child's inability to focus attention on the experience chart might be due to anticipation of the free play activity during recess fifteen minutes hence. Nonresponse to peers during the first hour might be caused by lack of breakfast or the fact that the child encountered a problem on the bus while en route to school.

The variance among and within pupils, coupled with the influence of environmental conditions on the behavior of individuals, complicates the process of evaluation. It also serves to accentuate the necessity of structuring the procedures for gathering evaluation data. Without information on the behavior of individual pupils, the teacher is ill prepared for the task of individualizing instruction.

Although attention has been given to assessing the effectiveness of individual units and their collective influence on the curriculum, the skills required to evaluate pupil performance are applicable regardless of what aspect of the curriculum is being evaluated. The organization of this chapter was designed to illustrate techniques for evaluating pupil performance and to relate these techniques to the process of evaluation within the framework of unit teaching.

## Evaluating the Composite Effects of Unit Teaching

The systematic approach for writing units and for developing a year's plan of work suggested in other chapters is evaluation-oriented. Each step requires teachers to make decisions regarding the appropriateness of content as well as the effectiveness of the activities they plan to employ. If they follow these steps, the opportunity for error through the individual units should be greatly reduced. Having completed instruction on the units included in the year's plan of work, the teacher should assess the collective effectiveness of the several individual units taught, in order to determine their contributions to the broader class curriculum goals. Teachers need to determine whether or not they accomplished through unit teaching those curriculum objectives allocated to unit teaching in planning the yearly instructional program. This is not to suggest that teachers ignore opportunities for daily evaluation of pupil performance or avoid evaluating the effects of individual units. Suggestions for evaluating pupil performance are directly applicable to evaluating instruction units. This section is intended to offer guidelines for an end-of-the-year evaluation of the overall effectiveness of the unit teaching program.

Although evaluation of the composite effects of unit teaching cannot be completed until the end of the school year, evaluation should be an ongoing process that requires the teacher to look routinely at pupil performance in reference to the content and skills being taught. A variety of techniques can be structured by teachers for this type of evaluation. Two alternatives will be illustrated. One focuses specifically on unit teaching and does not consider those curriculum aspects covered through other instruction methods. The second is a more comprehensive approach to evaluating the year's instructional program and includes provisions for assessing the total instructional program. The advantages of the former approach is that the teacher can develop an evaluation instrument directly from the work completed during the process of writing behavioral objectives for individual unit lessons. The more comprehensive approach requires that the teacher specify in advance the specific content, concepts, and skills to be included in the overall instructional program throughout the year regardless of the method that may be employed for teaching them. This approach, however, does have the advantage of offering the teacher more detailed information regarding the instructional program and the progress of individual children. It does not separate unit teaching from the other methods employed.

The goal of both approaches is to provide the teacher with objective data regarding the progress of individual children, along with an assessment of the collective class accomplishments during the year. This information can be used as a basis for planning subsequent instructional programs for the same children or for children with similar learning characteristics. The information can also be recorded in a form usable by other teachers who will have the same children in class at other times.

## Unit Evaluation Inventory Approach

This approach involves the development of an inventory that includes representative instructional objectives from the units taught during the school year. In other words, it is not necessary to include all instructional objectives. A sample of objectives that reflect the content covered will be sufficient for this type of evaluation. The inventory can be easily constructed by reviewing the lesson plans prepared for each unit during the year and listing the behaviorally stated instructional objectives according to the core areas, namely, arithmetic, social competencies, communication skills, health, safety, and vocational skills. This requires the teacher to make decisions about which core area the task called for in the objective represents. Having done this for each unit, the teacher has a check on the orientation of individual units by core area and can determine the degree of emphasis given to each core area through individual units. The check can also be applied to the total group of units taught during the year. These findings can be compared with the results of the preliminary steps for each unit and the year's plan of work discussed in Chapters 4 and 9.

The major difference, beside the emphasis on unit teaching, between this approach and the more comprehensive approach is that this one cannot be organized into final form until all the units have been developed. As a result, the teacher must develop a record-keeping system which later can be modified into an evaluation form.

If fifteen to twenty units are taught during the school year, the number of instructional objectives that could be recorded and applied to each child will be sizable. For this reason, teachers should select objectives representative of each unit rather than include all the instructional objectives developed through the lesson plans. Since the goal is to evaluate the composite contribution of unit teaching, it is not essential that each objective be included. The following steps are suggested for employing this approach.

1.  The performance of each pupil should be evaluated on the individual instructional objectives included in the various lesson plans. As teachers rarely develop all the units they plan to teach during the year in advance, it will be necessary that the performance of each child relative to the respective instructional objectives be recorded on the lesson plans, a note card, or in some other format. This information can later be transferred to the evaluation form.

2.  Select those instructional objectives you wish to include in the evaluation inventory. As previously mentioned, all instructional objectives can be

included; or if this represents too large a number, then a decision must be made on which instructional objectives are most representative of the units that have been taught.

3. Transfer the instructional objectives to a Unit Evaluation Inventory format (see Figure 12). The objectives can be stated in complete or abbreviated form. The important factor is that the statement of the objectives communicate the task for which the pupil's performance was evaluated.

4. Record the pupil's performance on the evaluation form.

The following two examples are suggested formats for recording the evaluation data. The examples are not inclusive of a year's plan of work in unit teaching. However, sufficient information is provided to illustrate the feasibility of this particular approach. The first example is designed for use with individual pupils, whereas the second applies to a class or a group of students.

### Individual Form

This form is self-explanatory. Teachers identify the core areas and list the instructional objectives which have been previously selected. They then record their assessment of the pupil's performance relative to each objective. If they have been careful to record the pupil's performance at the time of the learning experience, they merely transfer the evaluation data. If they have not routinely evaluated each pupil's progress, then it is necessary to structure situations that will allow them to assess performance in those areas specified in the instructional objectives. The column labeled "Unit Source" can be used to identify the unit from which the instructional objective was selected. This necessitates a number being assigned to each unit. The value of this feature is that it helps you gain a perspective on the contribution of individual units to the total unit teaching program.

Comments relevant to the child's performance on specific tasks, for example, interpersonal relations or manner of participation, can be recorded. Care should be taken to record only those comments that will be of assistance to you in revising your units for future students or helpful to teachers who will have the particular student in class the following year. The purpose of the comment section is to add flexibility to the format and to extend its use in the evaluation process.

Figures 12, 13, 14, 15, 16, and 17 illustrate the Individual Form.

| Core Area: __Arithmetic*__  Name: __Jane__ | HAS COMPETENCE | HAS LIMITED COMPETENCE | HAS NO COMPETENCE | |
|---|---|---|---|---|
| UNIT SOURCE — INSTRUCTIONAL OBJECTIVES | | | | COMMENT |
| 3 — Given the wage per hour and number of hours to be worked per week is able to estimate income. | | | | |
| 3 — Is able to set up a budget that takes into account income and necessary expenditures. | | | | |
| 3 — Is able to fill out the necessary forms for establishing a checking account. | | | | |
| 3 — Is able to write a check correctly and fill out the check stub accurately. | | | | |
| 1 — Given a road map, can determine distance between major cities. | | | | |
| 1 — Can identify map symbols and explain their meaning. | | | | |
| 1 — Can determine distance between cities on a map and estimate the travel time by car. | | | | |
| 6 — Given sales price and regular price on an item, can calculate amount saved. | | | | |
| 6 — Is able to compute the sales tax on items costing up to $1,000.00. | | | | |
| 6 — Can compute the money to be saved by buying items in quantity. | | | | |
| 8 — Is able to accurately change 25%, 50%, and 75% to decimals. | | | | |

*Selected from units taught at the junior high level.

**Figure 12. Unit Evaluation Inventory (Individual Form)**

| Core Area: Communication Skills* <br> Name: Betty | Has Competence | Has Limited Competence | Has No Competence | |
|---|---|---|---|---|
| **Unit Source** | **Instructional Objectives** | | | | **Comment** |
| 2 | Is able to write own name from memory in manuscript. | | | | |
| 4 | Is able to differentiate between color words and number words; for example, red, two, blue, three, six, white, and black. | | | | |
| 8 | Can correctly copy in cursive name and street name from manuscript form. | | | | |
| 9 | In listening to words read aloud, can differentiate between rhyming and non-rhyming words. | | | | |
| 8 | Is able to correctly demonstrate the use of a dial telephone. | | | | |
| 8 | Given a name, can locate the name in the telephone book. | | | | |
| 8 | Given a list of ten names, can place them in alphabetical order according to last name. | | | | |
| 10 | Given a topic, is able to write complete sentences of at least five words in length. | | | | |
| 11 | Given a work sheet with pictures of apples, oranges, bananas, and grapes, is able to write the appropriate name for each in recognizable form. | | | | |

*Selected from units for children in the 6-10 age level.

**Figure 13.    Unit Evaluation Inventory (Individual Form)**

| Core Area: Social Competencies* Name: Ann | | HAS COMPETENCE | HAS LIMITED COMPETENCE | HAS NO COMPETENCE | |
|---|---|---|---|---|---|
| UNIT SOURCE | INSTRUCTIONAL OBJECTIVES | | | | COMMENT |
| 1 | Is able to stand in line without bothering other children. | | | | |
| 1 | Given a description of behavior on the bus, is able to indicate whether it is appropriate or not. | | | | |
| 1 | Uses terms such as "please," "thank you," and "excuse me" at appropriate times. | | | | |
| 2 | When asked to participate in show and tell, does not share information about the family which is private. | | | | |
| 2 | Shares toys with classmates when there are insufficient toys for the group. | | | | |
| 4 | Voluntarily contributes to class discussion when the topic is familiar. | | | | |
| 5 | When asked to introduce a friend does so in an appropriate manner. | | | | |
| 7 | When directed to ask a question of two people engaged in a conversation, waits for an opportunity to say "excuse me" and to pose the question. | | | | |
| 8 | When using the telephone, keeps conversation short. | | | | |
| 10 | Is able to take correction without complaining or offering an alibi. | | | | |
| 12 | Given a set of verbal instructions on a task, is able to communicate them correctly to a small group. | | | | |

*Selected from units taught to a group of 6-10 year olds.

**Figure 14.   Unit Evaluation Inventory (Individual Form)**

| Core Area: ___Safety*___ Name: ___Joe___ | | HAS COMPETENCE | HAS LIMITED COMPETENCE | HAS NO COMPETENCE | |
|---|---|---|---|---|---|
| UNIT SOURCE | INSTRUCTIONAL OBJECTIVES | | | | COMMENT |
| 6 | Is able to demonstrate the safe use of a saber saw. | | | | |
| 6 | When asked to give a knife to another person, hands it to them with the handle first. | | | | |
| 7 | Given an illustration of an intersection, can explain the proper way to make a left-hand turn. | | | | |
| 7 | Is able to demonstrate the hand signals for stop, left turn and right turn. | | | | |
| 7 | When parking a car on a downhill slope, turns wheels toward the curb. | | | | |
| 5 | Fastens seat belt prior to starting the engine of a car. | | | | |
| 4 | Is able to explain why a person should not turn on a light switch while standing in water. | | | | |
| 4 | Given three extension cords with one in need of repair, can identify the one which is unsafe. | | | | |
| 4 | Can demonstrate the correct use of a fire extinguisher. | | | | |
| 5 | Can explain the correct procedure for putting out an electrical fire in the kitchen. | | | | |

*Selected from units taught at the secondary level.

**Figure 15.   Unit Evaluation Inventory (Individual Form)**

| Core Area: Health* <br> Name: Johnny | | Has Competence | Has Limited Competence | Has No Competence | |
|---|---|---|---|---|---|
| Unit Source | Instructional Objectives | | | | Comment |
| 1 | Can demonstrate the proper procedure for brushing teeth. | | | | |
| 2 | Given a menu for breakfast, lunch, and dinner, can identify which one is typically a breakfast menu. | | | | |
| 2 | Able to explain why some foods must be refrigerated. | | | | |
| 3 | Washes hands after using the rest room. | | | | |
| 4 | Wears warm clothing when playing outside during cold weather. | | | | |
| 5 | Can explain why he or she should stay home when ill. | | | | |
| 5 | Does not put objects such as pencils, crayons, and so on in mouth. | | | | |
| 7 | Can explain why meat should be cooked before being eaten. | | | | |
| 7 | Given several heads of lettuce, some of which are old, can identify which are fresh. | | | | |
| 7 | Is able to distinguish between fresh milk and milk that is sour. | | | | |

*Selected from units taught to a class of 6-10 year olds.

**Figure 16. Unit Evaluation Inventory (Individual Form)**

| Core Area: Vocational Skills*  Name: Betty | | Has Competence | Has Limited Competence | Has No Competence | |
|---|---|---|---|---|---|
| Unit Source | Instructional Objectives | | | | Comment |
| 1 | Is able to identify a source of community help in locating a job, that is, state employment agency, private agencies, and vocational rehabilitation office. | | | | |
| 2 | Is able to locate the employment office within a local industry. | | | | |
| 2 | Can demonstrate an appropriate procedure for inquiring about job opportunities at a local industry. | | | | |
| 2 | Is able to fill out a job application form accurately. | | | | |
| 3 | Can explain why it is important to be on time every day at a job. | | | | |
| 3 | Has obtained a social security number and keeps it accessible. | | | | |
| 4 | Is able to identify jobs that are generally within his or her ability. | | | | |
| 5 | Given an example of a job some distance from home, is able to decide a feasible plan for getting to and from work. | | | | |
| 8 | Able to demonstrate the use of a time clock. | | | | |

*Selected from units taught at the secondary level.

**Figure 17.   Unit Evaluation Inventory (Individual Form)**

## Group Form

An alternate format for the Unit Evaluation Inventory can be designed to accommodate the recording of group data, as shown in Figure 18. It has the advantage of reducing the number of forms the teacher must contend with, but it also eliminates the opportunity for recording comments on individual

Core Area: _Arithmetic*_

Ellen Smith's Class

| Unit Source | Instructional Objectives | John 1 2 3 | Joe 1 2 3 | Mary 1 2 3 | Sara 1 2 3 | Tom 1 2 3 | Austin 1 2 3 | Dick 1 2 3 | Bill 1 2 3 | Ann 1 2 3 | Judy 1 2 3 |
|---|---|---|---|---|---|---|---|---|---|---|---|
| 1 | Is able to demonstrate the use of cardinal numbers from one to ten. | | | | | | | | | | |
| 1 | Is able to demonstrate an understanding of terms such as up and down, on and under, front and back, etc. | | | | | | | | | | |
| 2 | Given a collection of 25 objects, can group them into five equal groups. | | | | | | | | | | |
| 4 | Given a group of ten objects and a group of eight objects, is able to identify the larger group. | | | | | | | | | | |
| 6 | Is able to rearrange objects on a flannel board into sets and indicate orally the numbers represented. | | | | | | | | | | |
| 7 | Given a quarter, dime, and nickel, is able to label them and indicate their value. | | | | | | | | | | |

1 = Has competency
2 = Has little competency
3 = Has no competency

*Selected from units taught to children at 6-10 age level.

**Figure 18.** Unit Evaluation Inventory (Group Form)

201

students. It has the additional advantage of providing an overview of the group's progress as well as an assessment of an individual's performance.

Because the listing of instructional objectives is the same as for individual forms, only one example is included. However, a teacher who chooses to use the group form rather than the individual form would need to develop an inventory for each core area.

## Comprehensive Skill Inventory Approach

In contrast to the Unit Evaluation Inventory, this inventory can be developed prior to the beginning of the school year. The basic feature of this approach is that it requires teachers to specify the skills and concepts they anticipate teaching during the school year. *The specification process discussed in Chapter 8 is compatible with this approach.* Many teachers find that this approach works best in the areas of arithmetic, reading, and language arts. However, it can be modified to accommodate subject matter such as social and vocational skills as well as motor skills. Since the skills are identified before being taught, they can be placed in sequential order within the form. This facilitates assessment and allows the teacher to illustrate graphically the progress of individual pupils as well as of the class as a group. It also enhances teacher evaluation of pupil performances as a routine daily practice.

While the Unit Evaluation Inventory approach focused specifically on unit teaching, this approach is designed to assist the teacher in assessing the overall impact of the instructional program. The emphasis is on the acquisition of skills and knowledge of pupils individually and collectively. Specific attention is given to a broad range of skills and knowledge, whether they were taught through unit teaching or other methods. Teachers electing to use this approach will find that the inventory can evolve from the planning they do prior to the opening of the school year. As decisions are made regarding what is to be taught and the manner in which the instruction will be organized, skills, concepts, and levels of understanding can be selected as the basis for evaluation.

The basic feature of the Comprehensive Skills Inventory approach is that it is representative of the total instructional program. This means that the inventory should accurately reflect what was or, if it is in the planning stage, what will be taught during the year. Obviously, the abilities of children in most classes vary considerably; thus, the inventory should be sufficiently comprehensive to accommodate the more able student as well as those who are less capable.

The development of a Comprehensive Skill Inventory involves many of the same tasks inherent in curriculum development. The process requires a knowledge of pupil needs and an awareness of their performance levels. The selected skills must parallel the curriculum, although the inventory itself need not be organized according to instructional patterns such as unit teaching, academic areas, social activities, or motor skills. The emphasis is on skill and content areas rather than teaching methodologies. Again there is nothing sacred about the format to be discussed, and teachers are encouraged to experiment with formats and procedures that best fit their personal teaching styles.

Many teachers find that even though they are committing a major portion of the school day to unit teaching, the evaluation of pupil progress is best approached from a subject frame of reference. This facilities evaluation of the total program inclusive of unit teaching and acknowledges the integrations of academic skills into the unit teaching aspects of the program.

As is true in any evaluation of pupil progress, the basic skills of arithmetic, reading, and language arts are more easily identified. They also lend themselves more readily to the establishment of evaluation criteria than do areas that are social in nature. If teachers are working from a prescribed curriculum or if they plan the instructional program in reasonable detail, the task of specifying evaluation criteria for the curriculum content is greatly reduced. The aim is to develop an inventory that is representative of the curriculum and includes items of sufficient specificity to yield evaluation information meaningful to the teacher regarding the performance of individual pupils and the class as a group.

For purposes of illustration, sample inventories have been developed for the areas of arithmetic, reading, and language arts. (See Figures 19, 20, and 21.) Inventories could also be developed for other areas, such as social competencies, science, and motor skills. The suggested format is very similar to the format of the Unit Evaluation Inventory. The major difference is the comprehensiveness of the skills, content, and concepts covered. Teachers wishing to make an account of what they feel was learned as a result of unit teaching or other instruction methods can include a column for noting the differentiation. Sample inventories for recording evaluation data on an individual and a group basis are included. Because of the similarities between the two forms, only one sample is included for the group procedure. (See Figure 22.)

Rather than use behaviorally stated instructional objectives to identify the selected curriculum content in the inventory, an abbreviated outline form has been used. This is done because teachers using this approach will most likely be working from a curriculum guide or will not have had an opportunity to develop the content into a lesson format inclusive of instructional objectives.

As with the Unit Evaluation Inventory, information acquired through the use of this procedure can be used to evaluate the contribution of unit teaching to the instructional program, to plan prescriptive teaching programs for individual pupils, as a basis for recording pupil progress, as a means for determining the need for curriculum revision, and as a source of information in providing feedback to students. It has the added advantage of being useful as a reference in determining the appropriate placement of children recommended for assignment to special classes. The child's performance of the skills included in the inventory can be measured and a decision made as to which class approximates his or her ability level. This, of course, would necessitate use of informal evaluation techniques plus a review of the child's previous school performance.

If all special class teachers in the school system utilize this approach, it can have a positive effect on the curriculum. Overlap and omissions become evident when comparisons are made among inventories for different classes. It is also possible to develop a single inventory of the total instructional program with teachers at various levels being concerned only with those skills appropriate to their respective classes. Since the skills and content can be ordered sequentially, the composite inventory can be subdivided according to the level of classes in the program. The difficult task is the initial development of the inventory. This, however, need only be done once and revised annually as the curriculum changes and as ability ranges shift in different classes.

## Reporting Pupil Progress

Having obtained evaluation-type data on the performance of individual pupils and on the general effectiveness of units taught, the teacher must make maximum use of the information acquired. Throughout this chapter, reference has been made to the use of evaluation data in the improvement of instruction and in curriculum development. Emphasis has also been given to the importance of providing immediate feedback to students. However, little mention has been made of the contribution of evaluation in reporting pupil progress to parents.

The periodic reporting of pupil progress to parents is a long established practice in our educational system. For the most part, it has taken the form of report cards, home visits, or parent-teacher conferences held within the confines of the school. The nature of the information voluntarily provided to parents by teachers during conferences varies considerably. The report card, however, has served to standardize, within school districts at least, the topics on which progress is reported to parents. In the case of special classes for the mentally retarded, there has been a tendency to devise report cards that differ from the form used in regular classes or to use the same format but omit items deemed inappropriate. Teachers of the mentally retarded, faced with the task of reporting the status of pupils to parents, frequently find they lack sufficient evidence of progress on which to report. Or they find that the data they do have tends to focus on what the child cannot do rather than on capabilities.

| Name: |
|---|
| Area: Language Arts* |
| Level: 6-10 C.A. |

| | Has Competence | Has Limited Competence | Has No Competence | Unit Instruction Other Methods | | |
|---|---|---|---|---|---|---|
| | Rating | | | | Source | Comment |
| **Verbal expression** | | | | | | |
| Expresses self clearly | | | | | | |
| Uses complete sentences | | | | | | |
| Spontaneously participates in discussion | | | | | | |
| Expresses ideas in sequence | | | | | | |
| Can verbally describe events | | | | | | |
| **Writing** | | | | | | |
| Knows purpose for writing | | | | | | |
| Reads manuscript writing | | | | | | |
| Writes capital and lowercase letters legibly | | | | | | |
| Writes a simple sentence | | | | | | |
| Writes short stories | | | | | | |
| Records in written form words from dictionary | | | | | | |
| Shows interest in cursive writing | | | | | | |
| Writes labels for pictures and things | | | | | | |
| Writes own name and address from memory | | | | | | |
| **Punctuation** | | | | | | |
| Uses period and question mark correctly | | | | | | |
| Can determine the need for a paragraph | | | | | | |
| Capitalizes appropriate words | | | | | | |
| Uses common abbreviations, e.g., Mr., Mrs., St., and states | | | | | | |
| **Listening** | | | | | | |
| Identifies common sounds | | | | | | |
| Identifies rhyming words | | | | | | |
| Can differentiate pitch | | | | | | |
| Follows directions | | | | | | |
| Attends to the speaker | | | | | | |
| **Spelling** | | | | | | |
| Spells personal words like name, community, days of week, etc. | | | | | | |
| Spells most words needed for writing | | | | | | |
| Identifies misspelled words at appropriate reading level | | | | | | |

*This inventory is by no means inclusive.

Figure 19.   Comprehensive Skills Inventory (Individual Form)

| Name: | | | | | | | | |
|---|---|---|---|---|---|---|---|---|
| Area:   Reading* | | | | | | | | |
| Level:   6-10 C.A. | | | | | | | | |

| | Has Competence | Has Limited Competence | Has No Competence | Unit Instruction | Other Methods | | | |
|---|---|---|---|---|---|---|---|---|
| | RATING | | | | | SOURCE | COMMENT | |

**Pre-reading**

Can sequence ideas
Shows interest in pictures
Describes pictures
Listens attentively
Imitates actions of teacher
Shows an interest in reading

**Visual discrimination**

Matches pictures with objects
Performs puzzles using geometric
    shapes
Recognizes letters
Adequate sight vocabulary

**Auditory discrimination**

Basic phonic skills

**Functional reading**

Reads crucial vocabulary
    words
Reads labels
Reads simple charts
Contributes to building experience
    charts
Has left-to-right orientation
Knows basic word attack skills

*This inventory is by no means inclusive.

**Figure 20.   Comprehensive Skills Inventory (Individual Form)**

| | Has Competence | Has Limited Competence | Has No Competence | Unit Instruction | Other Methods | | |
|---|---|---|---|---|---|---|---|
| Name: _____ | | | | | | | |
| Area: Arithmetic* | | | | | | | |
| Level: 6-10 C.A. | | | | | | | |
| | Rating | | | | | Source | Comment |
| I. Size and amount (Can differentiate between the following terms when given concrete objects to manipulate) | | | | | | | |
| A. large—small | | | | | | | |
| B. big—little | | | | | | | |
| C. long—short | | | | | | | |
| D. tall—short | | | | | | | |
| E. wide—narrow | | | | | | | |
| F. empty—full | | | | | | | |
| G. heavy—light | | | | | | | |
| II. Number skills | | | | | | | |
| A. Numbers one to ten | | | | | | | |
| 1. Counts one to ten by rote | | | | | | | |
| 2. Applies understanding of rote counting—one, two, three . . . ten | | | | | | | |
| 3. Writes numerals one to ten | | | | | | | |
| 4. Recognizes words "one" to "ten" | | | | | | | |
| B. Can identify plus and minus signs | | | | | | | |
| 1. Identifies and understands meaning of + and — signs | | | | | | | |
| 2. Can read words "plus," "minus," "add," "subtract" | | | | | | | |

*This inventory is by no means inclusive.

**Figure 21. Comprehensive Skills Inventory (Individual Form)**

Skill area: __Reading__

| SKILL | ANN 1 2 3 | BARB 1 2 3 | DICK 1 2 3 | JUDY 1 2 3 | BARRY 1 2 3 | BLAKE 1 2 3 | DON 1 2 3 | JOE 1 2 3 | SAM 1 2 3 |
|---|---|---|---|---|---|---|---|---|---|
| | | | | | | | | | |

OTHER INSTRUCTION

UNIT INSTRUCTION

1. Has competencies
2. Has limited competencies
3. Has no competencies

**Figure 22.  Comprehensive Skills Inventory (Group Form)**

If implemented, the procedures for evaluation discussed in this chapter will provide an ample base for reporting pupil progress. If teachers can put into practice the idea of criterion-reference evaluation, they have a ready-made resource of evaluative data that can be shared with parents. They can illustrate for parents examples of specific tasks and show them how their child fared on the item. If they have developed a Comprehensive Skills Inventory, they have a frame of reference for explaining to parents what has thus far been covered and what will be taught during the remainder of the year.

In other words, the by-product of routinely assessing pupil performance can be the creation of an information resource on individual pupils and class performance which can serve as input for your reporting system. Parents frequently do not understand what is implied by a report which says that Mary reads at the 3.1 reading level and is working at the 2.7 grade level in arithmetic. They seek meaningful information that tells them explicitly what Mary can or cannot do.

Report cards or conference guidelines that employ broad categories such as reading, arithmetic, social studies, science, and so forth, are not very helpful when attempting to communicate with parents. This is particularly true in terms of reporting pupil progress in areas covered through unit teaching.

## Summary

The evaluation of pupil performance is essential to the improvement of instruction. Unless teachers assess the effectiveness of their teaching efforts, their educational decisions are subject to considerable error. It is important for teachers to approach their daily instruction with an evaluation set that motivates them to look for evidence that their teaching is changing the behavior of their students.

Although formal evaluation procedures can be applied in assessing the performance of the mentally retarded, standardized tests for the most part are not designed to cover the content typically taught through units. However, this situation should not be used as an excuse for not evaluating the results of unit teaching. Skill inventories can be developed by teachers as a frame of reference for evaluating their instructional program. The type of inventory presented in this chapter builds on the use of criterion-reference evaluation techniques. These techniques are informal in nature. They require that teachers identify the behavior to be changed and establish a criterion level they will accept as evidence that the child has successfully performed the task. They then must allow the student to perform the task incidentally or structure a situation that requires him or her to perform the task under conditions that can be observed.

The results of evaluating pupil performance are necessary for individualizing instruction, helpful in revising curriculum, important as a source of feedback to students, and essential to the provision of needed input for reporting pupil progress to parents. The results of evaluation contribute to improved instruction.

**Exercise 14.** Develop a Unit Evaluation Inventory. Select three units written by yourself or other teachers. Select specific skills from these units and develop a Unit Evaluation Inventory using the following form.

## UNIT EVALUATION INVENTORY
### (Individual Form)

Core Area: _____

Name: _____

| UNIT SOURCE | INSTRUCTIONAL OBJECTIVES | HAS COMPETENCE | HAS LIMITED COMPETENCE | HAS NO COMPETENCE | COMMENT |
|---|---|---|---|---|---|
| | | | RATING | | |

**Exercise 15.** Develop Comprehensive Skills Inventory. Assume you are teaching a group of primary level mildly mentally retarded children. Develop a Comprehensive Skills Inventory in the area of language.

## COMPREHENSIVE SKILLS INVENTORY
### (Individual Form)

Name:_____

Area:_____ Level____

| | Has Competence | Has Limited Competence | Has No Competence | Unit Instruction | Other Methods | |
|---|---|---|---|---|---|---|
| | RATING | | | SOURCE | | COMMENT |

**Exercise 16.**   Develop a Comprehensive Skills Inventory. Assume you are teaching a junior high level group of mildly mentally retarded children. Develop a Comprehensive Skills Inventory in the area of arithmetic skills.

## COMPREHENSIVE SKILLS INVENTORY
### (Individual Form)

Name:_____

Area:_____ Level ___

| | Has Competence | Has Limited Competence | Has No Competence | Unit Instruction | Other Methods | |
|---|---|---|---|---|---|---|
| | RATING | | | SOURCE | | COMMENT |
| | | | | | | |

**Exercise 17.** Develop a Comprehensive Skills Inventory. Assume you are teaching a senior high level group of mildly mentally retarded pupils. Develop a Comprehensive Skills Inventory based on vocational skills.

## COMPREHENSIVE SKILLS INVENTORY
### (Individual Form)

Name:_____

Area:_____ Level___

| | Has Competence | Has Limited Competence | Has No Competence | Unit Instruction | Other Methods | | |
|---|---|---|---|---|---|---|---|
| | RATING | | | | | SOURCE | COMMENT |

**Exercise 18.**    Criterion for objectives. Describe a criterion measure for each of the following objectives.

1. Given four objects, the student will be able to order them according to size from smallest to largest.

2. Given specific information about a job vacancy, the student will be able to demonstrate correct procedures for applying for a job.

3. Using a real stove, the student will be able to determine accurately if the oven is heating according to the temperature dial.

## Bibliography

Barro, Stephen M. "An Approach to Developing Accountability Measures for the Public Schools." *Phi Delta Kappan* 52, no. 4 (December 1970).

Guba, Egon G. "An Overview of the Evaluation Problem." A paper read at the symposium on "The World of Evaluation Needs Reshaping." AERA Convention, February 1969.

Popham, W. James, and Husek, T. R. "Implications of Criterion-Referenced Measurement." *Journal of Educational Measurement*, Spring 1969.

Stephens, Thomas M. *Directive Teaching of Children with Learning and Behavioral Handicaps*. Columbus: Charles E. Merrill Publishing Company, 1970.


### Additional Selected References Related to Evaluation of Instruction

Drew, Clifford J.; Freston, Cyrus W.; and Logan, Don. "Criteria and Reference in Evaluation." *Focus on Exceptional Children* 4, no. 1 (March 1972).

Frank, A. R.; Retish, P. M.; and Crooks, F. C. "Developing a Skills Inventory." *Teaching Exceptional Children*, Winter 1971, p. 81.

Flynn, John T., and Garber, Herbert. *Assessing Behavior: Readings In Educational and Psychological Measurement*. Palo Alto: Addison-Wesley Publishing Company, 1967.

Gallagher, Patricia A. *Positive Classroom Performance Techniques for Changing Behavior*. Denver, Colo.: Love Publishing Company, 1971.

Grobman, Hilda. *Evaluation Activities of Curriculum Projects*. AERA Monograph Series on Curriculum Evaluation. Chicago: Rand McNally and Company, 1970.

Hall, R. Vance. "Responsive Teaching: Focus on Measurement and Research in the Classroom and the Home." *Focus on Exceptional Children* 3, no. 7 (December 1971).

Lovitt, Tom; Schaff, Mary; and Sayre, Elizabeth. "The Use of Direct and Continuous Measurement to Evaluate Reading Materials and Pupil Performance." *Focus on Exceptional Children* 2, no. 6 (November 1970).

Mercer, Jane R. "Crosscultural Evaluation of Exceptionality." *Focus on Exceptional Children* 5, no. 4 (September 1973).

Meyen, Edward L. and Hieronymus, Albert N. "The Age Placement of Academic Skills in Curriculum for the EMR." *Exceptional Children* 36 (January 1970).

———. "Evaluation, the Missing Link in Curriculum Development for the Mentally Retarded." *The Training School Bulletin* 65 (1968):3.

Minskoff, Esther H. "Creating and Evaluating Remediation for the Learning Disabled." *Focus on Exceptional Children* 5, no. 5 (October 1973).

Semmel, Melvyn I., and Thiagarajan, Sivasailam. "Observation Systems and the Special Education Teacher." *Focus on Exceptional Children* 5, no. 7 (December 1973).

Smith, Robert M. *Teacher Diagnosis of Educational Difficulties*. Columbus: Charles E. Merrill Publishing Co., 1969.

Steele, Sara M. *Contemporary Approaches to Program Evaluation: Implications for Evaluating Programs for Disadvantaged Adults*. Syracuse, N.Y.: Eric Clearinghouse on Adult Education, 1973.

STORY, ARTHUR G. *The Measurement of Classroom Learning*. Chicago: Science Research Associates, 1971.

WALKER, HILL M., and BUCKLEY, NANCY K. "Teacher Attention to Appropriate and Inappropriate Classroom Behavior: An Individual Case Study." *Focus on Exceptional Children* 5, no. 3 (May 1973).

# 8

# Organizing a
# Curriculum-Based Unit Plan

There has been a tendency among teachers who employ the unit teaching method to focus their efforts on constructing individual units. In doing so, they often overlook the educational gains to be derived from advanced planning of the relationships among units. For teachers who teach only an occasional unit, the former approach is sufficient. Their emphasis should be on designing the best experience possible within each individual unit. The situation changes, however, as the emphasis on unit teaching increases. If unit teaching comprises more than ten percent of the teacher's instructional program, then detailed attention should be given to the cumulative contribution of units to the curriculum. It is not only important to have a well-defined plan of what is to be taught through units, but it is also essential to be able to illustrate the relationship of instruction offered through units to the skills and concepts taught through other instructional modes.

Except for sparsely populated areas, most attendance centers include three or more classes per grade level. Even in Special Education programs, most attendance centers have several teachers with some assigned responsibility for teaching exceptional children. These circumstances are highly conducive to involving several teachers in the process of preparing unit plans. The trend in some districts to individualize instruction without regard to grade placement is also compatible with a team approach to structuring curriculum plans in terms of instructional units. This chapter will provide practical suggestions on how a district might engage groups of teachers in the process of systematically planning instructional programs that make extensive use of units. The following assumptions are made relative to the suggested procedures:

1. That units represent at least ten percent of the instructional program.

2. That two or more teachers have responsibility for teaching similar con-

This chapter is intended for teachers who allocate a substantial amount of instructional time to unit teaching and who are in a position where they can work cooperatively with other teachers in developing curriculum specifications for unit plans.

tent through units to groups of students with comparable learning characteristics.

3. That the district will provide participating teachers with resources for the planning process in the form of consultation, release time, and/or clerical support.

4. That the participating teachers recognize the importance of being able to account for pupil outcome resulting from unit teaching as well as from other dimensions of the curriculum.

### Implications of Unit-Based Curriculum

Several implications emerge as the emphasis on unit teaching increases. This is particularly true as the instructional time allocated to unit teaching approaches one-third to one-half of the curriculum. The obvious implication is that students will receive more of their education through unit teaching. Unless the total unit program is systematically planned, there is considerable risk that programs taught to individual students will not only lack sequence but may very well be characterized by omissions and redundancies. It is important that some form of curriculum planning process be employed that clearly details the curriculum outcome to be achieved and identifies what will be incorporated into units and what will be covered through other instructional modes.

The primary implications of an expanded emphasis on unit teaching are couched in the context of how effective a teacher is in the process of teaching units. There are, however, some implications that pertain to the teacher's role in curriculum development and to program management.

*Development Skills*    Unit teaching obviously involves a product: the instructional unit. If the experiences inherent in a unit are to be maximally appropriate to the students involved, it is advantageous if the teacher assumes major responsibility for constructing the unit. The net result is that the greater the emphasis given to units, the greater the need for development skills on the part of teachers. In programs where units will be extensively used, it is reasonable to take for granted that they can be shared among teachers. To implement an exchange of units assumes that the units follow a similar format and are well designed. If extensive use is to be made of units by several teachers, the district should employ a consultant or supervisor who is sufficiently skilled in unit construction to assist teachers in building units and coordinating the development process.

*Preparation Time*    As has been previously mentioned, it requires time to prepare good units. Although systematic procedures and experience in constructing units will reduce the required time, the more units one has to prepare, the more time one has to allow. However, the time demands are not in direct proportion to the number of units produced. What typically occurs in a program emphasizing unit teaching is that series of units are developed that can be adapted to various settings. The consequence is a better return on the teacher's time spent in developing units. Teachers can also cooperate in developing units. Cooperatively developed units often include more varied activities as a result of creativity evolving from teacher interaction in the development of an instructional product. Once a district or program has identified the sequence of skills, concepts, and information to be included and prepared a number of units, the time demands change. The emphasis shifts from preparing complete units to the planning of daily activities and the modification of preplanned activities.

*Curriculum Revision*   Because of the comprehensiveness of instructional units developed in accordance with the guidelines provided in this book, the unit format results in a more complete picture of what is included in the curriculum than do most other curriculum formats. It is possible to focus revision efforts on objectives, activities, resources, and general content. It is also possible to alter the internal activity sequence within a unit in order to accomplish revision. The latter, of course, would represent a simplified approach to curriculum revision.

*Content Control*   By design, instructional units specify content as well as teaching techniques. In many ways they are analogous to a text in that the experiences in which the students are to be involved are specified in advance. Thus, once the unit is prepared, there is a certain amount of control placed on the curriculum content. This is not to suggest that teachers will not alter activities during the process of teaching. But it is apparent that the intent of systematically planning a unit is to control content, that is, to be certain that relevant skills, concepts, and information are taught.

*Problem Detection*   Teachers experience a variety of problems in implementing instructional programs. Some of these relate to the behavioral characteristics of students, to student response to teaching style, and to the general features of the classroom climate. The typical approach to resolving an instructionally related problem is to focus on the teacher-pupil interaction. Granted, most such problems are process-related, but the content of what is being taught can also be the source of the problem. Because units describe content as well as technique, the unit represents an additional reference in seeking to resolve instructional problems. It is feasible to examine not only an activity but a complete unit or series of units to identify the factors contributing to instructional problems.

Although not necessarily implications of the approach, there are at least two other concerns that teachers need to be sensitive to when allocating a substantial portion of their instructional time to unit teaching. These concerns pertain to the relationship of *information* to *skills* in unit teaching. One of the major advantages of unit teaching is placing skill instruction in a relevant context. This is particularly significant in working with children who require a highly experiential approach. In many units there is a bona fide body of information that should be taught. In most cases this information provides the context or frame of reference in which skills and concepts are developed. However, there is frequently a tendency to overstress a unit's informational dimension. This occurs because it is much easier to identify information and to design activities for teaching units than to specify skills or concepts. This is more likely to become a problem when teachers develop a year's plan of work by themselves, as described in Chapter 9.

### "Givens" In the Development of Unit-Based Curriculum

Although few instructional programs are totally unit-based, some Special Education programs, particularly for mildly mentally retarded students, do implement what could be considered a unit-based curriculum. School districts considering establishing a unit-based curriculum should recognize that there is a set of features associated with unit-based curriculum that must be dealt with. The author has chosen to call these "givens." They have been derived from the author's observations of attempts to develop unit-based curriculum for special classes for the mildly mentally retarded. They should not be interpreted as criticism of the unit method but rather as concerns directed toward totally unit-based curriculum for any target student population. They should serve as cues for teachers in developing units generally.

1. *It is not feasible to develop a totally unit-based curriculum.* A unit-based curriculum is developmental in its orientation, and content must be identified, sequenced, and transformed into instructional units. As long as the teacher is effective in developing and teaching units, the approach works. However, students do have remediation needs. It is in the realm of correction or remediation that a unit-based curriculum falls short. It frequently becomes necessary to use prepared instructional programs in order to correct students' deficits. It would also be unreasonable to assume that sufficient experience could be built into units to accommodate teaching all reading and math skills. This is not to suggest that math and reading are not major goals of unit teaching. However, unless a district is in a position to invest heavily in curriculum development, it would be unwise to assume that teachers will be able to provide quality instruction in reading and math solely through unit teaching.

2. *Unless units can be meaningfully taught in sub-units, they are not sufficiently flexible as a curriculum design.*

Too often in programs where the curriculum is based primarily on units, those instructional units are the smallest elements in the curriculum. In other words, the only option for altering the curriculum by restructuring what has been developed is to reorder the sequence in which units are taught. The development steps described in Chapter 4 illustrate the concept of using sub-units. If this approach to constructing units is followed, units can be reconstructed using lesson plans, that is, objectives, activities, and resources, as the smallest curriculum element. Regardless of the development procedure followed, the format should allow for breaking units down into elements. The smallest element, however, must remain as a complete teaching activity. For example, it must indicate behavior(s) to be taught, the teaching strategy, and required resources. Typically, a unit comparable to a sub-unit, that is, a collection of planned lessons around a common theme, works best. New units can be developed as a result of rearranging sub-units. Also, sub-units can be selected from several units to supplement one another.

3. *Evaluating student progress through unit teaching requires constant monitoring.*

In contrast to teaching with a basic series where the emphasis is on specific skills (for example, math or reading), units of instruction are typically concerned with a broader range of behaviors. Skills are stressed in unit teaching, but considerable emphasis is also given to social development and information acquisition. Consequently, the teacher must sample a wider range of behaviors in determining the unit's successfulness. Techniques such as maintaining *Skills Inventories* (as illustrated in Chapter 7) are effective in assessing student achievement in individual units. A more difficult aspect of evaluating student progress as a result of unit participation relates to cumulative progress—that is, gains as a result of several units and outcomes resulting from incidental experience created by unit activities. When units constitute a major portion of the curriculum, considerable attention should be given to maintaining criterion-referenced skill inventories, anecdotal records, and observation systems in addition to the use of standardized achievement tests.

4. *Unit formats tend to become sacred the longer they are used.*

A major thesis of this book is that teachers should adhere to a systematic format in preparing units. A particular format has been suggested. Whenever units are to be used in a situation where several teachers are involved, the importance of a systematic and uniform format increases. Since the goal is to encourage all teachers to use a uniform format, all teachers should contribute to format decisions. However, in spite of the advantages of adhering to a common format within a district or program when units are to be shared, there is a tendency for an adopted format to become institutionalized and never changed. Situations do occur that call for format changes. Thus, the format should be reviewed periodically to determine its appropriateness for participating teachers. This does not mean that minor changes are encouraged to satisfy the unique desires of individual teachers. However, it is important to avoid negative teacher reaction to the format or procedures employed in developing units.

5. *Not every teacher can or wants to "teach units."*
Unit teaching places numerous demands on teachers. First, they must develop the units. Second, emphasis on group teaching techniques requires a wider array of teaching skills than do highly individualized remediation techniques. Basically, unit teaching involves the application of most good teaching techniques. Programs making extensive use of unit teaching should provide inservice training to participating teachers and appropriate teacher techniques. The hesitancy of some teachers to use units is generally related to a lack of experience with units and insufficient information on how to develop and/or teach them.

## Developing Specifications for a Unit-Based Curriculum

The same logic that supports the application of systematic procedures for developing units applies to the organization of units into a curriculum. Attention must be given to the identification and sequencing of skills and concepts to be included in units as well as to the determination of what units are to be taught and when. In essence, when the decision is made to allocate a substantial portion of instructional time to unit teaching, two types of planning tasks emerge. The first pertains to planning well-designed units for direct classroom application. The second planning task relates to developing an overall blueprint of unit instruction to which each individual unit contributes. Although individual teachers typically assume responsibility for developing units, the process of structuring an overall unit plan requires broader input and some centralized coordination. In circumstances where the teacher is not part of a larger group engaged in unit planning, a more restricted approach such as that suggested in Chapter 9 is appropriate. The restrictions for individual teachers developing unit plans are primarily a manpower problem. The suggestions included in the following discussion are appropriate regardless of the number of teachers involved. However, it is more feasible to carry them out with a broader talent and manpower base.

If your goal is to develop a long-term plan for unit teaching, that is, a year or more, you must develop a set of specifications that will serve as a frame of reference for the development of actual teaching units. It does not make much difference whether your goal involves unit development to teach language arts to elementary students in regular classes, mentally retarded students in special classes, or students assigned to resource rooms. You still have the same obligation for assuring the student a quality program. Unless a master plan is designed, there is considerable risk that there will be little sequence in the units taught and no assurance that the appropriate skills and concepts have been included. Detailed planning does not guarantee the student a quality education, but it does create a set of conditions conducive to providing quality instruction.

In any instructional program where teachers assume a major responsibility for developing instructional packages, planning increases in importance. Unless specific guidelines are provided, each unit, and ultimately the student's curriculum, becomes unique to the teacher. The net result is that the number of curricula implemented is equal to the number of teachers employed in a program.

*Specification Principles*

There are no set rules for developing specifications for a unit-based curriculum, but there are principles that warrant consideration. These principles can be used as evaluative criteria in determining the effectiveness of specifications for a unit-based curriculum. It should be kept in mind that the specifications are comparable to a set of blueprints that an architect might develop for a contractor. Just as the contractor builds the structure according to the specifications of the blueprint, so must the teacher construct units according to a set of specifications.

*The Unit Plan Specifications Should . . .*

. . . Be inclusive of the skills, concepts, and information considered essential to the target student population.

- Consider the total curriculum, not just the content to be covered by units.
- Apply various approaches to task, concept, and content analysis.

. . . Be in balance with the resources available for constructing units. The scope of the curriculum to be covered through unit teaching should represent an attainable development task.

- Every skill or concept included in the specifications must be incorporated in an instructional unit.
- The major resource required in operationalizing a curriculum unit is human talent. The major restriction placed on utilizing human talent is time.

- The specifications for a unit-based curriculum need not be transformed into units the first year. A time schedule should be established.

... Be in an organizational format that facilitates unit development by individual teachers and/or groups of teachers.

- Avoid using complex organizational formats and coding systems.
- The structure should allow for easy entry. The teacher should be able to locate specific content without conducting a time-consuming search of specifications.
- The format should provide for a cross-index between the specifications and the units developed for implementing them.

... Be in sufficient detail to minimize misinterpretation.

- The purpose of the specifications is to provide direction to teachers in preparing units. Unless the specifications are detailed, units may be developed that do not carry them out.
- The easiest approach to determining whether or not the specifications are sufficient detailed is to check their relattionship to the units developed by teachers in the program.

... Be applied as a curriculum-monitoring system in addition to being guidelines for unit development.

- The specifications represent what you feel should be included in the program. Thus, they serve as criteria for determining whether or not the curriculum has been implemented.
- Because the specifications are detailed and organized sequentially, they provide an excellent basis for revision.
- Specifications should be monitored constantly to determine the need for revision.

... Be applicable to alternative modes of instruction.

- Although the specifications are being prepared for unit teaching, they should not be unique to unit teaching. In other words, the teacher should be able to use the specifications as guidelines for other instructional techniques.
- This principle can be applied if the specifications are sufficiently detailed and systematically organized.

## The Specification Process

The various steps in preparing an instructional unit described in Chapter 4 represent a specification process at the unit level. The six steps represent guidelines for developing specifications to be followed in designing units of instruction. Given the identification of a unit topic, a teacher should be able to produce a quality unit if the steps are followed. In this chapter the emphasis is on developing specifications for a total curriculum or for that portion of the curriculum to be taught through units. The specifications become guidelines for a broad area of curriculum, not for a particular unit. Once the curriculum specifications are available, a teacher has a frame of reference for determining what skills and concepts should be included in unit instruction. In an ideal situation, curriculum specifications are available as a resource prior to preparing instructional units. In reality, few teachers participate in developing curriculum specifications. Consequently, units are designed without the guidance provided by a broader set of specifications. In terms of unit teaching, it is advantageous for teachers to be skilled in unit design prior to participating in the development of curriculum specifications. For this reason, the chapters related to unit development, which receives major attention, have appeared earlier.

Although it is highly desirable that curriculum specifications be developed in advance for all curriculum areas to be included in unit teaching, there is frequently not sufficient time for this activity. The specification process also can occur while the units are being implemented. In other words, as teachers prepare units, they are developing segments of the specifications for the broader curriculum area. The cumulative effect of teaching several units results in a form of specifications for the units taught. Under such circumstances, these specifications are not available for advanced planning. However, they can serve as the basis for specifications relative to subsequent groups of children. The problem is that the skills identified in the unit are organized around the unit topic. For maximum use as specifications, it will be necessary to sort out the skills and organize them according to the skill classifications rather than by unit topics.

## Skill Specification Process

One approach to developing curriculum specifications is to identify skills and concepts that are to be included in the curriculum, particularly those to be stressed in unit teaching, and develop what approximate scope and sequence charts. These can be designed using a behavioral-objective format or a skills-listing format. This approach works particularly well in the basic skill areas such as math and reading. However, in areas such as social studies, where content is less sequential, the process is effective, but it is more difficult to reach agreement on the skill placement and concepts sequence. Where units are used to teach or to supplement instruction in specific curriculum areas, the specification process may be restricted to that instructional area. In this circumstance, that specific instructional area would represent the skill classification shown as Step I in Figure 23.

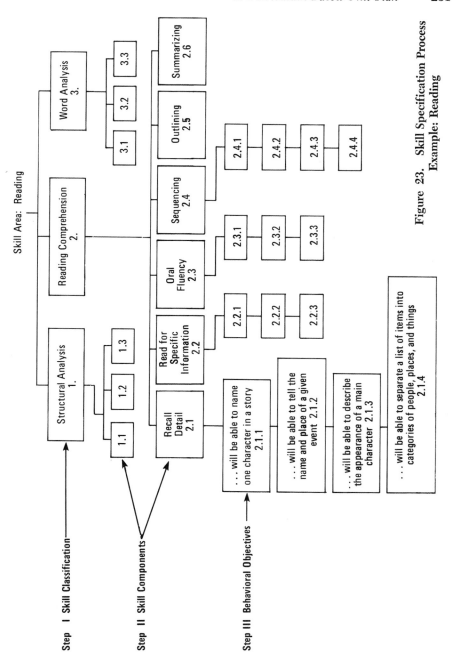

**Figure 23.  Skill Specification Process
Example: Reading**

However, special education teachers working with the mentally retarded assigned to special classes might elect to follow the core areas—arithmetic, social competence, communication skills, safety, health, and vocational skills—to represent the skill classification in Step I of Figure 23. Since the specifications constitute scope and sequence charts oriented around skill areas and not unit topics, the selection of skill classifications does not have a substantial influence on the units which will be developed later. The important concern is that the skill classifications be detailed and sequentially organized. At a minimum, they should include the skills and concepts to be covered through unit teaching. Remember that these specifications will be for a curriculum area and not a particular unit. In using the unit development steps described in Chapter 4, the teacher will refer to the specifications in selecting skills and concepts to be incorporated into units. As previously pointed out, the availability of curriculum specifications is a major resource to teachers during the unit development process. In programs where units will be used extensively, the development of curriculum specifications represents a staff development activity. The development of specifications will yield benefits in terms of teachers having a better concept of the content to be included in the curriculum and will also provide a quality control resource in terms of developing instructional units. Without curriculum specifications, teachers lack much-needed direction in terms of the decisions they must make regarding what to include in instructional units.

*Step I—Skill Classification Level*   This is the most general level in the specification process. There is no set group of skill classification headings. Keep in mind that this is the first of three steps in detailing specifications. If your skill classifications are too specific, for example, "addition facts," it is apparent that you will end up with a large number of skill classifications within the area of math alone. A more appropriate skill classification in math would be "basic operations" or "number concepts."

Examples of Skill Classification

| *Math* | *Reading* |
|---|---|
| Numbers and numerals | Structural analysis |
| Operations | Word analysis |
| Number concepts | Reading comprehension |
| Problem solving | Punctuation |
| Measurement | Sentence structure |

*Step II—Skill Components*   This step involves breaking the skill classification identified in Step I into more specific elements. Generally four to five skill elements will be sufficient. If you can only reduce the skill to two elements, then the skill classification is too specific. The skill component level provides a clear definition of what constitutes the skill classifications by breaking the classifications down into clearly described elements. Each component should represent a collection of skills or concepts. The cumulative effect of teaching the skills and concepts reflected in the skill components should comprise those skills and concepts implied by the skill classification.

## Examples of Skill Components

| *Math* | *Reading* |
|---|---|

1. Operations
   1.1 Properties
   1.2 Symbols
   1.3 Whole numbers
   1.4 Fractions
   1.5 Rational numbers

2. Measurement
   2.1 Weight
   2.2 Linear
   2.3 Volume

3. Numbers
   3.1 Cardinal numbers
   3.2 Ordinal numbers

1. Structural analysis
   1.1 Plural
   1.2 Singular
   1.3 Compound words
   1.4 Prefixes
   1.5 Suffixes

2. Oral language skills
   2.1. Comprehension of spoken word
   2.2 Picture interpretation
   2.3 Auditory memory
   2.4 Discrimination of sounds
   2.5 Rhyming
   2.6 Following directions

3. Reading comprehension
   3.1 Recall detail
   3.2 Reading for specific information
   3.3 Developing oral fluency
   3.4 Sequencing events
   3.5 Outlining
   3.6 Summarizing
   3.7 Classifying

*Step III—Behavioral Objectives*   This is the most specific level in the specification process. Although behaviorally stated objectives (see Chapter 6) are most effective since they can be directly applied in developing units, some teachers find an outline approach to be more commensurate with their planning style. The intent of this step is to develop a sequential list of behaviorally stated objectives for each skill component. This does not mean that every possible objective need be stated. However, the number of objectives should be sufficient to make clear the skills and concepts to be covered under the skill component. This can become an extremely time-consuming task if assigned to one person; a team approach should be used.

## Examples of Behavioral Objectives in Math

Note: The components are not in sequence; they were selected to illustrate the stating of objectives.

1. Number
   1.1 Ordinal numbers
       1.1.1 The student will be able to identify the first object in a set of five objects in response to directions from the teacher.
       1.1.2 The student will be able to designate the first and second desks in a row of five desks when asked to do so.
       1.1.3 . . . will be able to follow directions correctly when asked to take the last place in line.
       1.1.4 . . . will be able to point to the first, second, and third objects when shown a work sheet containing a series of objects.
       1.1.5 . . . will be able to identify the first, second, and last objects given a series of objects.

2. Operations
   2.1 Fractions
       2.1.1 The student will be able to distinguish a half of an object from a whole object.
       2.1.2 . . . will be able to divide a half circle into four quarter circles.
       2.1.3 . . . will be able to separate a set into four subsets each containing a set of 8, 2, or 16 objects.
       2.1.4 . . . will be able to identify that each subset is one-fourth of the whole set.
       2.1.5 . . . will be able to manipulate the parts of each geometric figure to form a whole when given several plane geometric figures divided into thirds.

## Examples of Behavioral Objectives in Reading

1. Reading Comprehension
   1.1 Recalling details
       1.1.1 The student will be

2. Oral Language Skills
   2.1 Rhyming
       2.1.1 The student will be

able to report the name of one character in a story.

1.1.2 . . . will be able to tell the time and place a given story took place.

1.1.3 . . . will be able to describe the appearance of the main character in a given story.

1.1.4 . . . will be able to tell what the character did, when asked to describe the main character.

1.2 Summary

1.2.1 The student will be able to separate a list of items into categories of people, places, or things.

1.2.2 . . . will be able to organize a set of statements into outline form, given direct statements from a story.

1.2.3 . . . will be able to summarize a given story in five sentences or less.

1.2.4 . . . will be able to synthesize the ideas, given two stories.

able to state two words that rhyme.

2.1.2 . . . will be able to identify the words that rhyme given two lines of poetry.

2.1.3 . . . will be able to state which words rhyme, given three stimulus words.

2.1.4 . . . will be able to tell if the words rhyme, given a group of ten words.

Once the specification process has been completed, teachers have a resource to refer to when teaching skills through units. The skills are organized and presented in three levels of specificity. The specifications also provide a basis for monitoring the curriculum in determining which skills have been taught, when, and in what sequence.

A numbering system is not essential, but it does help in organizing skills by levels. A numbering system has particular advantages when several teachers representing different grade levels are involved in developing or utilizing specifications. As has already been observed, a simple numbering system was used in the examples: 1. = classification level; 1.1 = component level; 1.1.1 = behavioral objective level.

## Application Specification Process

While skill specifications are helpful in preparing units, most units place considerable emphasis on information and social experiences. Specifications oriented toward skills do not provide teachers much direction in developing units relative to these dimensions of unit instruction. The same specification process employed for skills and concepts can be followed in detailing specifications that focus on applied content, that is, information, social skills, and the general application of skills. The only difference is that instead of task-analyzing skills, information or the application of skills is emphasized. There are some similarities in this process to the identifying of sub-units as described in Chapter 4 and in the strategies to preparing a year's plan of work in Chapter 9. The difference is in the organizational pattern in which the specifications are detailed. See Figure 24.

*Step I—Application Classification* This level is equivalent to a unit topic. However, the inclusion of a unit topic at this level does not necessarily mean that the same topic will be developed into a complete unit and taught as detailed in the subsequent specifications. The application components described in the following steps may be combined with application components from other units in the specifications to create the unit that is actually taught. For example, budgeting may be an application component under the classification of "money," and check writing may be an application component under the classification "home management." A teacher may select these two application components and organize them along with other components into a unit. This is the advantage of applying the specification process to the information dimension of curriculum in reference to units. It allows the teacher to examine unit topics that have been subjected to a modified form of task analysis.

### Example of Application Classification

Note:  Topics will vary depending on age level. They are grouped for illustration purposes by core area.

| *Arithmetic* | *Communication* |
|---|---|
| Measurement | Telephone |
| Time | Correspondence |
| Budget | Post Office |
| Money | Current events |

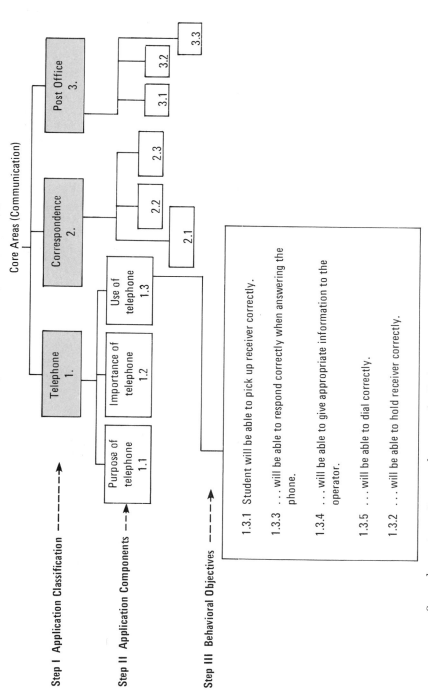

Core Areas (Communication)

**Step I Application Classification** ------->

Telephone 1.  |  Correspondence 2.  |  Post Office 3.

**Step II Application Components** ---->

Purpose of telephone 1.1  |  Importance of telephone 1.2  |  Use of telephone 1.3

2.1  |  2.2  |  2.3

3.1  |  3.2  |  3.3

**Step III Behavioral Objectives** ----->

1.3.1  Student will be able to pick up receiver correctly.

1.3.3  . . . will be able to respond correctly when answering the phone.

1.3.4  . . . will be able to give appropriate information to the operator.

1.3.5  . . . will be able to dial correctly.

1.3.2  . . . will be able to hold receiver correctly.

Space does not permit a complete example. Each core area could be developed into a set of specifications.

**Figure 24. Application Specification Process**

237

Taxes                           Newspaper
Salaries

*Social Competence*             *Health*
Home                            Food
Family                          Meal planning
Travel                          Health habits
Vacation                        Clothing
Community                       Weather

*Safety*                        *Applying for a job*
Traffic                         Planning your future
Automobile safety               Occupation
Safety on the job               Work responsibilities
Electricity                     Social Security

*Step II—Application Components*   The same process emphasized in the skill component step applies in breaking a unit down into components or sub-units. The goal is to identify major elements of the unit. There is one difference at this step between skills specifications and applications specifications—the number of application components versus skill components. While there may be only five or six skill components, a unit topic may break down into eight or ten application components.

### Examples of Application Components

Application Classification      1.  Citizenship (primary level)

Application Components              1.1  Respect for authority
                                    1.2  Respect for police
                                    1.3  Respect for fire department
                                    1.4  Respect of size
                                    1.5  Respect for property rights
                                    1.6  Care of public property

Application Classification      2.  Telephone (primary level)

Application Components              2.1  Purposes of telephone
                                    2.2  Importance of telephone
                                    2.3  Use of telephone
                                    2.4  Parts of telephone
                                    2.5  Telephone behavior
                                    2.6  Making personal calls
                                    2.7  Making emergency calls

| Application Classification | 1. Applying for a job |
|---|---|
| Application Components | 1.1 Source of job announcement |
| | 1.2 Contact people |
| | 1.3 Procedure to follow |
| | 1.4 Interview behavior |
| | 1.5 Completing form |
| | 1.6 Follow-up |

*Step III—Behavioral Objectives*   The only difference between the behaviorally stated objectives listed in the application specifications and in the skills specifications is in their sequence. In most skill areas, a sequence is built in to the skill acquisition; that is, skill A must be learned as prerequisite to learning skill B. However, in most units there is no set sequence for objectives related to information or social skills. In most cases it is a matter of building a logical sequence. This is not to suggest that the sequence is arbitrarily determined. But it should be noted that if different groups of teachers developed skill specifications, the final sequences of objectives could be very similar. For information or applied specifications, however, the sequence of objectives for a particular unit quite likely would not be similar. However, the sequences could easily be appropriate in both cases. When the emphasis is on information, the factors that tend to influence the sequence depend more on the teacher's preference for organization of content for purpose of instruction than on an inherent sequence from the perspective of the learner. This is highly defensible in the area of information and skill application.

The application specification process can be carried out for each core area. That is, a set unit topic can be selected in each core area. The process can be applied by age level. Topics should vary depending on the age or grade level of the target students.

## Examples of Behavioral Objectives

| Application Classification | 1. | Applying for a job |
|---|---|---|
| Application Component | 1.1 | Source of job announcements |
| Behavioral Objectives | 1.1.1 | Student will be able to select most appropriate newspaper for announcing current job openings. |
| | 1.1.2 | . . . will be able to locate want ad section. |
| | 1.1.3 | . . . will be able to locate em- |

ployment agency section in classified section of phone directory.

1.1.4 . . . will be able to contact known employers about possible job vacancies.

| Application Classification | 2. | Telephone |
|---|---|---|
| Application Component | 2.1 | Use of telephone |
| Behavioral Objectives | 2.1.1 | Student will be able to pick up receiver correctly. |

2.1.1 Student will be able to pick up receiver correctly.

2.1.2 . . . able to respond correctly when answering the phone.

2.1.3 . . . able to give appropriate information to the operator.

2.1.4 . . . will be able to dial correctly.

2.1.5. . . . will be able to hold receiver correctly.

## Summary

The specification processes presented in this chapter approximate the development of scope and sequence charts. Teachers devoting considerable portions of their instructional program to unit teaching are encouraged to develop specifications for at least that segment of the curriculum to be taught through units. Two approaches were presented. The first focuses on skills and the second on unit-related information or applied context. Once completed, the specifications represent a resource for teachers in planning units. They also serve as a reference for principals and/or supervisors concerned with monitoring curriculum. Because of the time required in developing specifications, a team approach is suggested. In situations where only one or two teachers are involved in unit teaching, a modified approach is described in Chapter 9 on developing a year's plan for work.

**Exercise 19.** (1) Using the guidelines presented in this chapter, prepare a Skills Specifications Chart in the areas of math and reading. Prepare the chart for a single grade level. If it is possible to complete the exercises in cooperation with other teachers, extend the scope to include three grade levels.

(2) Using the guidelines presented in this chapter, prepare an Application Specification Process. Select one core area. If it is possible to complete the exercises in cooperation with other teachers, extend the scope to include all six core areas for at least one age group. Specify the age or grade level. Also, if exceptional children are included in the target population, describe their primary characteristics.

# 9

# Developing a Year's Plan
# of Work for Unit Teaching

One of the most difficult tasks encountered by teachers in organizing their instructional programs is determining which aspects of the curriculum will be taught through units and which will be covered through other methods. While it may not be feasible to anticipate all of the experiences that will be provided through unit teaching during the year, a plan can be developed to represent the general content the teacher intends to cover using this method.

This chapter is designed for teachers who must do their own curriculum planning. If the teacher does not have access to resource people or if he or she teaches in a small attendance center with no other teachers teaching at the same level, it is still necessary to do long-term planning regarding unit instruction. At the same time, it is not reasonable to expect individual teachers to be as comprehensive in their planning as a team of teachers with access to many more resources. This chapter represents a modification of the more comprehensive approach discussed in Chapter 8. Whereas Chapter 8 applies to a team approach to curriculum planning, this chapter is oriented to planning by individual teachers.

A well-designed and effectively taught unit can independently make a significant contribution to a teacher's instructional program. However, few teachers limit their unit teaching to one or two units per year. Most will teach a number of units covering a variety of topics during the year. Collectively, these units may represent a major proportion of the learning experiences engaged in by the students. The topics selected for unit teaching as well as the pattern in which they are taught require careful consideration in developing a year's plan of unit work. An organizational plan facilitates communication with students, parents, fellow teachers, and administrators regarding the curriculum content to be covered through units. The process of preparing a plan requires the teacher to make decisions about both what is to be taught through units during the year and the general pattern in which units are to be taught.

Teachers working in a situation where no structured curriculum is available have fewer resources to rely on when making these decisions. On the other hand, teachers working from a well-designed curriculum must still make decisions about the sequence in which their units will be taught and the content to be covered through unit teaching. It is not practical to suggest the specific content that should be covered through units at any particular age level. The selection of unit topics and the determination of what will be included in selected units must take into consideration the established curriculum or what the teacher perceives as the curriculum. As pointed out in Chapter 3, academic skills as well as informational content can be effectively taught through units. Any restrictions on what can or cannot be taught through units are imposed by teachers themselves. This generally occurs when teachers feel other methods work better for them for certain curriculum facets. The most frequent restriction is to circumscribe unit teaching to encompass areas such as socialization, occupations, information on events, language development, and topics that allow for the application of basic skills taught through more formal approaches such as basal series.

Assuming that the teacher is skilled in writing units, the task of developing a year's plan of unit work becomes one of making decisions about which units will be taught during the year and how they can be organized to maximize their contribution to the instructional program. Teachers who elect to devote a major portion of their instructional program to unit teaching will find it helpful to make a basic plan for the units they anticipate teaching during the year. This does not mean that each unit will need to be written out in detail in advance. However, a blueprint for the year can be developed. Such a plan requires the teacher to make global decisions as to what will be taught through units. Having this type of information available, the teacher is then in a better position to proceed with developing individual units.

The year's plan of work should be viewed as a plan and not as a rigid schedule of units to be taught. They may be altered for a number of reasons. The teacher may decide to consolidate two or three areas of the plan into a single unit, or an event may occur that makes a topic planned for the future more relevant at the present.

A prerequisite to developing a year's plan of unit work is the determination of what is to be taught through teacher-made units and what is to be taught through subject-centered activities. If reading, language arts, and math, for example, are to be taught at specified times during the day and units employed for a short period of time to cover the related social content, then this will, of course, having a bearing on what is to be included in the year's plan of unit work. On the other hand, if major emphasis is to be given to unit teaching, the plan will need to reflect such emphasis.

As previously stressed, units can provide the framework in which the teaching of academic and social skills can be couched. The sequential aspects of these skills should not be altered because they are being taught through units. The informational aspects of units should also be presented sequentially. Teachers in ungraded situations who may have the same children for two or three years must avoid teaching the same concepts and information through repeated unit topics. Each teacher needs to have information on what other teachers are teaching relative to each unit topic. If all teachers in the system are working from a structured curriculum, no problems need arise. In the absence of such curriculum, the yearly plan of unit work proposed by each teacher can serve as a vehicle for communicating what each plans to teach through units during the school year. This makes the year's plan of unit work exceedingly important, particularly where heavy emphasis is being given to unit teaching and where no prescribed curriculum is available as a source of direction to the teacher in developing units.

Developing a year's plan of unit work according to the guidelines presented in this chapter is primarily an individual assignment to be carried out by each teacher. But the process should involve interaction with other teachers. When feasible, the plan should be developed prior to the beginning of the school year. Teachers can begin work on their plans as soon as they know the basic composition of their class. This will probably occur in the spring of the preceding year. The advantage of this timing is that the current year's instructional program is just ending and a firm base exists for making decisions on next year's program. Also, by knowing the units they plan to teach, teachers will be able to anticipate needed materials in time to order for the subsequent year.

While the year's plan of unit work should be geared to the teacher's particular class, the process of developing the plan can be broadened from an individual task to one that involves all special class teachers in a building or in the program. For example, teachers at the primary, intermediate, and junior high levels can collaborate in developing their plans. In many cases, the unit topics will be applicable to all or several of the levels represented in the program. The only differences will be in terms of what is taught under the umbrella of the topic. Having teachers from all levels involved facilitates communication and contributes to better decisions regarding what is to be taught about a particular topic at different age levels. This type of cooperative planning results in a generalized understanding, on the part of all teaching staff members, of the aspects of the curriculum being taught through units. It also encourages continuity and reduces redundancy. (See Chapter 8 for a discussion of team procedures.)

The manner in which a teacher organizes the daily program, as well as the number of units to be taught at one time, will also influence the plan of unit work. If teachers tend to teach two or three units in addition to other aspects of their program, they will likely base their plans on a larger number of unit topics than if they routinely teach only one unit at a time. In the latter situation, the unit topics are likely to be more general and fewer in number.

**Guidelines for Planning**

In developing a yearly plan for unit work, consideration should be given to formulating a plan that combines efficient curriculum coverage with explicitness. Frequently, the attention given to outlining curriculum content overshadows attempts to make the plan meaningful as a base for communicating the program. It is important that the plan be designed so that it reflects the scope of your unit work and does so in a manner easily understood by your principal, fellow teachers, and the parents of your pupils.

The following features are suggested as guidelines for developing a plan.

1. Select units that allow for teaching skills and concepts that represent major needs on the part of your pupils. This means that typically a teacher will find it necessary to teach more units from one core area than others. For example, if the class tends to be weak in arithmetic skills, a larger proportion of units that lend themselves to providing experience in arithmetic should be selected.

2. Select topics that are relevant and interesting to your group.

3. Select topics that are new to them. Avoid units which are repetitions of units studied in previous classes.

4. Select topics that convey meaning. In other words, in seeking more interesting topics, don't be lured into selecting humorous or vague titles merely for appeal. You can alter the title when teaching the unit. However, for purposes of your plan, stick with meaningful titles.

5. Select a plan format that is easily interpreted to your pupils. While pupil understanding is not the only criteria, it is helpful if students are aware of the general scope of the unit work for the year.

**Suggested Approaches**

A number of approaches can be employed in developing a year's work plan. Two approaches are offered as a point of departure for teachers in formulating their own approach. While teachers may wish to devise their own style, there is much to be said for uniformity within a school system. Agreement on a basic format will enhance communication on the instructional program. Teachers should be encouraged to explore several approaches prior to making a decision on the one to follow. The sample approaches are geared to two different teacher groups. The *continuum approach* is an example of how teachers who teach only one unit at a time might organize their yearly plan. The *core area approach* represents an example for those teachers who devote time to teaching two or three different units daily. The two illustrative approaches satisfy the five previously mentioned guidelines, yet they differ in order to meet the demands of the two teaching situations described.

Both approaches include the identification of unit topics plus a descriptive statement on the intended content. The content description can be in the form of a *brief outline* or in a series of *outcome statements* oriented toward pupil performance. If the teacher is skilled in writing objectives in behavioral terms, then outcome statements are recommended. However, if the teacher has not developed this proficiency, the formulation of outcomes for a large number of units would be a laborious task and would probably hinder the process of developing the unit plan. The outline form is recommended for most because it lends itself more readily to the planning task. It also is more compatible with the preliminary steps suggested for writing units in Chapter 4. The specification of outcomes in the form of behavioral objectives will take place when writing lessons. However, by the time teachers reach that stage, they will have completed the preliminary steps and be at a better state of readiness for writing objectives. At the plan level an outline form is sufficient.

The purpose of the content description is to indicate what is meant by the unit topic. In other words, a description is given of the general content to be covered and its level of complexity. For example, a teacher at the junior high level may describe the content of a unit on money as follows:

MONEY    (using outline format)

    a.  Services of the bank
    b.  Ways of saving
    c.  Establishing a checking account
    d.  Writing checks
    e.  Balancing a checkbook
    f.  Responsibilities that accompany a checking account

MONEY    (using outcome format)

    a.  Is able to explain the services of a bank.
    b.  Can describe the process of establishing a savings account, buying bonds, and purchasing savings certificates.
    c.  Is able to complete all steps necessary in establishing a checking account.
    d.  Can demonstrate the appropriate procedure for writing personal checks.
    e.  Is able to balance a checkbook accurately.
    f.  Is able to describe verbally the responsibilities of having a checking account.

At the primary level a teacher might also select the topic of money. The outline would likely reflect a concern for teaching coin and currency recognition plus an understanding of their values.

If teachers have a prescribed curriculum based on available curriculum outcomes, they would be well advised to follow the established pattern. If behavioral objectives are used in presenting curriculum content, then the task of developing the year's plan of work would be greatly facilitated by the use of outcome statements instead of the outline format. The task then becomes one of selecting outcomes from the prescribed curriculum and incorporating them under the appropriate unit topic. In this situation, the teacher is not called upon to construct the outcomes, as they are readily available from the prescribed curriculum. Few teachers will find themselves in this situation.

### Continuum Approach

The continuum approach assumes that a teacher will be basically teaching one unit at a time. The unit may last for several weeks, but no new unit will be introduced until the one presently being taught has been culminated. This type of plan is developed mainly by organizing selected units into a logical sequence and indicating the general content of each unit. The suggestions given below are steps to follow in developing a plan based on the continuum approach.

1. Identify the units you plan to teach during the year. Teachers should ask themselves the same kinds of questions at this point as suggested during Step 1 of the preliminary steps in writing units. (See Chapter 4.) In essence, if they develop a yearly work plan and are careful in unit selection, then most of the work for Step 1 in writing the unit has been completed. Basically, they must be guided in their selection by their knowledge of pupil needs and familiarity with units that have previously been taught. It is important to select unit topics that facilitate teaching the skills and concepts appropriate to the functioning level of the class. At the same time, the unit's informational aspects must also be meaningful to the pupils. Initially, the topics can be listed in random order. The emphasis at this stage is on the topic and content, not the order. The teacher is merely attempting to identify the units that should be taught during the year. During subsequent steps when the content is outlined, it may be that some unit topics can be merged. A logical order will also become apparent once the content has been outlined.

2. Briefly outline the content of each unit. The purpose is to include sufficient information to clarify the content coverage and to convey the intent of the unit to other teachers or administrators who may read the plan. In most cases, eight or nine major points will be adequate. It is advisable to have a colleague read two or three of your brief outlines to check on the meaning they convey. To be sure that the outline reliably conveys your intent, you may find that a more extensive outline is required. It is better

to be inclusive rather than to end up with a plan comprised of unit outlines that are too vague. The more complete the outlines are, the easier will be the task of developing them into teachable units later. An attempt should be made to organize the points in the outline sequentially.

3. Once the brief outlines have been completed, the major emphasis in terms of core areas should be apparent. In other words, a review of the outline should indicate whether the unit is strong in social competencies, communication skills, and so forth.

4. Organize the unit topics into a logical order. In reviewing the brief outlines, you can determine which units are most closely related. The intent is to organize the units so that the content of one unit serves as an introduction to the succeeding one. In addition to the relationship between unit topics, consideration must also be given to timing. Some unit topics are better taught in relation to certain seasons or events that regularly occur at specific times during the year. For example, a unit on the farm might be best taught in the spring or fall, while a unit on transportation could be taught at any time.

5. After the unit outlines have been developed and organized into sequence, the next step is to describe an activity designed to facilitate transition between units. The activity can be briefly described in a few sentences. You may not use the particular activity to make the transition when actually teaching the unit. However, the procedures enhance continuity.

*Examples of Continuum Approach*

The following are two sample plans for a year of unit work developed in accordance with the continuum approach. The *first* example utilizes an outline method of describing content. The *second* example is based on the outcome approach to presenting the content.

EXAMPLE 1:   CONTINUUM APPROACH USING AN OUTLINE FORMAT

(Developed for Mildly Mentally Retarded Children C.A. 6-10)

School Orientation (Social Competencies)*

1. The physical layout of the school.
2. Materials and their location in the classroom.
3. Rules in the school and the classroom.
4. Proper behavior in the classroom.

*Indicates the core area in which this unit was perceived by the teacher as being strongest.

5. Respect for other students' property.
6. Listening and speaking habits in the classroom.

## Courtesy (Social Competencies)

1. Respect for teacher and other elders.
2. Proper table manners.
3. Working and playing with others.
4. Use of telephone.
5. Care for toys and other property.
6. Responses to reprimands.
7. Behavior in public places.

## Jobs (Vocational Skills)

1. Responsibility for selected jobs in the classroom.
2. Assuming a fair share of work in the classroom.
3. Courtesy in regard to jobs.
4. Completing tasks according to schedule.
5. Importance of safety rules when doing job.
6. Neighborhood jobs the student can do.
7. Jobs the student can do in the home.

## Home and Family (Social Competencies)

1. Roles of different members of the family.
2. Student's role in helping with the housecleaning.
3. Jobs that can be delegated to the student which must be completed regularly, such as dishes, taking care of pets, and so forth.
4. Jobs the child can do in the yard.
5. Importance of assuming responsibility for a share of the work.
6. Planning family activities.
7. Rooms in the home and their uses.
8. Address and phone number.
9. Direction from home to school.
10. Safety at home.

## Citizenship (Social Competencies)

1. The meaning of citizenship in the home, school, community, state, and nation.
2. Need for good citizenship.
3. Respect for others and their property.
4. Respect for flag and other symbols of the nation.

5. Necessity for obeying rules, signs, and signals.
6. Respect for people in authority.

## Community Helpers (Vocational Skills)

1. Community helpers and their roles.
2. Role of police officers.
3. Role of firefighters.
4. The medical professions and their services to the community.
5. The librarian and the services the library provides.
6. Services of postal carriers.
7. Recognition of the different types of public transportation.
8. Kinds of help we can obtain from community helpers.

## Post Office (Communication Skills)

1. Purpose of the post office.
2. Knowing the location of the post office.
3. How mail is delivered.
4. Writing personal letters to friends.
5. Appropriate procedure for addressing envelopes.
6. Preparing packages for mailing.
7. Knowing where to buy stamps.

## Money (Arithmetic Concepts)

1. Recognition of coins and bills up to $10.00.
2. The value of coins to $1.00.
3. Ways of earning money.
4. Basic concept of saving.
5. Uses of money.

## Food (Health)

1. Recognition of selected fruits and vegetables.
2. Knowledge of where foods are grown.
3. Function of grocery store.
4. Basic classification of foods.
5. Reasons for needing well-balanced meals.
6. Foods needed daily for a good diet.
7. Ways to cook food.
8. Care for different kinds of food, such as refrigeration.
9. Importance of certain health habits in regard to food, such as brushing teeth after meals, washing hands before eating, and so on.

Health Habits (Health)

1. Importance of getting enough rest.
2. Necessity of seeing a dentist and doctor regularly.
3. Appropriate clothing for different types of weather.
4. Precautions needed to prevent the spread of communicable diseases.
5. Importance of regular exercise.
6. Importance of cleanliness.

Time (Arithmetic Concepts)

1. Purpose of a clock.
2. Telling time.
3. Reading a schedule.
4. Importance of promptness.
5. Days of the week.
6. Basic concept of budgeting time.
7. Reading a calendar.
8. Division of year into seasons.

Seasons (Health)

1. The four seasons of the year and the type of weather associated with each.
2. Safety rules to follow during each of the seasons.
3. Things to do at different times of the year.
4. Health rules to combat colds.
5. Proper clothing for each season.

Clothing (Health)

1. Importance of having clothing that fits, especially shoes.
2. Proper clothing to wear for certain occasions.
3. Selection of clothing that is appropriate for the season.
4. Necessity of changing clothes when they are wet.
5. Importance of changing underclothes regularly.
6. Caring for clothing.
7. Keeping clothes clean.
8. How clothes are made.
9. Responsibility for taking care of one's own clothing.

First Aid (Safety)

1. Necessity for treatment by doctor in severe injuries.
2. People to contact in case of injury.
3. Use of first-aid kit.

4. Treatment for minor injuries.
5. Necessity of cleanliness in the treatment of all injuries.
6. The danger of poisons, sharp objects, and fire.

Safety (Safety)

1. Safe places to play.
2. Necessity of safety habits to prevent accidents.
3. Safety rules necessary at school.
4. Rules of safety needed in the home.
5. Meaning of basic traffic and warning signals.
6. Safety rules needed on the playground.
7. Safety rules needed in traveling.

Transportation (Arithmetic Concepts)

1. Meaning of transportation.
2. Different types of transportation.
3. The concept of distance.
4. Importance of street numbers and how to use them.
5. Safety rules while using public transportation.
6. Safety rules for walking.
7. Purchasing tickets.
8. Behavior while using public transportation.

Telephone (Communication Skills)

1. Identification of different types of telephones.
2. Uses of the telephone.
3. Using the telephone directory.
4. Know good telephone manners.
5. The telephone for emergency calls.
6. Telephone for pleasure.
7. Good habits in using the telephone.

Playtime (Social Competencies)

1. Playing with other children.
2. Sharing and cooperating.
3. Activities appropriate to the particular setting.
4. Games and activities appropriate for different kinds of weather.
5. Good sportsmanship.
6. Following directions.
7. Safety at play.
8. Learning proper care of toys and other property.

Animals (Safety)

1. Animals commonly seen in the community.
2. Animals found on farms or found in the zoos.
3. Types of animals suitable for pets.
4. Handling of animals.
5. Care of animals.
6. Rules of safety applicable to handling animals.
7. Finding homes for lost animals.

Newspaper (Communication Skills)

1. The contents of the newspaper.
2. The newspaper as a source of information.
3. Locating different things in the newspaper.
4. Pictures contained and their messages in the newspaper.
5. The newspaper as a source of entertainment.
6. Importance of reading the newspaper.

## EXAMPLE 2: CONTINUUM APPROACH USING AN OUTCOME FORMAT
(Developed for Mildly Mentally Retarded Children    C.A. 6-10)

Family

1. Is able to describe the roles of family members.
2. Knows the names of the family members and is able to write them.
3. Is able to identify jobs in the home that are within his or her capabilities.
4. Understands the concept of "relative" and is able to name grandparents, uncles, and aunts.

School

1. Is able to recognize the school name.
2. Recognizes the teacher, principal, and school secretary and calls them by name.
3. Can locate classroom, restroom, principal's office, and nurse's office.
4. Adheres to school rules.
5. Participates in the fire drill by following directions from teacher.
6. Carries out assigned work tasks in the classroom.
7. Is able to identify classmates by name.

Money

1. Recognizes coins and currency by name and is able to indicate their value.
2. Can demonstrate making change up to combinations totaling five dollars.

3. Is able to compute accurately totals for expenditures up to ten dollars.
4. Can demonstrate an understanding of saving through role-playing exercises.
5. Can explain the services of a bank.
6. Is able to describe the major uses of money in supporting a family.
7. Is able to describe what is meant by earning money.

## Time

1. Can tell time accurately to a quarter of an hour.
2. Adheres to the school schedule by being on time.
3. Can identify different kinds of timepieces, such as watches and clocks.
4. Is able to write the days of the week in sequence.
5. Is able to write the months of the year in sequence.
6. Can demonstrate the appropriate method for setting a clock and watch.
7. Is able to estimate with reasonable accuracy the time required to perform a specific task.

## Seasons

1. Is able to list the seasons of winter, spring, summer, and fall.
2. Can describe the weather typical of each season.
3. Is able to explain the major activities that occur during each season, for example, planting, hunting, leisure activities, and so forth.
4. Is able to list the months in each season.
5. Recognizes the natural changes that occur in his surroundings during each season.
6. Is able to list the major holidays that occur during each season.
7. Is able to explain the organization and use of the calendar.
8. Can locate the date in the local newspaper.

## Grooming and Health Care

1. Practice good health practices related to washing hands before meals, working with food, and so forth.
2. Knows the services of the nurse, doctor, and dentist, and is able to describe what they do.
3. Changes clothing when soiled.
4. Is able to demonstrate appropriate procedures for brushing teeth.
5. Follows good health care practices when ill, such as having a cold.
6. Attempts to take care of clothing by using coatracks.
7. Is able to make simple repairs in clothing.
8. When given a choice of foods, will select food that is healthful.

Community

1. Knows name of community and state.
2. Is able to write name and address.
3. Can locate on a map the major community center such as a school, post office, parks, hospital, and so forth.
4. Obeys traffic signals.
5. Is able to locate designated places in the downtown area independently.
6. Can accurately give directions to a classmate on how to get to designated places.
7. Can describe the roles of community helpers such as police, firefighters, mail carriers, and so forth.
8. Is able to explain simple concepts related to community government.
9. Displays appropriate behavior while visiting places in the community.
10. Is able to list the recreational opportunities in the community.

Telephone

1. Is able to recognize different styles of telephones.
2. Can demonstrate correct use of dial phone.
3. Can recite home phone number.
4. Can demonstrate use of the telephone.
5. Can explain the use of the yellow pages.
6. Is able to obtain a new phone number not listed in the phone book from the operator.
7. Demonstrate good manners when using the telephone.
8. Is able to locate emergency numbers in the phone book.
9. Is able to demonstrate use of coin-operated telephones.
10. Can explain why use of the telephone costs money.

Transportation

1. Able to identify the most frequently used modes of transportation in the community.
2. Can demonstrate appropriate behavior when using public transportation.
3. Is able to explain the costs and can demonstrate payment procedures.
4. Can identify bus stops.
5. Is able to demonstrate good safety practices when using public systems of transportation.
6. Can explain the importance of transportation to the community and to the family.

Measurement

1. Is able to identify measuring instruments, such as scales, yardstick, ruler, tape measure, container, and so forth.

2. Can demonstrate accurate use of measuring instruments typically used at school and in the home.
3. Can calculate differences in measurements.
4. Knows own clothing sizes.
5. Can locate sizes on clothing.
6. Able to estimate basic length and quantity.
7. Can demonstrate computation of cost per measure, for example, cost per yard and per pound.

## Foods

1. Is able to recognize common foods and classify them as meats, fruits, vegetables, bread, and so forth.
2. Is able to describe how foods are derived and from what source.
3. Can demonstrate simple preparation of foods for eating, for example, washing fresh fruits, peeling vegetables, and so forth.
4. Can plan a basic menu given a group of foods from which to select.
5. Is able to differentiate foods with high nutrient value from foods with little value.
6. Can list foods normally found together in a supermarket.
7. Is able to explain why some foods must be refrigerated.

## The Newspaper

1. Knows the names of local papers.
2. Can identify the main section of the newspaper.
3. Is able to locate features such as the date and the weather.
4. Reads the paper when it is available.
5. Is able to locate information in the want ads section.
6. Can calculate the cost per week, month, and year.

## Weather

1. Is able to identify cues that suggest changes in weather.
2. Is able to read a thermometer accurately.
3. Can describe good safety practices under different weather conditions.
4. Dresses appropriately for weather conditions.
5. Is able to relate the need for moisture and sunlight to the growth of plants.
6. Is able to identify on a map the area of the country which has a warmer or colder climate than where student lives.

## Leisure Time

1. Plays fairly with classmates.
2. Can locate recreational areas in the community.

3. Knows leisure-type games that can be played indoors.
4. Practices sharing of toys with classmates.
5. Is able to give directions on how to play simple games.
6. Plays as a team member in sports.
7. Returns equipment and games to appropriate places when through using them.

### Supermarket

1. Can explain the purpose of the market.
2. Is able to locate the different departments in a supermarket.
3. Can explain the role of the checker.
4. Is able to select assigned items from the shelves.
5. Given the sale price and the regular price is able to calculate the difference.
6. Is able to describe how basic foods are obtained by supermarkets.
7. Can identify foods prepared locally.

## Core Area Approach

This approach involves organizing the year's plan of work according to the six core areas. Teachers planning to work on two or three units each day will find this approach most helpful. The process of selecting and describing the units to be included in your plan is similar to that suggested for the continuum approach. However, instead of sequencing the units in a logical order from the first to the last unit you anticipate teaching, categorize the unit topics according to core areas, that is, communication skills, arithmetic, social competencies, health, safety, and vocational skills. The order in which they are taught is determined by the current needs of the pupils and the appropriateness of the unit topic at the time another unit has been culminated. In the continuum approach previously discussed, the teacher established the order as a part of the plan. This is not feasible in this type of plan because it is difficult for a teacher to anticipate the amount of time required to teach each unit. The fact that more than one unit is being taught daily further complicates the task of trying to plan the units sequentially through the core area approach.

Consequently, some units will be taught over a four-week period of time, while others will require five or six weeks to complete. It is possible to accomplish sequence on a tract basis. For example, a teacher who plans to teach three units at different times during the day could develop a plan that groups the units into three general categories. A category might emphasize one or more core areas; the units within each category could be sequenced in a logical order. The teacher would then follow a pattern of introducing subsequent new units from a category, once a unit from that particular category had been completed. Another approach, which is probably more realistic, is to select the units and organize them by core areas. Once the units were grouped by core areas, the teacher would select those to be taught at a particular time by the relevance of the topic and its relationship to the unit being completed.

There is a certain amount of arbitrariness in the organization of units within this plan. Thus, teachers are reminded that the important criteria for teaching a unit are the needs of the student. The plan should not be so rigid that it interferes with this requirement.

The first two steps suggested in the directions for the continuum approach are applicable to the core area approach. To enhance the application of those steps unique to the core area approach, the first two steps are repeated.

1. Identify the units you plan to teach during the year. Teachers should ask themselves the same kinds of questions at this point as suggested during Step 1 of the preliminary steps in writing units. (See Chapter 4.) In essence, if they develop a yearly work plan and are careful in the unit selection, then most of the work for Step 1 in writing the unit has been completed. Basically, they must be guided in their selection by their knowledge of pupil needs and familiarity with units that have previously been taught. It is important to select unit topics that facilitate teaching the skills and concepts appropriate to the functioning level of the class. At the same time, the informational aspects of the unit must also be meaningful to the pupils. Initially, the topics can be listed in random order. The emphasis at this stage is on the topic and content, not the order. Teachers are merely attempting to identify the units that should be taught during the year. During subsequent steps when the content is outlined, it may be that some unit topics can be merged. A logical order will also become apparent once the content has been outlined.

2. Briefly outline the content of each unit. The purpose is to include sufficient information to clarify the content coverage and to convey the intent of the unit to other teachers or administrators who may read the plan. In most cases, eight or nine major points will be adequate. It is advisable to have a colleague read two or three of your brief outlines to check on the meaning they convey. To be sure that the outline reliably conveys your intent, you may find that a more inclusive outline is required. It is better to be inclusive rather than to end up with a plan comprised of unit outlines that are too vague. The more complete the outlines are, the easier will be the task of developing them into teachable units later. An attempt should be made to organize the points in the outline sequentially. The organization may change when you develop the unit but to the degree pos-

sible the outline of the content should reflect the scope and general manner in which you anticipate organizing the unit.

3. Having briefly described the unit content, you should organize the topics according to core areas. A review of the unit descriptions should readily reveal the emphasis of the unit. It is likely that more units will be listed under some core areas than others. The pattern of units of core areas should be representative of the needs of the pupils in the class. For example, if your pupil's major weaknesses are in the core area of communication skills, more units should be listed in this core area.

4. The final step is placing the unit topics within each core area in a logical order. Transitional activities are of less value in this approach since teachers will not likely teach the units in a prescribed sequence.

The following example of a year's plan of work utilizes an outline format. Since the outline format would differ only in the manner in which the content is presented, an example using outcome statements is not included. The reader is referred to the example for the continuum approach.

### EXAMPLE: CORE AREA APPROACH USING AN OUTLINE FORMAT

(Developed for Mildly Mentally Retarded Children   C.A.   10-14)

Core Area: Arithmetic

*Money*

1. Ways to earn money.
2. The use of money.
3. Recognition of coins and bills.
4. Value of coins and bills.
5. Making change for a dollar.
6. Correct use of cent and dollar sign.
7. Saving.

*Measurement*

1. Basic understanding of inch, foot, and yard.
2. Correct use of the ruler and yardstick.
3. Basic understanding of pint, quart, and gallon.
4. Basic understanding of one-half and full pound.
5. Correct use of the scale.
6. Basic understanding of dozen and one-half dozen.
7. Practical application of measuring tools.

*Time*

1. Days of the week.
2. Months of the year.
3. Seasonal changes.
4. Introduction of the calendar.
5. Simple daily record-keeping.
6. Concept of half and quarter.
7. Telling time.
8. Setting clock to correct time.

## Core Area: Communication Skills

*Post Office*

1. Purpose of the post office.
2. Location of the post office in the community.
3. Writing simple letters (invitations).
4. Addressing of envelopes.
5. Mailing of letters.
6. Sending of packages.
7. Buying of stamps.
8. Role of the postal carrier.

*Telephone*

1. Importance of the telephone.
2. Correct use of the telephone.
3. Identification of the parts and their use.
4. Telephone manners.
5. Making personal calls.
6. Making emergency calls.

*Current Events*

1. Daily use of the newspaper, date, and weather report.
2. Special news items of interest to the class.
3. News items pertaining to holidays.
4. Writing of a class newspaper.

## Core Area: Social Competencies

*Courtesy*

1. Introductions.

2. Saying thank you, please, excuse me, and so forth.
3. Respect for property rights.
4. Table manners.
5. Desirable behavior in public places.
6. Desirable behavior when using transportation facilities.

### Home and the Family

1. Members of the family.
2. Responsibility of each member.
3. Sharing.
4. Taking turns.
5. Rooms and their uses.
6. Shelter.
7. Care of the home.
8. Safety and the home.

### Community

1. Components of a community.
2. Acceptable social behavior when using community facilities.
3. Responsibility to the community.
4. Community helpers.

### Citizenship

1. Respect for authority.
2. Respect for the police department.
3. Respect for the fire department.
4. Recognition of certain signs and signals.
5. Respect of property rights.
6. Care of public property.

### Leisure Time

1. Good sportsmanship.
2. Inside games to play individually and in groups.
3. Group games to play outside.
4. Independent games to play outside.
5. Care of equipment.
6. Sharing.

Core Area: Health

*Food*

1. Identification of fruits and vegetables.
2. Association of name and food.
3. Understanding basic seven foods.
4. Understanding the foods important to specific meals.
5. Source of food.
6. Supermarket.
7. Health habits and food.
8. Manners.

*Health Habits*

1. Adequate amount of rest.
2. Dental care.
3. Cleanliness.
4. Good grooming.
5. Care of clothing.

*Clothing*

1. Type of clothing to wear according to the weather.
2. Kinds of clothes for summer, winter, and spring.
3. Change underclothing regularly.
4. Wear proper bed clothing.
5. Prevention of colds.
6. Play clothes, dress clothes, and work clothes.

*Water*

1. Importance of water.
2. Source of water.
3. Importance of washing hands.
4. Danger of drinking water from ponds, and so forth.
5. Health habits pertaining to public drinking fountains.

*Weather*

1. Awareness of seasonal changes.
2. The various kinds of weather occurring during each season.
3. The need for rain, snow, wind, sunshine, and so forth.
4. Awareness of safety hazards accompanying the different kinds of weather.

5. Health habits and weather.
6. Wear proper clothing according to the weather.
7. Weather report.
8. Role of the weather forecaster.
9. Months of the year—according to seasons.
10. Days of the week.

Core Area: Safety

*Safety and School*

1. Classroom safety.
2. Lunchroom safety practices.
3. Playground safety.
4. Use of equipment.
5. Care of equipment.

*Safety at Home*

1. Electrical hazards.
2. Danger of gas.
3. Care of toys.
4. Stairs and safety.
5. Rugs and slippery floors.
6. Poisons.
7. Refrigerators.
8. Fire safety at home.

*Bicycle Safety*

1. Traffic rules regarding bicycles.
2. Parking bicycles at school.
3. Care of bicycles.
4. Safe riding habits.

*Traffic Safety*

1. Importance of traffic laws.
2. Understanding traffic signs, lights, and signals.
3. Correct use of crosswalks.
4. Looking both ways before crossing the street.
5. Playing in the street.
6. Toys in the street.
7. Obeying the police officer.

Core Area: Vocational Skills

*Jobs at Home*

1. Kinds of jobs which can be done at home.
2. Completing a job.
3. Following directions.
4. Responsibility for doing the same job daily.

*Earning Money*

1. Allowances and how they are earned.
2. Types of jobs for which youth can earn money.
3. Responsibility for earning pay.
4. Saving principles.

## Summary

The development of a year's plan of work requires the teacher to anticipate pupils' needs and to structure a blueprint for unit teaching. While the plan is not rigid, it does serve as a frame of reference in developing the instructional program. It is particularly helpful in communicating with parents, pupils, principals, and fellow teachers regarding the content to be covered. The approach presented in this chapter is oriented toward the teacher who must do curriculum planning without the benefit of resource people. Although the approach is very general compared to the strategies discussed in Chapter 8, the individual teacher using this approach will be able to construct an organizational plan for unit teaching.

**Exercise 20.**   Continuum Approach. Select twenty unit topics applicable to the class you are teaching or to the age level you plan to teach and develop a Year's Plan of Work using the continuum approach. Describe your units in outline form.

**Exercise 21.**   Core Area Approach. Using the units included in Exercise 20, develop a Year's Plan of Work using the core area approach. Describe your units using outcome statements.

# 10

## Seatwork and Unit Teaching

In spite of the wide array of instructional materials available on the commercial market, most teachers find it necessary to develop many of their own supplemental materials. The majority of teacher-made materials are used by students in independent study situations or in small group activities approximating peer teaching. The development of seatwork experiences is not an easy task. It is particularly difficult for those teachers working with mentally retarded children. The major problem encountered in designing seatwork for the mentally retarded relates to their inability to work independently. This characteristic of the retarded learner is generally accompanied by the inability to sustain attention for very long periods of time and difficulty in following directions. As noted by teachers of regular classes, these behaviors are characteristic of many children whose learning problems are unrelated to mental retardation. These characteristics, however, do place the teacher in the position of having to invest additional effort in designing seatwork experiences with attention-holding features and in the structuring of verbal and written directions within the comprehension level of such pupils.

Teachers also face a situation similar to the development of criterion-referenced evaluation techniques. They have to have a specific objective in mind for the seatwork activity, be sensitive to the child's ability level, and structure the activity so that the child understands what is expected. Provisions must also be structured for making feedback on performance available to the pupil. When these conditions are considered along with the learning characteristics of the mentally retarded and the amount of time devoted to seatwork activities, the necessity of teacher planning becomes apparent. Too often teachers do not have sufficient time for planning seatwork activities or view such activities as noninstructional. Teachers who require pupils to engage in poorly designed seatwork activities run the risk of discouraging children from participating in independent activities or of creating a situation in which the experiences are primarily "busy work," not contributing to the instructional program. These circumstances frequently result in management problems or poor attitudes toward learning on the part of pupils.

For the purposes of unit teaching, seatwork will be defined as *activities in which students can engage independently or in small groups with a minimum of teacher supervision*. They may take the form of committee assignment on projects, individualized work sheets, or various media such as film strips, Language Masters, audio tapes, single loop films, or peer-conducted exercises. While the term "independent activities" is probably more appropriate than "seatwork," the latter term is used to differentiate classroom activities from field trips or other activities engaged in by students informally or formally outside the classroom.

Viewed within this context, seatwork activities can serve several purposes. They can be used as a vehicle for extending the teaching of skills and concepts initiated through unit lessons. Used in this manner, the seatwork activities can be incorporated within the lesson presentation or employed at the conclusion of the lesson. They can be designed as behavior reinforcers. If the tasks are geared to the ability level of the pupil and relevant to the content of the unit currently being worked on, the experience can provide the learner with meaningful feedback. This in turn becomes a means of reinforcement. They can also be organized to make use of novelty features that hold attention but do not interfere with the learning experiences built into the activity. In this case, the form of the activity serves as a diversion for the learner even though the content of what is to be learned through the activity is compatible with what is being taught through units or other aspects of the curriculum.

The application of previously learned skills and concepts is an important use of seatwork. Used in this fashion, the activities are not intended to teach a skill or concept, but rather are utilized as a means of providing practice in applying skills or concepts in which the learner has some competency but is not as proficient in the particular skill as the teacher would like. This is differentiated from practice for the sake of practice. There may be occasions when the teacher will ask pupils to engage in drill exercises. When making such a decision, teachers should give serious consideration to the effect that this request might have on the motivation of the pupils. If they can demonstrate to the pupils the necessity for completing the task or if it can be presented to them within a context that holds their attention, then it can probably be carried out without negative effects.

An important but indirect contribution of well-designed seatwork is in the area of behavior management. While some teachers use seatwork activities as a means of keeping students busy and diverting their attention from disruptive activities, seatwork can be used in a positive manner in behavior management. If the seatwork activity is designed as a learning experience geared to the ability level of the pupils, and perceived by them as relevant, then the chances are increased that they will pursue the activity with a minimum of teacher supervision. This allows the teacher time to give individual attention to other pupils and/or to prepare for a subsequent learning experience.

## Tips on Planning Seatwork Activities

1. Identify the particular skill or concept you are attempting to reinforce or teach through the activity. If the activity relates to a specific unit or lesson, be sure the relationship of the activity to the lesson is obvious to the student.
2. Analyze the task from the perspective of determining what type of activity would be most appropriate for the task. Avoid extensive reliance on paper-and-pencil activities that take the form of drill exercises. Vary the type of activities used during the day as well as within particular units.
3. Estimate the amount of time required for your pupils to complete the activity. You may find it necessary to vary the nature of the activity or its scope in order to accommodate the different ability levels represented in your class.
4. In formulating the directions to be given students, use vocabulary words you know they understand. In some cases, verbal directions will be sufficient; however, when feasible, both verbal and written directions should be provided. Use questions or illustrations to check their understanding of directions.
5. If the activity is a group project, be sure that all participants understand their roles.
6. Review the activity to make certain that all needed materials and equipment are available. If media equipment is to be used, check the students' ability to operate them.
7. Although seatwork is intended as an independent activity, remain accessible so that you can provide help when needed.
8. Decide in advance how and when you will provide feedback to the students. If they are to receive a grade, inform them when the assignment is made.

## Use of Commercially Prepared Work Sheets

A number of commercial firms are marketing prepared work sheets in the form of ditto masters. For the most part, these are developed around unit themes such as weather, measurement, and time, or they are designed as review exercises for the development of basic skills. While teachers should not rely on them entirely, there are advantages in using commercially prepared work sheets. For example:

1. They can be purchased in advance and thus are accessible when needed.
2. They are generally legible and reflect a professional appearance.
3. They are relatively inexpensive considering the time required on the part of teachers to develop their own work sheets.
4. They generally employ varied styles of type and use better illustrations than most teachers can develop within the time available to design seatwork activities.

While there are times when the influence of these advantages will cause teachers to employ commercially prepared work sheets, there are certain cautions to be considered. Teachers must be selective in the work sheets they choose to use. Not much is gained if the work sheet does not offer the experiences they want to provide the students. Many teachers find it helpful, when developing a unit, to review available commercially prepared work sheets on the unit topic and decide in advance which ones would probably be appropriate in supplementing specific lessons to be included in the unit. They are then in a position to anticipate the number and kinds of seatwork activities they must develop through their own efforts.

In using commercially prepared work sheets, you may find that some are too comprehensive and/or attempt to include too many different concepts within the same activity. Teachers should be alert for these problems and either modify the work sheet or develop their own. It is difficult to anticipate the effectiveness of a particular work sheet with individual students. Consequently, if a work sheet containing several concepts is to be used, teachers may find it necessary to conduct the activity as a group exercise rather than as an independent activity.

If teachers find a set of commercially prepared work sheets for a unit they will be teaching, in addition to reviewing the individual work sheets in terms of the number of concepts presented and the organization of the exercises, they should also check the series to see whether work sheets on the same concept are presented at different levels of difficulty. They may find, for example, that work sheets are available regarding the use of the ruler for measuring to an accuracy of one inch; however, no exercises are available for more precise uses of the ruler. In this case, they might choose to use the one that is available and develop additional work sheets on the same concept but at a more difficult level. When reviewing a series of prepared work sheets on a topic, teachers should not assume that the sequence in which the work sheets are ordered is necessarily sequential in terms of prerequisite skills required to perform the tasks. They will need to make their own decisions regarding the sequence in which they will use the work sheets if they adopt the entire series.

Commercially prepared work sheets can be effectively employed in unit teaching if the teacher is selective and does not depend upon them as the only source. Because of the convenience of commercially prepared work sheets, teachers must guard against their overuse in the classroom. Many teachers have tended to use such work sheets to the extent that they become the dominant type of independent activities engaged in by their students.

## Evaluation of Seatwork Activities

Just as it is important for the teacher to know whether or not the child has learned a particular concept, it is important to know if the child has failed or succeeded at an assigned seatwork activity. The child's need for feedback also is as important in seatwork activities as it is in testing situations. Evaluation of seatwork activities extends beyond the assessment of pupil performance on a particular task. If teachers are to make maximum use of seatwork activities in structuring learning experiences for children, it is important for them to obtain information about the effectiveness of particular activities as well as information regarding their own efficiency in designing seatwork experiences.

### *Evaluating Pupil Performance*

1. Be sure pupils understand how their participation will be evaluated; in other words, what you are expecting from them in the way of performance. In the case of work sheets, the type of response desired is relatively obvious. However, in terms of group activities your objectives may be less obvious. Give them some indication of how their participation will be evaluated.
2. Monitor the participation of pupils in the activity while it is in process. Some students may not understand the directions and consequently will be unable to pursue the task unless additional directions are offered.
3. If work sheets are being used, correct the papers and provide feedback as soon as possible. When grading papers, look for recurring errors that reflect a skill deficiency.
4. If the child's paper is below your expectations, check to make sure he or she understood.
5. Frequently, teachers find that there is insufficient time available to grade papers and provide immediate feedback to students. When this occurs, there are alternatives which can be employed by teachers to facilitate the correcting of papers and the subsequent provision of feedback to students relative to their performance. For example:
   a. In group activities, individual pupils can be given the correct responses and serve as a group leader or teacher substitute.

b. Work sheets can be designed to include the key so that students can grade their own papers.

c. Papers can be exchanged with peers for purposes of grading.

d. Correct responses can be recorded on the chalkboard or on experience charts and grading done as a group exercise.

When keys are provided or when peers grade each other's papers, checks should be made at the time of grading to identify systematic errors. To avoid embarrassment resulting from grades becoming public knowledge, spend time early in the year working on attitudes. Try to establish the idea that when correcting someone else's paper, we are helping them and that the paper is theirs. Thus, the grade is also their private property. Granted, this attitude may not be easy to achieve. There will be situations in which it will be in the best interest of some children if peers are not used in evaluating work sheets. On the other hand, if the teacher is doing a good job in planning seatwork activities, the evidence of children failing them routinely should be greatly reduced.

### Evaluating Teacher-Designed Seatwork Activities

Criteria for assessing the effectiveness of seatwork activities include the degree to which the activity carries out the instructional objectives and the benefit derived by pupils through participation. There are questions which the teacher can pose as an informal technique for assessing the seatwork activities employed in the instructional program.

1. Is the activity meaningful and functional; is the skill used in a situation as close as possible to the way it would be utilized in real life?

2. Does the activity really require the use of the skill or reinforce the important concept? Make sure the activity reinforces the skill you intend and not just the skills of cutting, pasting, copying, and so on.

3. Does the activity require too many other skills in addition to the one being emphasized? Are any of these secondary skills too difficult?

4. Can the students do the activity independently; is it within their ability range and experiential background?

5. Are materials, supplies or equipment needed for the activity available in sufficient quantities for the particular classroom situation?

6. Will the activity require the students to think; is it challenging enough?

7. Does the activity allow students to use problem-solving techniques in a meaningful way?

8. Is the activity reasonably interesting, attractive, and varied?

9. Is the amount of teacher preparation time required to develop and produce the activity within reason?

10. Will the activity engage the students in independent work for a sufficient period of time, or will it take too long to complete?
11. Can the activity be done quietly if other instruction is taking place in the classroom?[1]

As you accumulate evaluation information on seatwork activities over a period of time, it will become apparent that your class responds better to some types of activities than they do to others. The response pattern is likely to vary from group to group. In some cases, students prefer certain activities because of specific inherent features. If you can identify these features, it may be possible to capitalize on them by incorporating them into other activity forms. You may also find that your students' preference is influenced by your enthusiasm for a particular activity. Be alert for this situation because you may unconsciously be causing some activities to fail because of your personal preference for others. While you may not be able to alter your behavior, you should at least attempt to identify why some activities work and others do not.

## Summary

Student participation is essential to effective unit teaching. The alert teacher will find no shortage of opportunities for engaging students in unit work. However, the nature of their involvement must not be restricted to group discussion or completing work sheets comprised of drill exercises. Teachers must be creative in varying the type of seatwork activities used. They must also approach the development of seatwork with the perspective that such activities are instructional in nature and are an inherent part of unit lessons. Just as the teacher needs feedback from students on their reaction to seatwork assignments, they need information from the teacher on their performance.

1. Reprinted by permission from *Developing Appropriate Seatwork for the Mentally Retarded,* Special Education Curriculum Development Center, University of Iowa (Iowa City, April 1969). Supported in part by grant from U. S. Office of Education Project No. 6-2883.

**Exercise 22.** Creating and Categorizing Seatwork Activities. Write a behavioral objective for a unit lesson. In a "brainstorming" fashion generate as many seatwork activities as you can that would be applicable to teaching the objective. Having done this, categorize your activities according to the following types.

a. Work sheet
b. Group project work
c. Use of media
d. Individual projects

Now select one activity from each category and develop the activity at two levels of difficulty.

**Exercise 23.**     Writing Directions. Assume you are teaching a unit on foods to a group of fifteen children at the primary level. Further assume that you plan to use the following work sheet as a means of providing the pupils with experience in associating the names of fruits and vegetables with illustrations. Write directions for the exercise that convey to the students what they are to do.

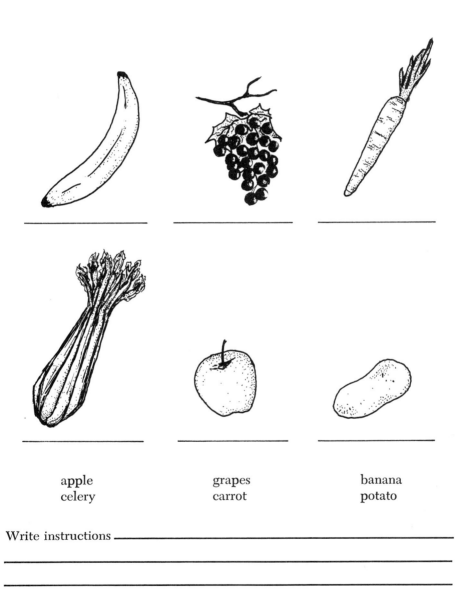

| | | |
|---|---|---|
| apple | grapes | banana |
| celery | carrot | potato |

Write instructions _____

**Exercise 24.** Correcting Work Sheets. Using the following example of a work sheet, design and/or describe three ways in which the work sheet could be corrected by students independently or as a group.

## Coins

Write the name of each coin in the space provided.

How many nickels make a quarter? .........................
How many pennies make a dime? .........................
How many pennies make a quarter? .........................
How many quarters make a half dollar? .........................

Write the following values using numbers.

Three dollars .........................
Four dollars and thirty cents .........................
Ten cents .........................
Eight dollars and forty-six cents .........................
Fifteen dollars .........................

**Exercise 25.**  Identifying Concepts. List the different concepts included in the following example of a work sheet.

---

U.S.D.A. Grade 'A' Pearl Brand
Young 6 to 8Lb. Sizes

# HEN
# TURKEYS............$2.79
Each

---

# TURKEYS
U.S.D.A. Grade 'A' Pearl Brand

7Lb. Average
Each............$2.79

---

1. How big are the turkeys that are advertised? ....................................................
   (Is this saying the same thing in two different ways?)
2. How much do the turkeys cost per pound? ....................................................
3. Is there any difference in the brand in the two ads? ....................................................
4. Could some turkeys weigh more than 7 pounds? ....................................................
5. Could some turkeys weigh less than 7 pounds? ....................................................
6. Is it important to check the weight of each turkey that you buy? ................

BIBLIOGRAPHY

Special Education Curriculum Development Center. *Developing Appropriate Seatwork for the Mentally Retarded.* Iowa City: University of Iowa, 1969.

ADDITIONAL SELECTED REFERENCES RELATED TO THE
DEVELOPMENT OF SEATWORK

CHEYNEY, JEANNE S. "It Worked for Me." *Grade Teacher* 85 (January 1968):33.

CHRISTOPLOS, F. "Programing for Children With Learning Disabilities." *Journal of Learning Disabilities* 2 (1969):45-48.

DARROW, HELEN FISHER, and VAN ALLAN, R. *Independent Activities for Creative Learning.* New York: Bureau of Publications, Teacher's College, Columbia University, 1961.

DETERLINE, W. A. *An Introduction to Programmed Instruction.* Englewood Cliffs, N.J.: Prentice-Hall, 1964.

FRANK, ALAN R. "A Study of Selected Variables in the Preparation of Seatwork for the Mentally Retarded." Unpublished doctoral dissertation, University of Iowa, 1970.

FUCHIGAMI, ROBERT Y., and SMITH, ROLAND F. "Guidelines for Developing and Evaluating Seatwork Materials for Handicapped Children." *Education and Training of the Mentally Retarded* 3, no. 3 (October 1968).

GREENMAN, GLADYS. *Independent Work Period.* Washington, D.C.: Association for Childhood Education, 1941.

JORDAN, LAURA J. "Effective Seatwork for the Educable." *Education and Training of the Mentally Retarded* 3, no. 2 (April 1968).

KIRK, S. A., and JOHNSON, G. O. *Educating the Retarded Child.* Boston: Houghton-Mifflin Co., 1951.

McKIM, MARGARET S., and CASKEY, HELEN. *Guiding Growth in Reading in the Modern Elementary School.* New York: Macmillan Co., 1963.

OTTO, CAROL C. "The Tape Recorder as an Aid in Teaching Slow Learners." *Wisconsin Journal of Education,* January 1967.

RAINEY, D. S., and KELLY, F. J. "An Evaluation of a Programed Textbook With Educable Mentally Retarded Children." *Exceptional Children* 34 (1967): 169-74.

RASMUSSEN, MARGARET, editor. *Homework.* Washington, D.C.: Association for Childhood Education International, 1963.

# Appendix

## EXPERIENCE CHART EASEL
## DIRECTIONS FOR BUILDING*

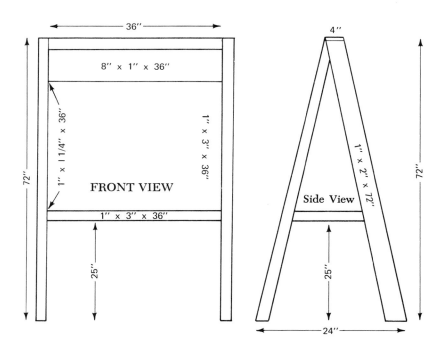

FRONT VIEW

8″ x 1″ x 36″

1″ x 1 1/4″ x 36″

1″ x 3″ x 36″

1″ x 3″ x 36″

36″

72″

25″

Side View

4″

1″ x 2″ x 72″

72″

25″

24″

## LIST OF MATERIAL

4 - 1″ x 2″ x 72″ legs
4 - 1¼″ x 1″ x 36″ back base for sides
4 - 1″ x 3″ x 36″ back base and front base
2 - 1″ x 8″ x 36″ top back base
1 - 1″ x 4″ x 36″ top cap

2 - 32¾″ x 42½″ x ½″ cellotex or chalkboard
1 - 14½″ x 34″ x ¼″ plywood or hard board for storage area bottom
4 - 6″ heavy duty clipboard clips

8 - ½″ x 36″ quarter round trim

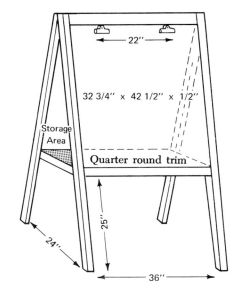

22″

32 3/4″ x 42 1/2″ x 1/2″

Storage Area

Quarter round trim

25″

24″

36″

*Designer unknown.

73